THE WORLD'S GREAT
marques

SMITHMARK

THE WORLD'S GREAT
marques

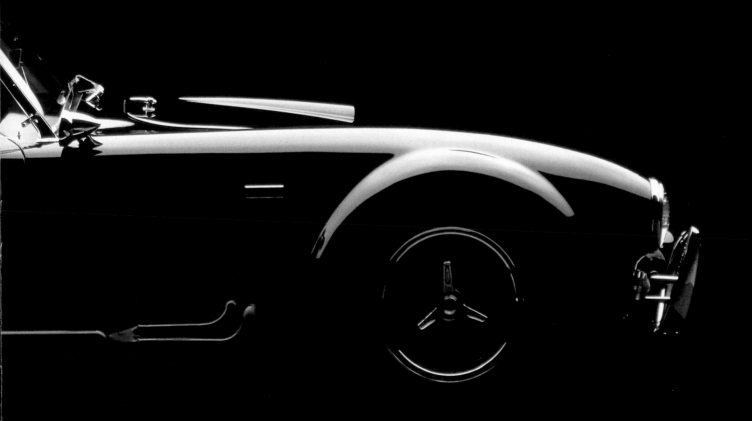

© Aerospace Publishing 1991

This edition published in 1992 by SMITHMARK Publishers Inc.,
16 East 32nd Street, New York, NY 10016.

SMITHMARK books are available for bulk purchase for sales
promotion and premium use. For details write or call the
manager of special sales, SMITHMARK Publishers Inc.,
16 East 32nd Street, New York, NY 10016; (212) 532-6600.

Printed in Hong Kong

ISBN: 0-8317-9302-3

Pictures were supplied by: Aerospace, BMW, Chevrolet, CW Editorial,
Daily Telegraph Picture Library, Ian Dawson, Mirco Decet, Martyn
Goddard, Haymarket Publishing, Ian Howetson, Vic Huber, Ray Hutton,
John Lamm, Ludvigsen Associates, Mercedes, Andrew Morland,
National Motor Museum, Nissan, Luke Parminter, Pininfarina SpA,
Porsche, Quadrant Picture Library, Rex Features, Road & Track,
Peter Robain, Robert Harding Picture Library, Peter Sessler,
Tony Stone Worldwide

Production manager: Alastair Gourlay
Production editor: Chris Marshall
Design: Mick McCarthy

*Previous pages: An AC Cobra 427. A seven-liter V8 engine gave the
427 astonishing power — and speed.
(Tony Stone Worldwide/Ken Fisher)*

CONTENTS

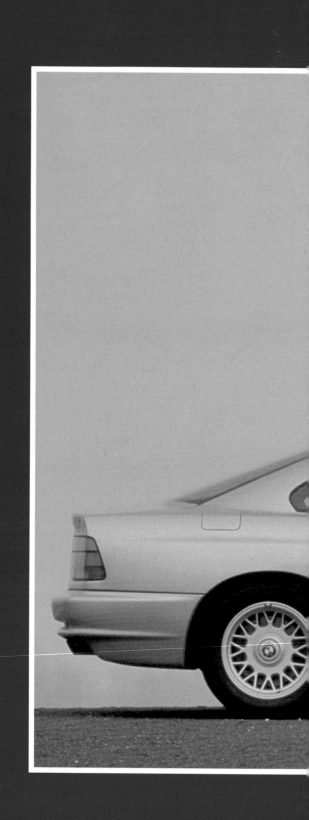

BMW 850i

Take a state-of-the-art five-litre V12 engine producing 300 bhp, add it to a striking two-door coupé body, and you have guaranteed performance. The 850i offers even more than that; it's also a showcase of advanced technology.

The BMW 850i is a contender as the best Grand Tourer in the world. It competes with cars that have been around for some time: the Jaguar XJ-S, Porsche 928 and Mercedes 560 SEC are the obvious examples, but it stands alone, at the head of the pack purely because of its technical brilliance. Though there was some confusion when the car was first launched and many thought that they would be seeing a BMW to take on Ferrari or Lamborghini, the truth was less exotic, but stunning nevertheless.

See one on the road, and you'll give an unequivocal vote of approval for a shape that is quite exquisite. From the driver you'll get even more, for the BMW 850i – practical supercar, delight to look at and to drive though it is – is also a technological *tour de force*.

The 850i is motivated by a five-litre V12 developing 300 brake horsepower and a maximum torque of 332 lb ft. That's enough to power it from a standstill to 60 mph in 7.2 seconds. Top speed is electronically limited, to around 160 mph for environmental and political reasons, but un-governed examples are claimed to have reached 180 mph with ease. It's an environmentally friendly 180 mph too as, naturally, it has a three-way catalytic converter.

The car bristles with technical innovations:

Speed electronically controlled to 160 mph

for a start, it is the first production car to use multiplex wiring, a system whereby one wire and 'intelligent' switches replace much of the conventional, complex and messy normal wiring loom. This not only reduces weight but also improves the reliability of the electrical circuits – an important feature in a car where electronics play so vital a role.

It is the first car to offer a 12-cylinder engine *and* a six-speed manual gearbox in one package. A four-speed automatic switchable gearbox (between sport, economy and manual) is also available, although the enthusiastic driver will prefer the manual for its flexibility and the access it gives to the full range of engine power and performance.

The rear axle is a highly sophisticated multi-link device which eliminates the usual compromise between ride and handling that is the bugbear of modern, high-performance car designers. The problem lies in the fact that as the chassis is tuned to give a sharper response, so the ride becomes harsher and less comfortable. On the 850i the integral rear axle is of an elasto-kinematic design (achieved by manipulating the rigidity of rubber mounts and their interaction with other components), which allows for maximum tyre contact with the road whatever the driver is doing. Whether the car is accelerating, braking or cornering and almost regardless of the road surface, the handling remains impressive and the ride smooth and comfortable. This system is also known as 'Passive Rear-Wheel Steering'.

The car features Automatic Stability Control (ASC), which eliminates wheelspin on all surfaces by cutting the throttle as soon as the driving

ing the ignition. As a safety feature the system is more effective than the old mechanical limited slip differential. Because the throttle is electronically controlled, it doesn't matter what you do with your right foot should the car start to slide; the ASC+T will automatically compensate without your lifting off. It gives greater traction in ice and snow, particularly useful if only one side of the car is on the slippery surface. It doesn't make the car foolproof but it takes a lot of the worry out of driving in poor conditions.

Think of any advanced feature, and this car has it: regenerating bumpers, a service interval monitor which means that the car decides when it needs a service, an on-board computer with a full systems check, cruise control, automatic air-conditioning with a particle filter to stop pollen and other particulates entering the car (it has its own 'nose' which decides when air needs to be recycled and when to admit outside air). The windscreen wiper pressure is speed-related, there's a compact disc player with boot-mounted changer, electrically operated rear blind, auto-dipping rear view mirror – all these feature on the 850i either as options or as standard equipment depending on the market where it is sold. All contribute to the car's technological prowess and enhance its pre-eminent position among its rivals.

It is only as you approach the car that you start to appreciate the BMW's sheer presence. It is less than 15 ft long but nearly six feet wide, and four and a half high, which gives it a powerful, almost mean look. It is best in dark colours as well, the modern lines being uncluttered with impedimenta and everything looking custom-made.

You know it's a BMW immediately, which is good marque marketing, but it is a very understated car. There is nothing pretentious or overtly brash about it, it is elegant and harmonious in line and proportion. From the front it looks predatory; from the rear the four, square tail pipes give the immediate image of immense power.

As you open the door, the window drops slightly, opening the seal between it and the frame, and there is plenty of room to get in as the steering wheel seems a long way away. Close the door and the window slides back to its closed position; switch on and the steering wheel moves back into the pre-memorised position (the front seats and external mirrors operate on the same

reliable memory).

After settling in and luxuriating in the cockpit for a while, enjoying the almost aircraft-like feel of the close surrounding instruments, starting the engine is a reminder that there are 300 eager horses under the hood. Deciding whether to drive them through a manual or an automatic box is really a philosophical question: on the one hand there is the active control of the manual system; on the other there is comfort and effortless driving with the auto box. The sensible option is, of course, to choose the latter, if only because of today's traffic conditions, and with the switchable box the sports element is still in evidence. But the true sportsman will choose the manual (and the optional and rather stiffer M-technics suspension), even though it isn't strictly necessary.

It's the chassis, though, which moves the 850i away from its competitors. It sets standards that few others reach, and the adoption of the Automatic Stability Control means that at least a driver will have its reassurance, even when conditions do not favour the full force of 300 bhp and all that torque.

No superiors and very few equals . . .

The 850i is no exotic, even though it can match the energy of many an Italian supercar. Though room in the rear is restricted, research has shown that few 850i owners will use those seats for anything other than a briefcase, but there is room for four adults for a brief journey, two adults and two children for a longer time, or two adults with enough luggage for a long journey.

Perhaps the beauty of the 850i is that it offers the advantages of all BMWs whether 3-, 5- or 7-Series. But the 850i will make its own mark in the world of special motor cars, because anyone who has spent time with the car, or any owner with enough wisdom to choose this model over other makes and models, will quickly come to know and respect the power, performance and perfection of design that make up this discreetly packaged car, a true supercar dressed as a saloon. They will know that it has no superiors and few, if any, equals.

The enjoyment of an 850i comes from the feeling of technical superiority and exceptional competence as well as the car's suitability for everyday use. There is only one disadvantage – not only does it cost a great deal of money, but worldwide production for the next three years is all spoken for. Pools win or not, you couldn't get a new one even if you had the money!

wheels start to lose grip. On the manual version, this is linked with the brakes and is called ASC+T, the 'T' standing for Traction. It's a truly advanced system which uses the familiar technology of electronic ABS to provide traction control too. The ABS sensors detect wheelspin on any wheel, and if it's a driven wheel the ASC+T system reacts incredibly quickly to decrease the torque applied to that wheel. The system can do that in three ways, by applying the brake to that wheel alone (which is the quickest way), by reducing the throttle opening, or finally by retard-

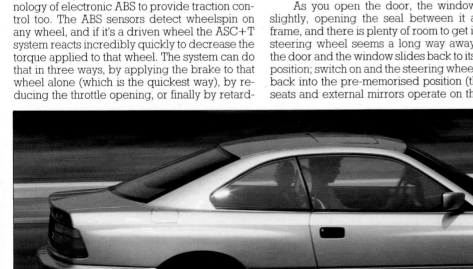

BMW 850i

According to BMW, to view the 850i coupé as a kind of updated 6-series coupé would be a mistake. The 850i was designed to take BMW into the very highest realms of the sports and coupé market.

The intention was to combine the refinement of the V12 used in the 750i saloon with a dramatic coupé body to give what BMW hoped would be an unrivalled combination of technical merit and prestige. With features like a six-speed manual gearbox, and ABS allied to traction control, not to mention a new, sophisticated rear suspension design in addition to that V12 engine, BMW were confident that their flagship coupé would stand above their Mercedes, Porsche, Jaguar and Ferrari rivals and help the company gain a bigger slice of a market expected to reach 80,000 customers by 1995.

Automatic window-lowering

As you open the 850i's door, the window is automatically lowered by a fraction. This mak door easier to close, as you are not trying to compress all the air in the car.

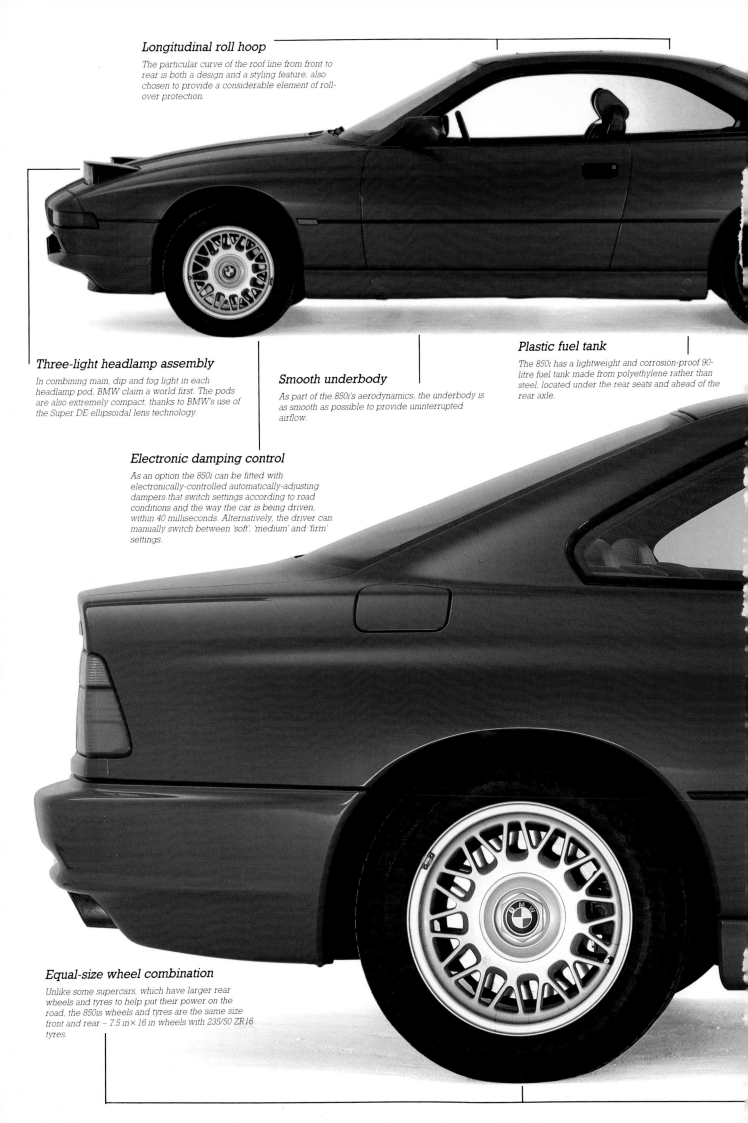

Longitudinal roll hoop

The particular curve of the roof line from front to rear is both a design and a styling feature, also chosen to provide a considerable element of roll-over protection.

Three-light headlamp assembly

In combining main, dip and fog light in each headlamp pod, BMW claim a world first. The pods are also extremely compact, thanks to BMW's use of the Super DE ellipsoidal lens technology.

Smooth underbody

As part of the 850i's aerodynamics, the underbody is as smooth as possible to provide uninterrupted airflow.

Plastic fuel tank

The 850i has a lightweight and corrosion-proof 90-litre fuel tank made from polyethylene rather than steel, located under the rear seats and ahead of the rear axle.

Electronic damping control

As an option the 850i can be fitted with electronically-controlled automatically-adjusting dampers that switch settings according to road conditions and the way the car is being driven, within 40 milliseconds. Alternatively, the driver can manually switch between 'soft', 'medium' and 'firm' settings.

Equal-size wheel combination

Unlike some supercars, which have larger rear wheels and tyres to help put their power on the road, the 850is wheels and tyres are the same size front and rear – 7.5 in × 16 in wheels with 235/50 ZR16 tyres.

Above left: The rear lights wrap around to give an almost seamless look to the rear, while the four exhaust outlets are a sure sign that there's more than a straight-six engine under the bonnet.

Above: High-speed cornering is drama-free in the 850i, thanks to BMW's Automatic Stability Control plus Traction system (ASC+T), which eliminates wheelspin.

Left: The 850i has the advantage of variable suspension setting: the dampers adjust automatically to hard, medium or soft, depending on functions such as road speed, acceleration and steering angle. The driver can also override the automatic system and manually select the setting required.

Driving an 850i: *Safety fast*

Below left: From the side, the 850i is sheer aerodynamic elegance. The drag coefficient is an excellent 0.29, far better than the previous 6-Series coupé and all the current BMWs. It's one very good reason why the 850i would run on past 170 mph if the engine were not deliberately restricted to 'only' 300 bhp.

As soon as you get into this BMW you know it's a car that can think for itself. Just open the door and the glass automatically drops slightly, so that the air pressure inside is lowered to make it easier to close the door . . .

You know it's a car that's going to take care of you. The rear axle is designed to 'forgive': it shrugs off driving errors and allows drivers to take autobahn bends or twisting country roads with fervour equalled by peace of mind. Even a car weighing nearly two tonnes can be responsive and agile if it's engineered correctly.

It does take time, though, to get completely in tune with the 850i. Its width requires some mental adjustment, and the steering and chassis some familiarity before one feels completely at ease. But even before you reach that point you know that if a patch of ice or damp causes wheelspin, the 850i simply cannot slide sideways; wheelspin has been eliminated, and all the driver knows of the potential drama is the flashing light on the dashboard that tells him the electronic masterpiece that is the 850i is working correctly. It's fast – very fast indeed – but never furious.

PERFORMANCE & SPECIFICATION COMPARISON	Engine	Displacement	Power	Torque (lb ft)	Max speed	0-60 mph	Length (in/mm)	Wheelbase (in/mm)	Track front/rear	Weight total (lb/kg)	Price (1991)
BMW 850i	V12, overhead-cam	4988 cc	300 bhp 5200 rpm	332 lb ft 4100 rpm	161 mph 259 km/h	7.2 sec	188.2 in 4780 mm	105.7 in 2684 mm	61.2 in 61.4 in	4149 lb 1882 kg	£59,500
Ferrari Mondial t	V8, quad-cam, 32-valve	3405 cc	300 bhp 7700 rpm	238 lb ft 4200 rpm	156 mph 251 km/h	5.6 sec	166.5 in 4229 mm	97.8 in 2484 mm	59.0 in 62.2 in	3300 lb 1497 kg	£62,500
Jaguar XJ-S	V12, overhead-cam	5344 cc	278 bhp 5250 rpm	298 lb ft 3000 rpm	152 mph 245 km/h	7.7 sec	188.0 in 4775 mm	102.0 in 2591 mm	58.6 in 59.2 in	3861 lb 1751 kg	£36,200
Mercedes 500SL	V8, overhead-cam, 32-valve	4973 cc	326 bhp 5500 rpm	332 lb ft 4000 rpm	157 mph 253 km/h	5.9 sec	176.0 in 4470 mm	99.0 in 2515 mm	60.4 in 60.0 in	3902 lb 1770 kg	£66,000
Porsche 928 GT	V8, quad-cam, 32-valve	4957 cc	330 bhp 6200 rpm	317 lb ft 4100 rpm	169 mph 272 km/h	5.6 sec	177.9 in 4518 mm	93.3 in 2369 mm	61.0 in 60.0 in	3494 lb 1585 kg	£64,496

BMW 850i Data File

BMW's reputation has been built on producing cars with a definite sporting image. Before World War II, the first example of that was the superb 328 convertible, which was years ahead of its time. After the war BMW took a long time to re-establish themselves, and their first sporting car was the V8 507 convertible, which was very expensive and consequently built in very limited numbers. The right way to combine a sporting heritage with saloon car production was to produce a coupé; the first BMW coupé, the 3200 CS, appeared in 1962, and there have been coupés in BMW's lineup ever since. The best known have been the 3.0 CSL and, more recently, the 6-Series cars such as the 635.

The 635 coupé was extremely popular and a very hard act to follow. To be an advance it had to have a better engine than BMW's excellent inline six-cylinder, and that meant using BMW's V12 developed for its top-of-the-line 750i saloon in a shorter coupé body. The result first appeared at the Frankfurt Motor Show in 1990.

Styling

'Form follows function' is the principle that lies behind all BMW styling, and on the 850i this can be seen by the aerodynamic streamlining and the conspicuous care given to every component's design. Every detail has been carefully tested in a wind tunnel to achieve the best result and to avoid any impression of being 'added-on'.

From the front, the BMW 'kidney' grille is clear, and, together with the air inlet and the exterior light strip, gives the car a stretched impression. The extended styling of the car forms a wedge shape from the flat front to the rear, while the bumpers are integrated into the smooth flow of the body surfaces.

The roof structure has no 'B' pillars,

which gives an impression of lightness – a characteristic of BMW coupés – while offering good all-round visibility and emphasising the elegance of the stretched body shape.

Side surfaces flare slightly and discreetly round the wheel arches, while the light alloy wheels use a cross-spoke design.

These design characteristics are followed inside with a spacious and logical arrangement of the control panels and their functions. An example is the control panel for the windows being in the door panel and the multi-information display, radio, air conditioning and the on-off switch for the ASC system being in the centre console.

Below left: The interior follows the usual BMW standards of excellent ergonomics, with the instruments and controls angled towards the driver.

Below: The front seats are electrically operated, and the driver's seat has a memory system to adjust to as many as three regular drivers.

Rear axle

The 850i's rear axle is a complex design intended to provide both anti-dive under braking and anti-squat under acceleration. At the same time it was designed to eliminate camber changes under hard cornering, while avoiding the nastier consequences of roll-steer and the rear-wheel steering effects caused by the driver lifting off abruptly while cornering. At the same time the design had to be compact enough to allow room for large fuel tanks to feed the V12 and for the catalytic converters.

Both the upper and lower wishbones have very rigid mounting bushes, which prevent the assembly twisting under braking and acceleration, as do conventional rubber bushes. The harder bushes do

not produce the penalty of a harsh ride because the suspension assembly is mounted to the body on more compliant bushes.

Whereas some cars have either active or passive rear-wheel steering designed to minimise understeer (by turning the rear wheels to sharpen turn into a corner) the 850i's passive system is designed to overcome the oversteering tendency that abrupt lift-off in a corner brings. Bias built into certain of the bushes means a load reversal will result in both rear wheels turning fractionally to generate under-rather than oversteer.

If that's not enough to satisfy the sporting driver, he can opt for the available stiffer set-up from M-technics.

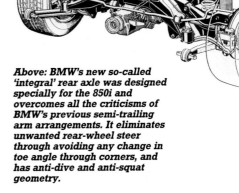

Above: BMW's new so-called 'integral' rear axle was designed specially for the 850i and overcomes all the criticisms of BMW's previous semi-trailing arm arrangements. It eliminates unwanted rear-wheel steer through avoiding any change in toe angle through corners, and has anti-dive and anti-squat geometry.

SPECIFICATION
BMW 850i

ENGINE

Type:	V12, overhead-cam
Construction:	light alloy block and heads; seven main bearings, iron-coated pistons running in alloy block
Bore×stroke:	3.3 in×2.9 in (84 mm×75 mm)
Displacement:	4988 cc
Compression ratio:	8.8:1
Valve gear:	two valves per cylinder operated via rockers and hydraulic tappets by single overhead camshaft per bank of cylinders
Fuel system:	Digital Motor Electronics fuel injection
Ignition:	electronic
Maximum power:	300 bhp at 5,200 rpm (PS Din)
Maximum torque:	332 lb ft at 4,100 rpm

TRANSMISSION

Type:	six-speed manual or four-speed automatic

Ratios:		manual	automatic
	1st	4.25:1	2.48:1
	2nd	2.53:1	1.48:1
	3rd	1.68:1	1.00:1
	4th	1.24:1	0.73:1
	5th	1.00:1	
	6th	0.83:1	
Final drive ratio:		2.93:1	3.15:1

BODY/CHASSIS

Type:	integral steel monocoque with two-door coupé body

RUNNING GEAR

Steering:	recirculating ball, 3.4 turns lock-to-lock
Suspension:	front: independent with MacPherson struts, coil springs, telescopic dampers and anti-roll bar rear: BMW 'integral axle' with double wishbones and one longitudinal control arm per side, coil springs, telescopic dampers and anti-roll bar
Brakes:	ventilated discs front and rear, 12.8-in (324-mm) diameter
Wheels:	cast alloy, 7.5 in×16 in
Tyres:	235/50 ZR16

DIMENSIONS AND WEIGHT

Length:	188.2 in (4780mm)
Width:	73.0 in (1854 mm)
Height:	52.8 in (1341 mm)
Wheelbase:	105.7 in (2684 mm)
Track:	61.2 in (1554 mm) front; 61.4 in (1560 mm) rear
Kerb weight:	4,149 lb (1882 kg)

PERFORMANCE

Acceleration:	0-30 mph 2.9 sec
	0-40 mph 4.1 sec
	0-50 mph 5.3 sec
	0-60 mph 7.2 sec
	0-70 mph 9.0 sec
	0-80 mph 11.0 sec
	0-90 mph 13.5 sec
	0-100 mph 16.7 sec
	0-110 mph 20.0 sec
	0-120 mph 24.8 sec
	0-130 mph 29.3 sec
Standing ¼ mile:	15.3 sec (96 mph)

Acceleration in gear (automatic)	mph	third	second
	30-50	4.4	3.5
	40-60	5.1	3.6
	50-70	5.7	3.6

Maximum speed:	161 mph (259 km/h)
Overall fuel consumption:	14.4 mpg
Price (1991):	£59,500

Performance figures from AUTOCAR

BMW 850i kindly supplied by BMW (GB) Ltd

speed

ic design is
ooling air
d to avoid

Self-regenerating bumpers

The 850i's bumpers can naturally withstand heavy impacts, but with lesser ones (up to 6 km/h) the bumpers will always 'regenerate' and regain their original shape with no paint damage.

Concealed headlight washer jets

The washer jet nozzles automatically rise through water pressure when the headlight washers are activated.

BMW 'kidney' radiator grille

The one thing that was absolutely fixed about the design of the new BMW 850i coupé was that it should retain the hallmark of that distinctive 'kidney' BMW radiator grille, even if it were used in its most abbreviated form.

Speed-dependent wipers

In addition to folding away for aerodynamic efficiency, the windscreen wipers' intermittent speed across the screen automatically varies according to the speed of the car.

Superb aerodynamics

Without using any add-on aerodynamic aids, BMW have created a shape with an extremely low Cd of only 0.29. Lift is equally low front and rear to help ensure directional stability at speed.

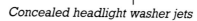

Air intakes close at high

At the front of the car the aerodyn... such that at high speed the flow of through the radiator grille is restri... unnecessary drag.

Left: The 'eyebrows' over the wheel arches follow the style pioneered by one of BMW's rivals, Porsche, with the 944.

Above: The low sloping bonnet gives no clue to the presence of a big, front-mounted five-litre V12 engine.

Left and below: The contrast in shape and style between the 750i (left) and the 850i (below). The saloon looks elegant enough until matched against the coupé. Despite being six inches shorter than the saloon, the 850i manages to create an impression of length, thanks to the long curves of front and rear screens.

Above: The amount of room in the rear makes the 850i fit somewhere in between a full four-seater and a 2+2.

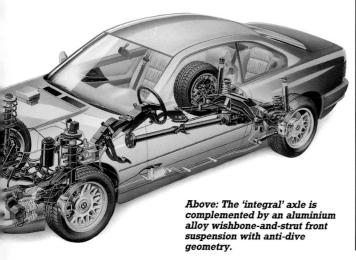

Above: The 'integral' axle is complemented by an aluminium alloy wishbone-and-strut front suspension with anti-dive geometry.

Engine

BMWs were long renowned for the smoothness of their six-cylinder overhead-cam engines. The only way to improve on that for their top-of-the-range supercars was to double up on the six and create a V12. The engine was conceived at a time when only Jaguar had a mass-production V12.

The engine first appeared in the 750i saloon, and needed only the minimum of changes (to the throttle housing and the route of the fuel lines) to allow it to fit under the 850i's lower bonnet.

Heads and block are all made in aluminium alloy, with the pistons running directly in the block rather than in iron cylinder liners, as used by some other manufacturers. To allow the pistons to run direct in the alloy block they are iron-coated, while the cylinder bores are silicon-coated. The pistons actually run on the silicon crystals cast into the alloy, a layer of the very hard crystals being exposed by acid etching the bores to remove a layer of the surrounding alloy. It's a process that's been around for many years, but it is now perfected.

It's a short-stroke design (84 mm × 75 mm), which helps keep engine height down and contributes to smooth running, as does a crankshaft running on seven main bearings.

A single chain-driven overhead camshaft is used for each bank of cylinders, operating two valves per cylinder in trapezoidal-shaped combustion chambers via rockers and hydraulic tappets. Hydraulic tappets are maintenance-free and also contribute to smooth engine running, as the tappets should never be out of adjustment.

The quoted power output of 300 bhp at 5,200 rpm, along with 332 lb ft of torque at 4,100 rpm, hardly does the engine justice, as it is deliberately limited to give the car a theoretical top speed of 'only' 155 mph, although some magazine testers have achieved higher speeds. Much more power is easily available!

Above: The under-bonnet view of the 850i is neat and tidy, with the cast-alloy intake pipes the most obvious feature. Those intake pipes are in fact far longer than they look, as they continue under the central cover to feed the opposite bank of cylinders. This can be seen most clearly in the engine cross-section diagram (far right). The length of the inlet tracts is thus maximised to give the most efficient breathing possible. Power output is 300 bhp at 5,200 rpm and the maximum torque of 332 lb ft is produced at 4,100 rpm.

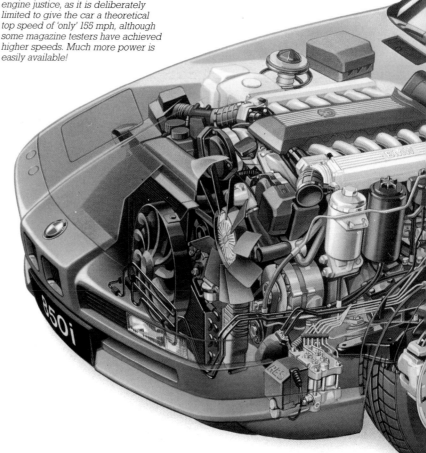

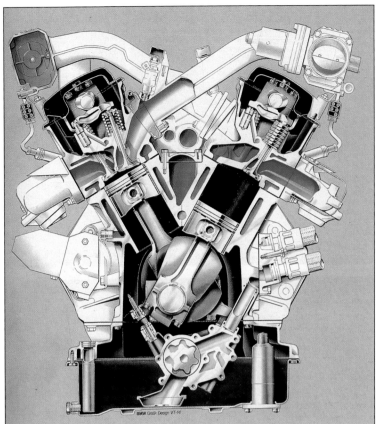

Above: The exploded diagram shows the workings of BMW's five-litre V12 engine. It's the first V12 from a mass producer since Jaguar introduced theirs back in 1971. The BMW engine has the pistons running direct in the block, which is of 'AlSil6Cu4Mg' aluminium alloy. The iron-coated pistons actually run on the hard silicon crystals (the 'Si' in the alloy spec), which are exposed by acid etching the bores. Chain drive, rather than the more common belt drive, is used for the single overhead camshafts.

Right: Only two valves per cylinder are used, both operated by the same camshaft via rockers and hydraulic tappets. The valve angle is very narrow, with the combustion chamber almost flat.

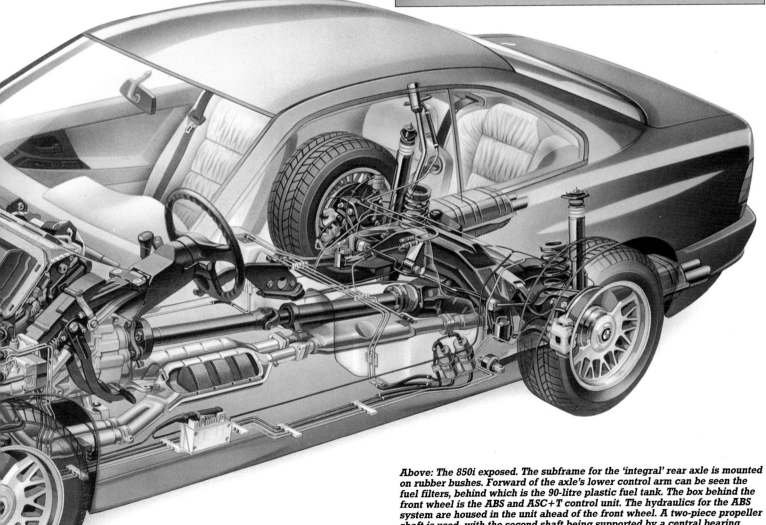

Above: The 850i exposed. The subframe for the 'integral' rear axle is mounted on rubber bushes. Forward of the axle's lower control arm can be seen the fuel filters, behind which is the 90-litre plastic fuel tank. The box behind the front wheel is the ABS and ASC+T control unit. The hydraulics for the ABS system are housed in the unit ahead of the front wheel. A two-piece propeller shaft is used, with the second shaft being supported by a central bearing mounted to the chassis. With so much power to spare, the engine runs an old-fashioned viscous coupling cooling fan from the crankshaft, although there is a supplementary electric fan mounted ahead of the radiator. Above and behind the alternator is the easily accessible oil filter, while the canister next to that is the power-steering fluid reservoir.

Mercedes 500 SL

Mercedes-Benz have always been in the forefront of technological innovation, and the SL convertibles have always been fast, comfortable cars. The latest model – the 500 SL – combines both traditions.

T he 500 SL is the flagship of the sporting end of the Mercedes range. It is the most powerful and expensive model in a three-car family which has taken the SL philosophy into the 1990s – and it should, thanks to Mercedes' long-life design policy, see the SL theme through towards the 21st century.

Two illustrations of the 'design-to-last' philosophy are the facts that this is only the fourth generation of SLs since the original 300 SL went into production in 1954, and that it had been fully 10 years in the design process before Mercedes were ready to launch it at the Geneva Motor Show in March 1989.

The car is positively bristling with high-technology features and is an exceptional example of the superb engineering for which Mercedes are most famous. The 500 SL is described by Mercedes as a sports car in the old SL, or *Sport Leicht*, tradition; but in character the 'Light' part of the definition long ago gave way to luxury.

The design team, led by Bruno Sacco, who worked on the 500 SL for so long, described it as "the most difficult and challenging task we have ever faced". Even that may be something of an understatement.

Highly refined, yet still very sporty

As a car conceived in the 1970s, designed through the 1980s and expected to last through the 1990s, in markets worldwide, the 500 SL had to score very high on safety features and very low on pollution and consumption – or as low on the latter as could be expected of any car weighing over 4,100 lb and capable of 155 mph. It also had to be styled so that it looked fresh and distinctly 'modern', while remaining recognisably Mercedes and recognisably SL, but so that it wouldn't

look corny or boring in years to come. So the stylists aimed for "a timeless appeal – modern and fresh, but without fads which could quickly render the concept out-of-date in a world of rapidly changing aesthetics". That intention was complicated by the fact that, like previous SLs, this car was to be offered with both detachable hard-top and folding soft-top roofs.

Mercedes' decision to go for a modern design but with a touch of tradition cannot really be considered a compromise, however, since the new car was to be engineered almost from scratch, with no expense or production effort spared in finding the *best* solutions rather than just the easiest or the least costly ones.

In the end, the 500 SL has one of the most complex and safest unit chassis/body structures Mercedes have ever built – and not just for the occupants in the event of an accident, but for other vulnerable road-users too. It has an engine which, while derived from one already familiar in

Mercedes 500 SL

Since the mid-1950s, there has always been a sporting SL model in the Mercedes range. The latest example comes with a choice of three different engines – a 12-valve straight-six, a more powerful 24-valve version of the six-cylinder engine, and the five-litre 32-valve V8 which is fitted to the 500 SL version. The solidly-built 500 SL is clearly the top of the range. It's no lightweight, but its powerful engine gives it the performance to keep up with all but a handful of the world's most exotic cars.

Removable hard top

With the hard top fitted, the SL is as cosy as any saloon. Lift the roof into place, press the electric roof-locking switch, plug in the heated rear window, and the car is ready for winter motoring.

Automatic gearbox

Six-cylinder SLs (the 300 SL and the 300 SL-24) can have either a five-speed manual gearbox or a four-speed automatic. With the 500 SL, the automatic unit is fitted as standard and there is no manual option.

Automatic damper adjustment

There are four different damper settings, ranging from hard to soft. An electronic system automatically adjusts the damper settings according to the road surface and the way the car is being driven.

the 500 saloon and coupé ranges (and even in the older 500 SL), was comprehensively upgraded for the new-generation sports car and given masses of both power and character. It has a highly refined yet still very sporty multi-link suspension, and brakes with an anti-lock system which is also used to control wheelspin. And the 500 SL features some stunning high-tech solutions to problems other manufacturers probably hadn't even thought about before. The seats, for instance, not only incorporate fully automatic adjustment, but even carry the entire belt system. There is a rear roll-over bar which normally folds flat but will spring up automatically and instantly if an imminent accident is sensed; there is ride-height control for the suspension, and the facility to vary the parameters of the anti-skid electronics when snow chains are used.

Above: Even the mirrors have been developed to give minimum aerodynamic drag and the least possible wind noise.

Fast, beautiful and luxurious

There is also the versatility of open-topped, soft-topped or hard-topped motoring, all as part of the package, and all worked at the touch of a single button. To detach the hard top, all that is necessary is to put the transmission selector into 'Park', switch on the ignition (or have the engine running), detach the simple plug-in connector for the heated rear screen, and pull back the red switch in the centre of the console. The roof unlocks and, with the help of a friend (it isn't light enough for one person to handle), it can simply be lifted off and stored in the garage. Putting it back is just as easy: line up the catches, hit the switch, and simply connect the plug. The soft-top operation is even easier: put the car in 'Park' with the power on, move the switch, and the roof (with the help of 15 hydraulic motors, 45 hydraulic lines, 17 micro-switches and a central control unit) unclips itself and retreats under a neat metal cover behind the cockpit – all well within 30 seconds. Push the switch the other way and it whirrs smoothly back up; you don't even need to

Below: The soft top folds down to stow away out of sight underneath a hinged cover.

disturb yourself enough to touch a clip.

With the soft top down, too, so long as there is only the driver and a front-seat passenger in the car, there is the option of a fine, soft-mesh net which fits inside the erected roll-over bar and all but eliminates draughts from behind, for high-speed, fresh-air motoring of the finest kind – helped by the amazingly powerful heating and air-conditioning system to keep the cabin cosy.

If the 500 SL has any problem at all, it is really only one of definition. This is a very fast car, very beautiful, and as luxurious and well-appointed as the most exotic limousine – for two people at least. Yet Mercedes do still call it "a true sports car". Underneath all the pampering refinements, it undoubtedly *is,* but it is just as well to think of it as the thing that Mercedes worked very hard to achieve: a true SL.

Below: With the metal hard top in place, the 500 SL is as well-insulated as any saloon car.

Top: In profile, the latest model in the SL family shows its ancestry. The fluted rear light lenses and squared-off boot line are similar to those on the previous SL shape.

Above: The padded steel roll-over bar will spring up automatically to protect the passengers if the car is involved in an accident. The driver can also raise the bar at any time by operating a hydraulic mechanism.

Driving the 500 SL: *startlingly quick*

At the heart of the 500 SL is a wonderful V8 with the utmost smoothness and refinement for cruising, but a strong and sporty note when it is extended. It has immense flexibility at most speeds, is very responsive to the throttle, and is superbly matched by the smooth-changing four-speed automatic transmission. That also reacts instantly to pressing the throttle hard enough to ask for kick-down, and both 'Sport' and 'Economy' modes hold the up-changes late on full throttle, while 'Economy' moves the part-throttle changes to lower revs.

For such a heavy car, the 500 SL is startlingly quick, showing how well the power is spread and how well the gear ratios are chosen. It will reach 60 mph in almost exactly six seconds and 100 mph in just 14, with a top speed artificially limited to around 155 mph so as not to contravene the law. It has a marvellously comfortable ride for a sporting car, but also superb grip and handling thanks to the well-damped, softly-sprung suspension and fine geometry. The anti-wheelspin control, which reduces the possibility of provoking oversteer by clumsy use of too much power, delights some drivers – albeit at the expense of frustrating others!

PERFORMANCE & SPECIFICATION COMPARISON	Engine	Displacement	Power	Torque (lb ft)	Max speed	0-60 mph	Length (in/mm)	Wheelbase (in/mm)	Track front/rear	Weight total (lb/kg)	Price
Mercedes 500 SL	V8, quad-cam, 32-valve	4973 cc	326 bhp 5500 rpm	332 lb ft 4000 rpm	157 mph 253 km/h	5.9 sec	176.0 in 4470 mm	99.0 in 2515 mm	60.4 in 60.0 in	4167 lb 1890 kg	£70,090 (1991)
BMW 850i	V12, overhead-cam	4988 cc	300 bhp 5200 rpm	332 lb ft 4100 rpm	161 mph 259 km/h	7.2 sec	188.2 in 4780 mm	105.7 in 2684 mm	61.2 in 61.4 in	4149 lb 1882 kg	£59,500 (1991)
Ferrari 348 tb	V8, quad-cam, 32-valve	3405 cc	300 bhp 7000 rpm	224 lb ft 4000 rpm	163 mph 262 km/h	5.6 sec	166.5 in 4229 mm	96.5 in 2450 mm	59.0 in 62.2 in	3300 lb 1497 kg	£74,587 (1991)
Nissan 300 ZX	V6, quad-cam, 24-valve, twin-turbo	2960 cc	280 bhp 6400 rpm	274 lb ft 3600 rpm	155 mph 249 km/h	5.6 sec	178.1 in 4525 mm	101.2 in 2570 mm	58.9 in 60.4 in	3485 lb 1581 kg	£30,650 (1991)
Porsche 911 Turbo	Flat-six, overhead-cam, turbo	3299 cc	320 bhp 5750 rpm	332 lb ft 4500 rpm	167 mph 269 km/h	4.7 sec	167.3 in 4249 mm	89.4 in 2271 mm	56.4 in 58.7 in	3216 lb 1459 kg	£74,580 (1991)

'Trademark' air outlets

The slatted air outlets just behind the front wheels were deliberately styled to look like the air vents on the front wings of the classic 300 SL, which was introduced in 1954.

Fold-away hood

The car comes as standard with a removable hard top and a folding soft top. The soft top goes up or down at the touch of a button. In just 30 seconds, an electro-hydraulic mechanism folds the hood down and stows it underneath a metal cover.

Roll-over bar

A tubular steel roll-over bar will protect the occupants in the event of a serious accident. If the car crashes or starts to overturn, the roll-over bar automatically springs up in three-tenths of a second.

Chassis and body

At first glance, the base which bristles with so much technology looks much like any modern pressed-steel platform chassis with a unit body, but in most aspects of this car it has been refined to a very high degree. Mercedes designed it (with the help of the most modern computer systems) to provide maximum safety for its occupants and even for any pedestrian or other road-user it might come into contact with. It is all-new, with twice as much light alloy as the last SL family – almost five per cent of the body weight. The floor and frame use high-strength steel with large reinforcing sections and a particularly strong attachment for the windscreen pillar area, which acts as a front roll-over bar. The front and rear incorporate large controlled-crush structures, and the doors, door pillars and locks are all designed to resist side impacts. An additional cross-member at the windscreen base deflects part of any side-impact force

to the opposite side of the car, and several features of the door and shell design are to prevent the doors either springing open or jamming closed in the event of an accident. Steering-column movement is limited by an additional cross-member under the dash, and in an accident the pedals would swing forward to limit injuries to legs and feet. There is even a thick foam cushion below the footwell carpets to absorb the energy of a passenger bracing him/herself against the floor. The smooth, steeply-sloping nose isn't just handsome and aerodynamic; with its smoothly rounded corners and deformable wing tops, it is designed to be kind to pedestrians or cyclists.

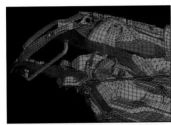

Below and right: Computer-aided design techniques were used to calculate the stresses on the 500 SL's body.

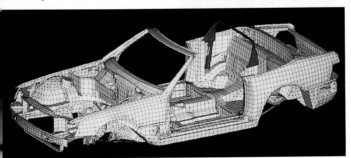

Engine

The five-litre all-aluminium V8 engine for the 500 SL is derived from the V8 used in the S-class saloons and coupés, but with some very desirable uprating, for significantly more power and torque. It has a stronger block and a new crankshaft and connecting rods, but most of the changes are in the cylinder heads. These have been altered from two valves per cylinder to four, with two camshafts per bank driven by duplex chains, plus hydraulic tappets for silent, self-adjusting operation. The new heads also have very steeply-angled exhaust valves, to help minimise the width of the engine. The inlet camshaft has electronically-controlled, fully-automatic variable timing, to vary the valve overlap and give optimum performance and refinement at all speeds and under all operating conditions. The adjusting mechanism is incorporated into the camshaft

gears and controlled by the injection management in relation to engine speed and load. At low speeds the timing is set to give smoother running, fewer emissions and better fuel consumption; at medium speeds it changes to improve torque; and at high speeds it adopts maximum overlap for maximum power. From 4973 cc, with a compression ratio of 10.0:1 and Bosch electronic injection, the V8 produces 326 bhp at 5,500 rpm (which is over 80 bhp more than the old two-valve) and 332 lb ft of torque at 4,000 rpm (up by 37 lb ft). A four-speed automatic transmission is standard, and is widely regarded as one of the best of its kind; it has dual modes (modifying the change-up points at the touch of a neat switch on the console) and a very tall final drive ratio, which, with a direct top gear, allows a long-legged 28 mph per 1,000 rpm for relaxed cruising.

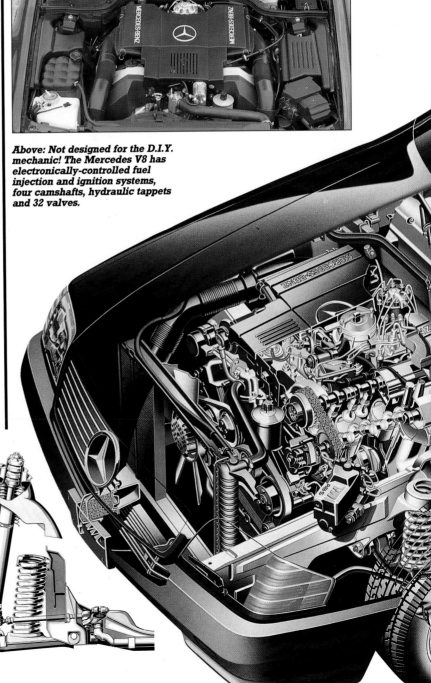

Above: Not designed for the D.I.Y. mechanic! The Mercedes V8 has electronically-controlled fuel injection and ignition systems, four camshafts, hydraulic tappets and 32 valves.

Suspension and brakes

Mercedes' suspension design has come a very long way since the days of the original 'Gullwing' SL family of the early 1950s. The 500 SL uses a complex strut system at the front, with lower wishbones and an anti-roll bar, with the coil springs and dampers mounted apart from each other – rather than, as is almost universal elsewhere, co-axially. The rear also uses separate coil springs, gas-filled telescopic dampers and an anti-roll bar, with location by the well-proven Mercedes multi-link system, with five control links per side and an optional self-levelling feature. The geometry incorporates anti-dive at the front and anti-squat and anti-lift at the rear, where there is also a small amount of

compliance in the bushing to promote stabilising rear-wheel toe-in when the SL is cornered hard. Steering is by power-assisted rack and pinion, and, as is traditional for Mercedes, the steering wheel is much too big. The brakes have solid rear discs and ventilated front discs which are almost a foot in diameter and work with four-pot calipers. ABS is standard and the wheel-locking sensors also double up to act as wheelspin sensors for an 'Acceleration Skid Control'.

Below: The rear suspension (left) uses five links to control wheel movement, and a limited-slip differential to reduce wheelspin. At the front (right) there are ventilated disc brakes and rack-and-pinion steering.

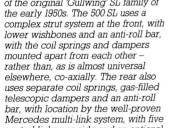

Catalysed exhaust

The car's emissions pollute the atmosphere as little as possible because there is a catalytic converter in the exhaust system. There is also a sensor which monitors the exhaust gases and adjusts the injection and ignition systems to give the lowest emissions.

Electronic speed limiter

Although there is enough power to make the car go faster, the top speed is electronically limited to around 155 mph because of safety considerations, such as the ability of the tyres to run at sustained very high speeds.

Variable inlet timing

The inlet camshafts automatically rotate to one of two different positions. At medium engine speeds, the inlet valves open earlier, helping the engine to give more torque. When the engine is idling, and when it is running at more than 4,500 rpm, the camshafts open the inlet valves slightly later.

Integral seat belt

The seat belt is built into the seat, so that the belt is always at the correct angle however the seat is adjusted. Each seat has five electric motors to move it fore and aft, and to adjust the backrest, the head restraint and the upper seat belt mounting point.

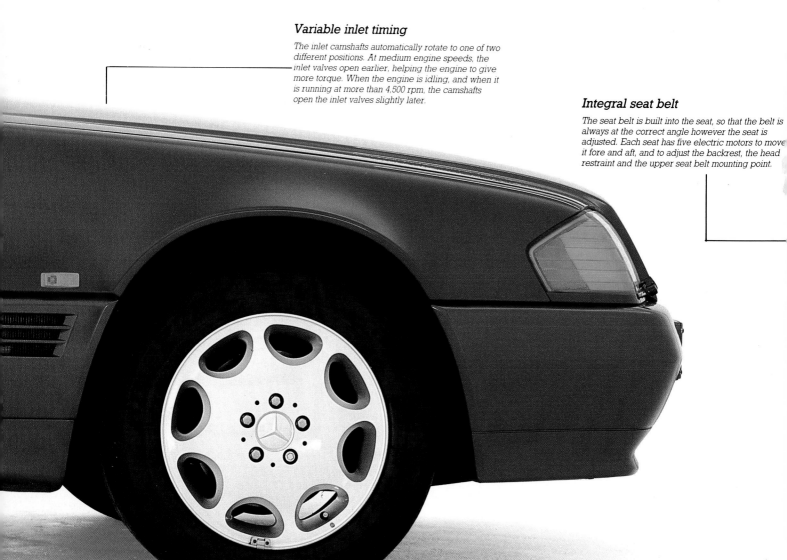

SPECIFICATION

1991 Mercedes 500 SL

ENGINE

Type:	V8, quad-cam, 32-valve
Construction:	light-alloy block and heads, five main bearings
Bore × stroke:	96.5 mm × 85.0 mm
Displacement:	4973 cc
Compression ratio:	10.0:1
Valve gear:	four valves per cylinder operated by twin overhead camshafts per bank of cylinders
Fuel system:	multi-point fuel injection
Ignition:	electronic
Maximum power:	326 bhp (DIN) at 5,500 rpm
Maximum torque:	332 lb ft at 4,000 rpm

TRANSMISSION

Type:	four-speed automatic	
Ratios:	1st	3.87:1
	2nd	2.25:1
	3rd	1.44:1
	4th	1.00:1
Final drive ratio:	2.65:1	

BODY/CHASSIS

Type:	unitary body/chassis assembly

RUNNING GEAR

Steering:	recirculating ball, power-assisted
Suspension:	front: independent with MacPherson struts and anti-roll bar rear: independent with multi-links, coil springs, telescopic dampers and anti-roll bar
Brakes:	ventilated discs front, solid discs rear
Wheels:	light-alloy, 8 in × 16 in
Tyres:	Dunlop D40 225/55 ZR16

DIMENSIONS AND WEIGHT

Length:	176.0 in (4470 mm)
Width:	71.3 in (1812 mm)
Height:	51.3 in (1303 m)
Wheelbase:	99.0 in (2515 mm)
Track:	60.4 in (1535 mm) front, 60.0 in (1523 mm) rear
Kerb weight:	4,167 lb (1890 kg)

PERFORMANCE

Acceleration:	0-30 mph 2.3 sec		
	0-40 mph 3.4 sec		
	0-50 mph 4.7 sec		
	0-60 mph 5.9 sec		
	0-70 mph 7.5 sec		
	0-80 mph 9.4 sec		
	0-90 mph 11.6 sec		
	0-100 mph 14.0 sec		
	0-110 mph 16.5 sec		
	0-120 mph 20.4 sec		
Standing ¼ mile:	14.4 sec		
Standing km:	25.3 sec		
Acceleration in gear:	mph	fourth	third
	60-80	–	4.2
	80-100	–	4.5
	100-120	7.8	–
	120-140	9.1	–
Maximum speed:	157 mph (253 km/h)		
Overall fuel consumption:	16.2 mpg		
Price (1991):	£70,090		

Performance figures from AUTOCAR & MOTOR

Mercedes 500 SL kindly supplied by Mercedes-Benz (United Kingdom) Ltd

Mercedes 500 SL Data File

There has been an SL (*Sport Leicht* or Light) in the Mercedes-Benz line-up since 1954 – the era of the 190 and 300 SL (the famous 'Gullwing'). The 190 and 300 SL were followed by a new generation of SLs in the early 1960s. Even by the introduction of this range in 1963 the 'Light' part of the SL equation had become a misnomer, as the weight of the sporting six-cylinder cars had grown considerably. In 1972 came the next generation of SLs – a large family that encompassed 340, 450, 380, 500 and 560 SL models, again with six-cylinder overhead-cam engines or aluminium-alloy V8s. This generation of cars lasted from 1972 until 1988 and was well overdue for a change by the time the present generation of SLs appeared. In addition to the 500 SL, the new range included two three-litre models – the 300 SL and the 300 SL-24 with, as its name suggests, 24 valves. Design and development lasted as much as 10 years because the brief was to produce as modern a car as possible, but one in the SL tradition and with recognisable links to the preceding generations. When the new 500 SL appeared, at the 1989 Geneva Motor Show, all those objectives had been realised.

Above: Mercedes design their cars with pedestrian safety in mind. There are no sharp edges at the front to injure people in an accident.

Styling

In styling the SLs, Bruno Sacco's team faced the challenge of following the best modern aerodynamic and safety thinking while evoking an SL line dating back to the 'Gullwing' of 1954. They aimed for a 'timeless' look, fresh and modern but without gimmicks. A long nose and squat roof line (hard and soft top) emphasise the power and give a hint of aggression, while the steeply-sloping grille starts a distinct wedge profile for optimum airflow. The three-pointed star on anodised louvres establishes the Mercedes identity, and the small vents in the wings evoke earlier SLs. The low aprons, contoured mirrors, recessed handles, near-flush glass and dirt-deflecting screen pillars all contribute to style with efficiency.

Above: The wind tunnel shows how the air flows smoothly over the car, making it more comfortable for the passengers when the top is down.

Below: A four-speed automatic gearbox is standard on the 500 SL. Note the built-in loudspeakers in front of the door pillar.

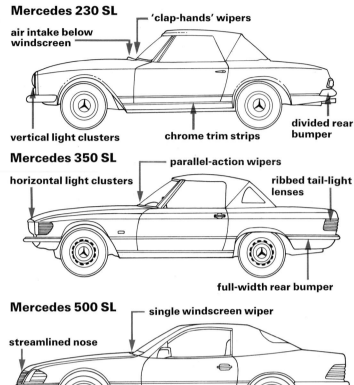

Mercedes 230 SL — 'clap-hands' wipers, air intake below windscreen, vertical light clusters, chrome trim strips, divided rear bumper

Mercedes 350 SL — parallel-action wipers, horizontal light clusters, ribbed tail-light lenses, full-width rear bumper

Mercedes 500 SL — single windscreen wiper, streamlined nose, air outlet, auxiliary lights in spoiler

Above: Like most other systems on the 500 SL, the hood is power-operated. The driver just pushes a button to make it go up or down.

High-tech trimmings

Basic engineering apart, two things above all underline just how committed Mercedes were to using modern technology. First, the seats not only incorporate a huge range of electrical adjustment but also the complete seat-belt system. They are built onto an immensely strong magnesium frame, and have five motors for 10-way adjustment, and pneumatic locking for the backrest tilt. The belts are built in because there are no true rear-door pillars to set the top belt mounting at the ideal height; the top mount on the seat adjusts automatically as the headrest is raised and lowered. The other high-profile feature is the automatic roll-over bar at the rear of the cockpit. If the car is about to have an accident, this springs up automatically in about 0.3 seconds – controlled by a network of sensors which detect sudden deceleration, over-large roll angles or severe suspension movement.

Below: The seat belt is built into the frame of the seat itself.

Below: A powerful hydraulic ram raises the roll-over bar.

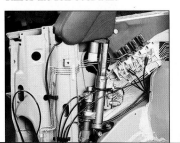

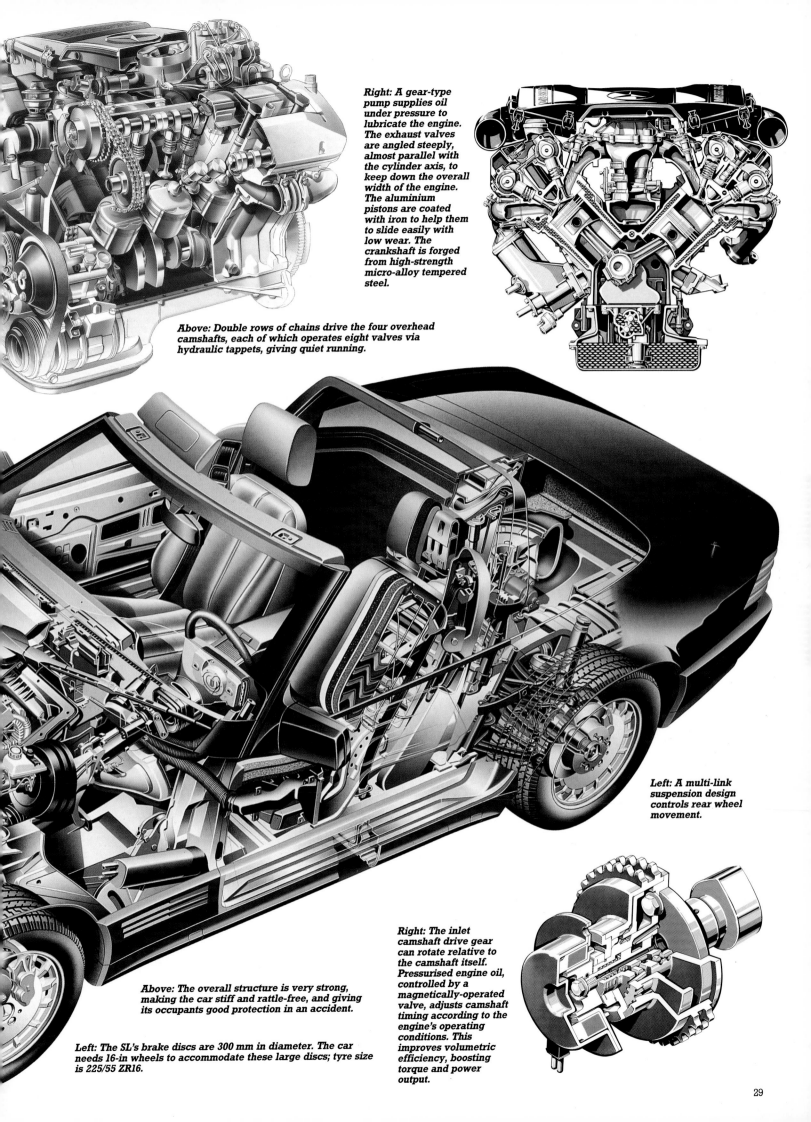

Right: A gear-type pump supplies oil under pressure to lubricate the engine. The exhaust valves are angled steeply, almost parallel with the cylinder axis, to keep down the overall width of the engine. The aluminium pistons are coated with iron to help them to slide easily with low wear. The crankshaft is forged from high-strength micro-alloy tempered steel.

Above: Double rows of chains drive the four overhead camshafts, each of which operates eight valves via hydraulic tappets, giving quiet running.

Left: A multi-link suspension design controls rear wheel movement.

Above: The overall structure is very strong, making the car stiff and rattle-free, and giving its occupants good protection in an accident.

Left: The SL's brake discs are 300 mm in diameter. The car needs 16-in wheels to accommodate these large discs; tyre size is 225/55 ZR16.

Right: The inlet camshaft drive gear can rotate relative to the camshaft itself. Pressurised engine oil, controlled by a magnetically-operated valve, adjusts camshaft timing according to the engine's operating conditions. This improves volumetric efficiency, boosting torque and power output.

Porsche
911 Turbo

Porsche's 911 Turbo was an unruly interloper among the supercar elite – stunningly quick, superbly engineered, but bad-mannered due to its anachronistic rear-engined layout. For 1991 it grew faster still, but more sophisticated too.

Dr Ernst Fuhrmann's original prediction in the early 1970s that it would be difficult to sell 500 911 Turbos (type 930) showed he was a better engineer than corporate strategist and was soon refuted in the marketplace.

Porsche needed to manufacture 500 of the Turbos during 1975 in order to race the type 934 and 935 derivatives the following year, but so rapturous was the public response that 1,300 were sold in the first 24 months! Demand has continued unabated, and some 15,000 of them will have been made in Zuffenhausen by the end of 1991.

Porsche's engineers wanted to offer the Turbo as a spartan, lightweight road-racer, a successor to the Carrera RSR 3.0, but Dr Fuhrmann reasoned that the customers, wealthy as they must be, would demand a luxury model. The Turbo was offered with leather upholstery, electric windows and air conditioning at an initial price of DM67,850 – nearly double the price of a 2.7-litre 911.

Porsche's goal was to dominate the World Championship for Manufacturers, the so-called 'silhouette formula' which came into being in 1976. The Group 5 racing car development, the 935, won the first title in 1976 after a tough battle with BMW, then dominated the series over the next three years.

The 935's crowning glory was to win the Le Mans 24 Hours in 1979, the Kremer K3-prepared car being the first production-derived car to win the classic for many a year, and the last. With equal ease the Group 4 derivative, the 934, so dominated the Grand Touring class that the European series was abandoned by the FIA at the end of 1978, and has never been revived.

Porsche's Turbo model has a platinum-plated pedigree, but what sort of car is it? Curiously old-fashioned in some ways, it's almost the antithesis of such modern rivals as the Ferrari Testarossa, the Lamborghini Diablo and even the Chevrolet Corvette ZR-1.

The German contender can never shake off the fact that the basic design was created over 25 years ago, even though a modernisation was carried out in 1988 and the latest, fastest, version appeared in 1991. Even the current model is unfashionably narrow inside the cabin, the windscreen is more upright than is usual nowadays, and the once-handsome dashboard is now a mess of switches and knobs that need to be learned, as a newly-blind person learns to read braille.

That's the first reaction, and it's a turn-off to some people with more than £70,000 to spend. But patience is rewarded. Just hear the solid 'thump' as the doors are closed. Just smell the leather upholstery . . . just flick the gear lever around, to appreciate what is now one of the most precise shifts in the sports car industry.

The new chassis, a modification of the greatly developed chassis used on the 911 Carrera 2, offers some benefits that aren't noticed straightaway. Extra space was afforded to move the 13-litre dry-sump oil tank forward, alongside the gearbox, and that released space for a fully-efficient exhaust system with three-way catalytic emission controls.

Significantly faster than before

The Turbo's weight rose, inevitably, by 10 per cent to 3,216 lb but this was offset by a gain of 20 horsepower, to 320 bhp. In the emission-controlled markets, however – most of the world, nowadays – the gain is greater, up to 315 from a previous 285 bhp, and the Turbo is significantly faster than before.

Polyurethane front and rear body sections improve the Turbo's aerodynamics and promote the 'family' look, in common with the 928 S4 and the four-cylinder 968, and the wheel diameter

Left: At the front, the latest 911 Turbo's elegantly remodelled looks give it a 'family' resemblance to other recent Porsches, including the mighty 959. The deep, body-colour bumper with neatly integrated wrap-around side/turn lights produces much purer lines than those of the old-style Turbo.

has now crept up to 17 inches, with the fitting of classic-looking forged-alloy rims shod with uni-directional, ultra-low-profile tyres.

Initially, the engine is a disappointment. The noise level is extremely low, the famous flat-six being partially encapsulated, then finally muffled by heavy silencing and an efficient, all-metal catalyser. Nor does the engine feel very flexible below 3,000 rpm, despite the promise of the written specification.

The brakes are simply astonishing . . .

Where conditions allow a full-throttle exercise, it's fascinating to see how quickly the white needle flicks around the face of the tachometer, transforming this luxurious cruiser into a lusty thoroughbred that wouldn't be disgraced if let loose on a racetrack.

When a four-speed gearbox was all that customers could have, it was offered as a virtue – so much torque, you see, you don't need to change gear very often . . . The introduction of the five-speed transmission can now be judged as an unmitigated blessing, closing up the spread of ratios and enhancing the sporting nature of the Turbo.

Power steering and power brakes would have been greeted as an abomination two decades ago, but so refined are the systems that

they suit the nature of the Turbo perfectly. The steering is extremely responsive and well-weighted, by no means featherweight, while the ABS-assisted, Brembo-calipered brakes are simply astonishing for their sheer power. The wide wheels and tyres offer levels of adhesion far beyond the normal limits on public highways, but the high bump-thump factor gives unwelcome harshness at low speeds.

That's easier to come to terms with now, as the 911 Turbo's other traditional faults have been smoothed away and many almost eliminated. The ergonomics may be as poor as always but the performance, which is the heart of the 911 Turbo, is far easier and safer to exploit, to the extent that the Turbo is now a far more usable supercar than some of its more exotic but more temperamental Italian rivals.

Above: The new back end has smoother, Carrera 2/4-style lines, too – apart from the wing.

Below: On the 1991-model Turbo, Porsche have tamed the rear-engined and naturally oversteering chassis' habit of brutal rear-end breakaway – so much so that the car now understeers gently until severely provoked, and lets go more controllably even then.

Porsche 911 Turbo

Larger intercooler

Above the engine, under that large tail, is mounted the KKK turbocharger's intercooler. It's larger than that used on the previous turbo and takes up most of the underbonnet space above the traditional flat-six's large cooling fan.

There has been a 911 Turbo in the Porsche line-up since the mid-1970s. Since then the basic design has been significantly revised and improved, with a view to making it more refined and sophisticated, safer and more user-friendly. The latest move in this policy of constant improvement is the 1991 Turbo. Although the current model shares the same basic rear-engined layout as all the preceding 911 Turbos, it is different in several important respects, most notably in having a chassis derived from that in the 911 Carrera 2. This makes the 911 Turbo's massive power output far more safe to use.

Air-cooled engine

Like all 911 power units before it, the latest 911 Turbo engine is air-cooled. There are no cooling problems, despite the engine being mounted at the rear and despite the greater underbonnet temperatures that are generated by a turbocharged powerplant.

'Whale-tail' rear spoiler

Although the rear spoiler is smaller and far less obvious than on previous 911 Turbos, it's still a large device capable of generating considerable rear downforce.

Rear-wheel steer

The latest chassis incorporates passive rear-wheel steer (rather than the active system of cars like the four-wheel-steer Honda Prelude). It's designed to keep the car more stable, both on the straight and through corners.

Above: Thanks to the 911's rearward weight bias, traction has always been a strongpoint, so the Turbo is more at home among ice and snow than most supercars. Even in its new, more civilised guise, however, with 320 bhp on tap it demands respect on slippery surfaces. On a dry road, let alone an icy one, lifting off the power abruptly will still result in lurid, tail-sliding oversteer, albeit not so uncatchably sudden as was once the case.

Driving the Turbo: *fast; less furious*

Silken the new 911 Turbo may be, but accelerating fiercely with the windows down confirms that it makes all the right noises! Snapping the throttle open is to command the launch of the car towards a far horizon in one breathtaking surge. First gear is good for 44 mph, reached in a mere 2.5 seconds, and second gear can see 76 mph. Sixty mph, the magic figure for road-testers, is reached in just 4.7 seconds, 100 mph in 11.4 seconds and 125 mph in 18 seconds. A standing quarter-mile can be accomplished without undue drama in just over 13 seconds.

In the right conditions, the determined driver will be able to see 170 mph on the speedo and he will not have to wait that long . . . Nor will he be worried about the car's hitherto fearsome behaviour. The latest revisions to the long-established design have produced a car that actually understeers at all the speeds most drivers use and has to be provoked into the oversteer that used to hang like a sword over 911 Turbo drivers. But if you still feel such performance is too much, there is the security of ABS-controlled Brembo disc brakes which bring you to a standstill from 60 mph in under three seconds and in a space of just 36 yards.

PERFORMANCE & SPECIFICATION COMPARISON	Engine	Displacement	Power	Torque (lb ft)	Max speed	0-60 mph	Length (in/mm)	Wheelbase (in/mm)	Track front/rear	Weight total (lb/kg)	Price
Porsche 911 Turbo	Flat-six, overhead-cam, turbo	3299 cc	320 bhp 5750 rpm	332 lb ft 4500 rpm	167 mph 269 km/h	4.7 sec	167.3 in 4249 mm	89.4 in 2271 mm	56.5 in 58.8 in	3216 lb 1459 kg	£74,580 (1991)
Chevrolet Corvette ZR-1	V8, quad-cam, 32-valve	5727 cc	375 bhp 5800 rpm	370 lb ft 4800 rpm	171 mph 275 km/h	5.6 sec	178.5 in 4534 mm	96.2 in 2443 mm	60.0 in 62.0 in	3519 lb 1596 kg	£58,995 (1990)
Ferrari Testarossa	Flat-12, quad-cam, 48-valve	4942 cc	390 bhp 6300 rpm	362 lb ft 4500 rpm	171 mph 275 km/h	5.2 sec	176.6 in 4485 mm	100.4 in 2550 mm	59.8 in 65.4 in	3675 lb 1667 kg	£115,500 (1991)
Honda NSX	V6, quad-cam, 24-valve	2977 cc	274 bhp 7000 rpm	210 lb ft 5300 rpm	162 mph 261 km/h	5.2 sec	173.4 in 4405 mm	99.6 in 2530 mm	59.4 in 60.2 in	3020 lb 1370 kg	£55,000 (1991)
Mercedes 500 SL	V8, quad-cam, 32-valve	4973 cc	326 bhp 5500 rpm	332 lb ft 4000 rpm	157 mph 253 km/h	5.9 sec	176.0 in 4470 mm	99.0 in 2515 mm	60.4 in 60.0 in	4167 lb 1890 kg	£70,090 (1991)

Porsche 911 Turbo Data File

P orsche's 356 model was a truly difficult act to follow. The company's reputation was founded on the four-cylinder sports car line, originally based on the Volkswagen Beetle (itself designed pre-war by Professor Porsche, assisted by his son 'Ferry'), although the VW ancestry was quickly despatched.

Dr Ferry Porsche commissioned the 356 replacement, and the earliest drawings by his son Ferdinand ('Butzi') date back to 1956. The type 7, as it was known at Zuffenhausen, would continue to offer 2+2 seating and a very sporting demeanour, but it would be quicker, quieter and more sophisticated.

Its heart would be a brand-new six-cylinder engine, air-cooled and with dry-sump lubrication. As before, the cylinders would be horizontally opposed, to keep the centre of gravity as low as possible.

The 901 was first seen at the Paris Motor Show in October 1963, but Peugeot claimed a right to the zero middle digits and the car went into production in September 1964 as the Porsche 911. Its first competition outing was at the Monte Carlo Rally in January 1965, when Herbert Linge and Peter Falk won the Grand Touring category and finished in fifth place overall.

Although the 911 was first and foremost a road car, it was homologated both as a GT car and as a Touring car (911T) and often won both categories in the same event in the 1960s. It was as much at home in rallies as on the tracks, as three Monte Carlo Rally successes show.

The significant developments in the 911's evolution were the introduction of the 911S (1966), the 2.2-litre engine (1969), the 2.4-litre engine (1971), the 2.7 Carrera RS (1972), the Carrera 3.0 and the Turbo (1974), the Turbo 3.3 (1977), the 911 Cabriolet (1982), the Carrera 3 (1983), the Carrera 4 (1988) and the Carrera 2 (1989).

Above: 911 Turbo styling changed little from the earliest 1970s cars to the last, prior to the complete updating in late 1990.

Styling

Ferdinand Alexander 'Butzi' Porsche is not rated as one of the world's top automotive stylists, but his 911 design has stood the test of time. The greatest compliment of all was paid by the Porsche company in 1988 when the 911 Carrera 4 model was introduced, a quarter of a century after the 901 made its debut at Frankfurt. Given the chance to change everything, Porsche chose to keep the style virtually unchanged. "Our customers would not have forgiven us if we made major changes," said Porsche's chairman of the time, Heinz Branitzki.

The width has increased, of course, with the fitment of modern tyres. The original 911 model ran on 4.5-in rims and 165-section tyres, and had an overall width of 63.4 inches. The

modern Turbo has 7-in wide rims at the front, 9-in at the rear, on 205- and 255-section tyres. Not surprisingly, the overall width of the 911 'flagship' model has increased to 69.8 inches.

Superficially the cars of 1964 and 1991 are very similar in appearance, although very few parts would be interchangeable. Above the waist, though, the cars are almost identical, save for the specification of the glass, and the fixing of swivelling quarter-lights. Optional for many years, the 'black look' (i.e., no chrome or brightwork) is now de rigueur.

Below: Latest and previous-pattern 911 Turbo noses together show the change in the frontal styling.

Above: There's no separate air dam in the new front design (seen already on the Carrera 4 and 2); the bumper simply extends downwards into an integral spoiler/apron with air intakes.

Below: The new Carrera 2/4-style Turbo (lower drawing) looks much less fussy than the 1974 Carrera RSR that set the original trend.

1974 Porsche 911 RSR

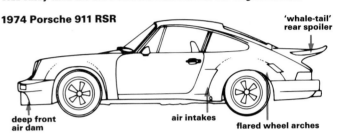

'whale-tail' rear spoiler

deep front air dam

air intakes

flared wheel arches

1991 Porsche 911 Turbo

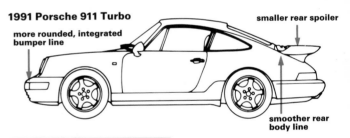

more rounded, integrated bumper line

smaller rear spoiler

smoother rear body line

Above: The wing houses the intercooler, hence the vents.

Below: Under that bulging rear arch lurks a 255/40 ZR17 tyre.

Below: Inside the 911 Turbo, fittings and trim are of excellent quality, but control and instrument ergonomics are still poor.

SPECIFICATION

1991 Porsche 911 Turbo

ENGINE

Type:	flat-six, longitudinally rear-mounted
Bore × stroke:	97 mm × 74 mm
Displacement:	3299 cc
Compression ratio:	7.0:1
Valve gear:	two valves per cylinder, operated by single overhead camshaft per bank of cylinders
Fuel system:	Bosch K-Jetronic fuel injection with single KKK turbocharger boosting at a maximum of 0.75 bar
Ignition:	electronic
Maximum power:	320 bhp at 5,750 rpm
Maximum torque:	332 lb ft at 4,500 rpm

TRANSMISSION

Type:	five-speed manual, with limited-slip differential	
Ratios:	1st	3.15:1
	2nd	1.79:1
	3rd	1.27:1
	4th	0.97:1
	5th	0.76:1
Final drive ratio:	3.44:1	

BODY/CHASSIS

Type:	integral chassis/body with two-door coupé body

RUNNING GEAR

Steering:	rack and pinion, power-assisted
Suspension:	front: independent front with MacPherson struts, lower wishbones and anti-roll bar rear: independent with semi-trailing arms, coil springs and anti-roll bar
Brakes:	ventilated discs; 12.6-in (320-mm) diameter front, 11.8-in (299-mm) diameter rear
Wheels:	cast-alloy, 7 in × 17 in front, 9 in × 17 in rear
Tyres:	205/50 ZR17 front, 255/40 ZR17 rear

DIMENSIONS AND WEIGHT

Length:	167.3 in (4249 mm)
Width:	69.8 in (1773 mm)
Height:	51.5 in (1308 mm)
Wheelbase:	89.4 in (2271 mm)
Track:	56.5 in (1434 mm) front, 58.8 in (1493 mm) rear
Kerb weight:	3,216 lb (1459 kg)

PERFORMANCE

Acceleration:	0-30 mph 2.0 sec
	0-40 mph 2.7 sec
	0-50 mph 3.7 sec
	0-60 mph 4.7 sec
	0-70 mph 6.0 sec
	0-80 mph 7.8 sec
	0-90 mph 9.5 sec
	0-100 mph 11.4 sec
	0-110 mph 13.9 sec
	0-120 mph 16.7 sec
	0-130 mph 20.0 sec
	0-140 mph 24.8 sec
Standing ¼ mile:	13.3 sec

Acceleration in gear:	mph	fifth	fourth	third
	30-50	10.7	7.1	4.4
	40-60	10.0	6.1	3.5
	50-70	9.0	5.9	3.1

Maximum speed:	167 mph (269 km/h)
Overall fuel consumption:	15.1 mpg
Price (1991):	£74,580

Performance figures from AUTOCAR

Porsche 911 Turbo kindly supplied by Porsche (Great Britain) Ltd

-litre six-cylinder turbo

ough Porsche had a new 3.6-litre twin-spark
ne available, it was decided that the old 3.3-litre
ne could provide adequate power. In its latest
, with a single KKK turbocharger, it produces
e power than before – 320 bhp at 5,750 rpm.

Ultra-low-profile tyres

To help tame the 911 Turbo's near-170-mph
performance, it's fitted with extremely low-profile,
high-performance tyres, of 205/50 ZR17-section on
the front wheels and wider 255/40 ZR17-section on
the back.

Power-assisted steering

Although the bulk of the 911 Turbo's weight is over
the rear wheels, the front tyres have become so
large on the current model that power assistance is
needed to help the steering.

Front-mounted spare wheel

The spare wheel is carried at the front, helping to
balance (albeit fractionally) weight distribution. With
the engine being air-cooled, there's not even a
radiator to offset the weight of the rear-mounted
powerplant.

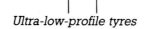

Ventilated discs all round

The 911 Turbo has braking that wouldn't disgrace an
endurance racing car. Its disc brakes are huge
affairs, the fronts with a diameter of over a foot, and
ventilated to provide good performance under the
hardest use. ABS is standard.

Chassis

Until recently, the 911 models have had a reputation for difficult handling. As fast as Porsche's engineers wrung improvements out of the chassis, other cars came along to set new standards, often at a fraction of the cost.

The location of the six-cylinder engine, overhung behind the rear wheels, continued Porsche's pre-war philosophy and had some advantages, for instance in traction, but it was always a battle to make the car vice-free and safe for less experienced drivers. The original 911 was so tricky that the designers even resorted to putting lead in the front body recesses, to improve weight distribution.

Extending the wheelbase by 57 mm in 1968 was a significant development, while Pirelli's famous P7 tyre was developed specifically for the 911 Turbo model. It was unavailable for the first few months of Turbo production in 1975 and the early versions, on rounded Cinturato tyres, were decidedly difficult to handle.

The original philosophy of long suspension travel and narrow tyres as a means of controlling camber change took a long time to die, and the Cinturato-equipped Turbo was probably the last really wild Porsche.

A further increase in wheelbase, with the 3.3-litre model in 1977, made a minor contribution to handling improvement, although the main purpose was to introduce a new, quieter, clutch disc centre, and to allow for the extra weight of the intercooler.

There matters rested until the current Turbo (type 964) was introduced in 1991. It is based on the Carrera 2 chassis platform, which has very different suspension, using MacPherson struts with coil springs at the front and a much more sophisticated semi-trailing-arm design at the rear.

Below: A 911 body assembly makes its way through the paint shop at the Stuttgart factory; Porsche build-quality is second to none.

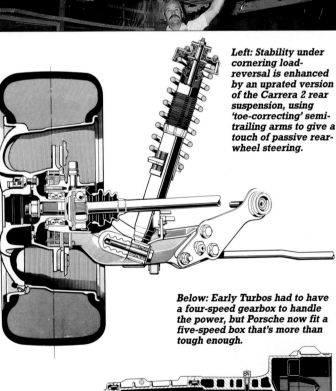

Left: Stability under cornering load-reversal is enhanced by an uprated version of the Carrera 2 rear suspension, using 'toe-correcting' semi-trailing arms to give a touch of passive rear-wheel steering.

Below: Early Turbos had to have a four-speed gearbox to handle the power, but Porsche now fit a five-speed box that's more than tough enough.

Engine

With a rating of 320 bhp (235 kW) from 3299 cc, Porsche's Turbo engine is by no means highly-stressed. It is, however, a supremely practical power unit which delivers a huge chunk of power smoothly from 3,000 rpm to 6,500 rpm, guaranteeing maximum overtaking capability with the minimum of fuss.

Porsche's six-cylinder 'boxer' engine has proved to be the most versatile power unit of modern times. In the space of 27 years it has been developed from two litres and 130 bhp to 3.6 litres with double the original power, 260 bhp, in the Carrera 2 and 4 models, without the benefit of turbocharging.

It has powered an airship, and is fully certificated to power light aircraft. With turbochargers, the flat-six has yielded more than 800 bhp and won countless championships around the world, most significantly 10 class victories at Le Mans.

The technology of turbocharging was learned by Porsche's Weissach engineers in CanAm racing, with the flat-12 917-10 and 917-30 sports car

engines, and it was one inevitable step from there to the application of turbo techniques to passenger cars.

The introduction of the Porsche 911 Turbo (type 930) caused a minor sensation at the Paris Motor Show in October 1974. A single KKK turbocharger boosted the power of the three-litre engine to 260 bhp, despite a lowered compression ratio of 6.5:1, and the car was brutally fast despite the fitment of a four-speed gearbox (the torque figure of 253 lb ft at 4,000 rpm was simply too much for the 911's five-speed transmission).

Three years later, in the autumn of 1977 (for the 1978 model), the engine capacity was increased to 3.3 litres and the power to 300 bhp, while the torque figure rose to 304 lb ft. The cylinder bore was increased from 95 to 97 mm and the stroke from 70.4 to 74.4 mm, for a capacity of 3299 cc.

The addition of an intercooler to the specification, underneath the 'whale-tail' wing on the engine cover, cooled the charged air and improved thermal efficiency, and the compression ratio was increased to 7.0:1.

There were no other significant changes until the current version, based on the Carrera 2 chassis, was introduced in 1991.

Left: On the 911 Turbo production line, meticulous final assembly of the light-alloy, air-cooled 3.3-litre flat-six is done by hand.

Above: For many years 911s used struts with torsion-bar front springs. Nowadays, you find conventional coil-spring MacPherson struts, with lower wishbones, a substantial anti-roll bar and negative-offset geometry. As ever, the result is firm springing and high roll stiffness.

Above: The negative-scrub-radius geometry combines with a new, power-assisted steering rack damp out the excessive road-surface feedback that was a minor flaw of previous 911s. The power assistance enables the steering ratio to be kept high without the wide, 205/50-section front tyres now fitt making it excessively heavy, and still gives good sensitivity.

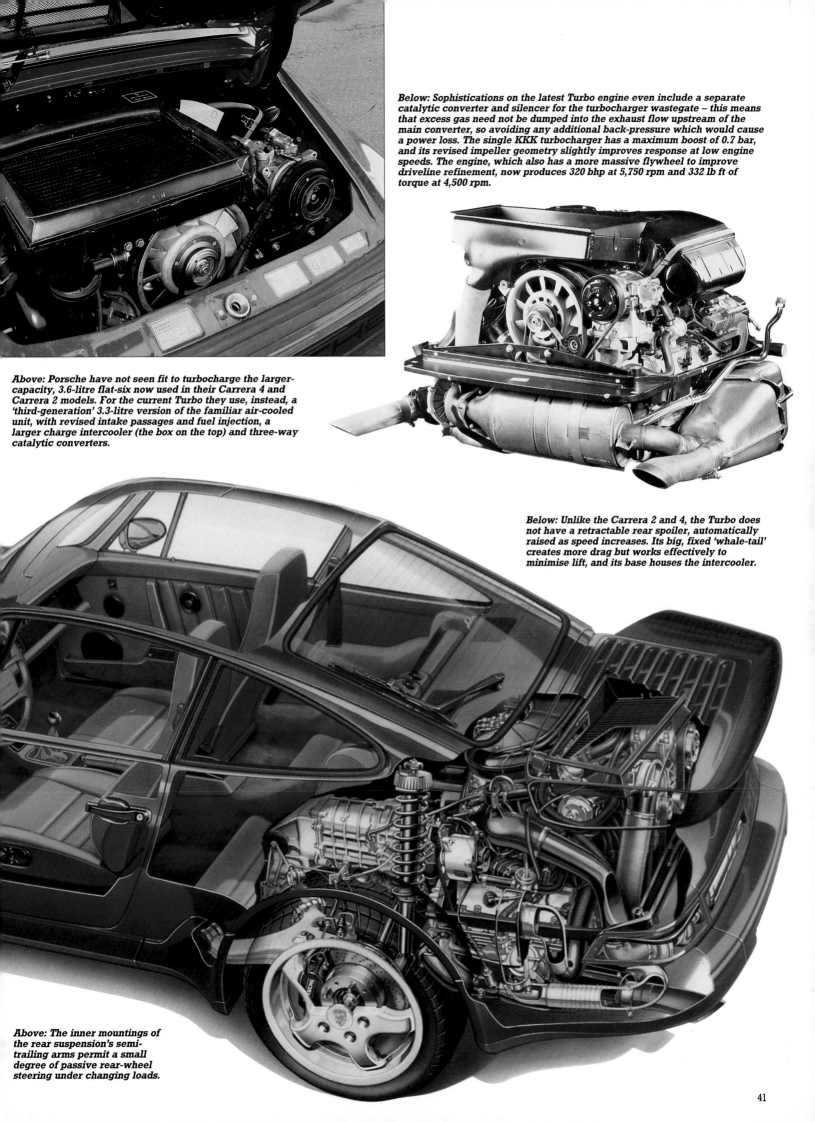

Below: Sophistications on the latest Turbo engine even include a separate catalytic converter and silencer for the turbocharger wastegate – this means that excess gas need not be dumped into the exhaust flow upstream of the main converter, so avoiding any additional back-pressure which would cause a power loss. The single KKK turbocharger has a maximum boost of 0.7 bar, and its revised impeller geometry slightly improves response at low engine speeds. The engine, which also has a more massive flywheel to improve driveline refinement, now produces 320 bhp at 5,750 rpm and 332 lb ft of torque at 4,500 rpm.

Above: Porsche have not seen fit to turbocharge the larger-capacity, 3.6-litre flat-six now used in their Carrera 4 and Carrera 2 models. For the current Turbo they use, instead, a 'third-generation' 3.3-litre version of the familiar air-cooled unit, with revised intake passages and fuel injection, a larger charge intercooler (the box on the top) and three-way catalytic converters.

Below: Unlike the Carrera 2 and 4, the Turbo does not have a retractable rear spoiler, automatically raised as speed increases. Its big, fixed 'whale-tail' creates more drag but works effectively to minimise lift, and its base houses the intercooler.

Above: The inner mountings of the rear suspension's semi-trailing arms permit a small degree of passive rear-wheel steering under changing loads.

41

Ferrari F40

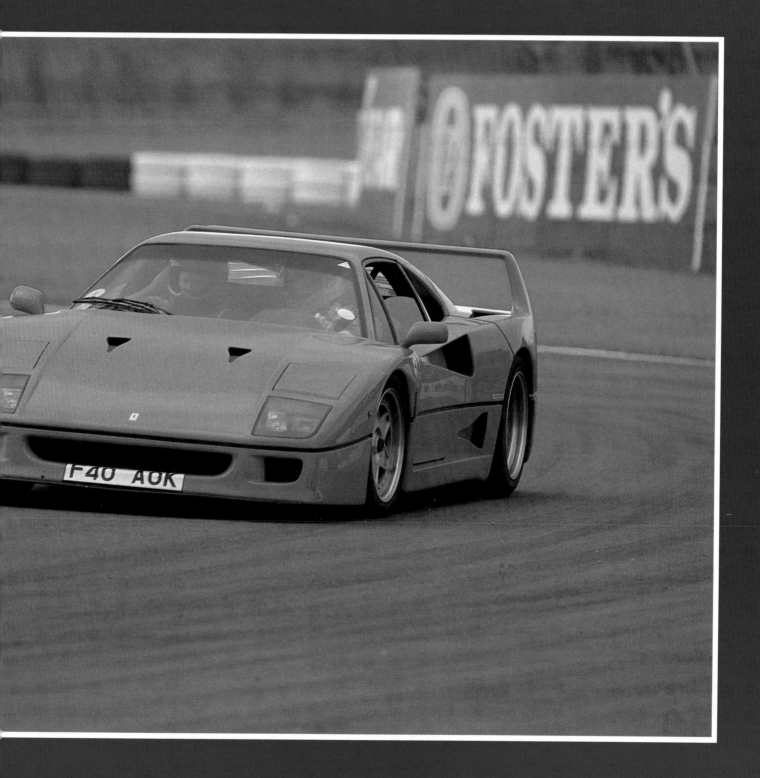

Enzo Ferrari wanted to build a special car to celebrate the 40th anniversary of the very first Ferrari, which left the factory in 1947. The resulting 200-mph F40 set new standards for supercar performance.

A mid all the euphoria that greeted the Ferrari F40's launch four years ago, there was a gentle undercurrent of reservation. In comparison with the technologically masterful 959, went the argument, the F40 was an unadventurous concept being sold at an ambitious price. How could Ferrari claim to be at the forefront of high-performance car design when the F40 did not even have anti-lock brakes, let alone four-wheel drive?

Ferrari had set out not to create a technological tour de force, but to build the most pure track-inspired sports car the world had ever seen. The F40 contains state-of-the-art engineering that has been directed towards the single-minded aim of packing prodigious power into a lightweight car. Thanks to the advanced use of composite materials (including carbonfibre) for its body and chassis, it weighs little more than a ton. On this super-rigid platform sits a twin-turbocharged 2.9-litre V8 engine producing 478 bhp. That made it the most powerful production engine ever developed for a road car before the Lamborghini Diablo appeared on the scene.

. . . power output of 478 bhp at 7,000 rpm

The F40 is a direct descendant of the 288 GTO, Ferrari's first attempt to build a limited-edition supercar. Launched at the Geneva Motor Show in 1984, the GTO – which took its name from the famous *Gran Turismo Omologato* model of the early 1960s – was a fascinating hybrid of road and race technology inspired by FISA's new Group B racing regulations, but, as it turned out, was never raced by the factory nor its customers.

The GTO's tubular steel chassis was nothing special, but parts of the body benefitted from knowledge gained in Formula 1 by Dr Harvey Postlethwaite, the English designer who gave Ferrari its first composite Formula 1 chassis in 1982.

The most advanced application of Postlethwaite's expertise was the bulkhead between engine and passenger compartment. Formed of an aluminium honeycomb core clad on each side with a layer of Kevlar/glassfibre composite, this bulkhead acts as a rigid structural member, an insulating barrier and a firewall. Kevlar/Nomex composite, a remarkable blend of lightness and strength, was used for the roof panel, the rear deck and the front luggage lid; this last piece, weighing only seven pounds, is so light that it cannot be slammed shut.

The GTO had its motor mounted longitudinally, Formula 1 style, in line with a five-speed transaxle extending behind the rear axle line. A pair of Japanese IHI turbos, chosen in preference to the German KKKs used in Formula 1 because of their performance across the full engine range, endowed the GTO's engine with formidable punch; an output of 400 bhp at 7,000 rpm made it the most powerful roadgoing car Ferrari had ever produced and gave figures of 0-100 km/h (62.1 mph) in 4.9 seconds, the standing quarter-mile in 12.7 seconds and a top speed of 189.5 mph. At around £90,000 a time, it proved to be so easy to sell the 200 cars required for Group B homologation that Ferrari yielded to temptation and built a few more, the final total running out at 278.

This level of interest so amazed Ferrari's senior executives that the decision to build an even more awe-inspiring successor was made a few months later.

On the face of it, the F40 was developed in a remarkably short time, just over a year elapsing between the official go-ahead and the car's press

Above: Even in the wet, the F40 can be driven safely at speeds which would see most cars spinning off into the scenery.

launch on 21 July 1987. In fact, most of the work had already been accomplished on an interim car called the GTO Evoluzione.

The F40 engine differed from the GTO's in having a wider bore of 3.23 in and shorter stroke of 2.74 in to produce even more 'over-square' dimensions. Maximum boost pressure was reduced to 1.1 bar, and with emission controls the F40's power output settled at 478 bhp at 7,000 rpm – enough to make it Ferrari's most powerful production engine ever.

That power output was not hampered by weight. The F40's body is made up from 12 pieces of Kevlar/carbonfibre/glassfibre composite.

Three times more rigid, yet weighs less

The chassis is a separate unit that essentially takes the form of a simple steel spaceframe incorporating bonded composite panels to endow greater strength. The complete structure, Ferrari reckons, is three times more rigid than a conventional steel frame would have been, yet weighs 20 per cent less. Tubular steel forms a passenger cage with outriggers to carry the engine/gearbox and suspension.

The F40 can exceed 200 mph in top gear, and cover the standing quarter-mile in 11.9 seconds. With off-the-line acceleration of 0-100 mph in 8.8 seconds and 0-150 mph in 18.5 seconds, it is no wonder that it has become the most sought-after of modern Ferraris.

Below: Ferrari developed conventional winding side windows which can be specified as an alternative to the sliding type seen above.

Right: At speed, the F40's aerodynamic shape keeps it glued to the road.

Ferrari F40

Many early Ferrari production cars could also be used in competition; there was a very thin dividing line between the two roles, particularly with models like the 250 GT SWB. Over the years, Ferrari road cars became luxury, very high-speed, sports cars rather than the competition machines the marque had started with. The F40 was a return to Ferrari's roots in being as much of a racing car as modern regulations would allow on the road, as well as a celebration of 40 years of Ferrari production. The F40 was a development of a genuine racing car, the 288 GTO, albeit one which never raced. . .

Oil-cooler air exit

The shark-like vents at the back of the F40 enable the cooling air ducted to the oil coolers to escape.

Ground-effect technology?

The rear styling of the F40 gives the impression that — there are two underbody venturis, or tunnels, to create extra downforce, as found on Group C endurance racers. In fact the F40's downforce is generated by the upper body profile and rear wing.

window echoes an idea ni Miura, which also had difference is that the

Brake cooling duct

The lower, NACA, duct ahead of the rear wheel is just one of 13 on the F40. It feeds cooling air to the large rear vented disc brakes.

Inverted aerofoil rear wing

Downforce at the rear of the F40 is created with the use of an inverted aerofoil-section rear wing. It looks like an integral part of the whole rear structure but is a separate piece bolted to it.

Slatted rear wind

The slatted Plexiglass re first seen on the Lambor a slatted engine cover. F40's is transparent.

Three-litre twin-turbo V8 engine

The F40 is powered by a mid-mounted V8 with four valves per cylinder, four belt-driven overhead camshafts, twin IHI intercooled turbochargers and a huge power output of 478 bhp at 7,000 rpm.

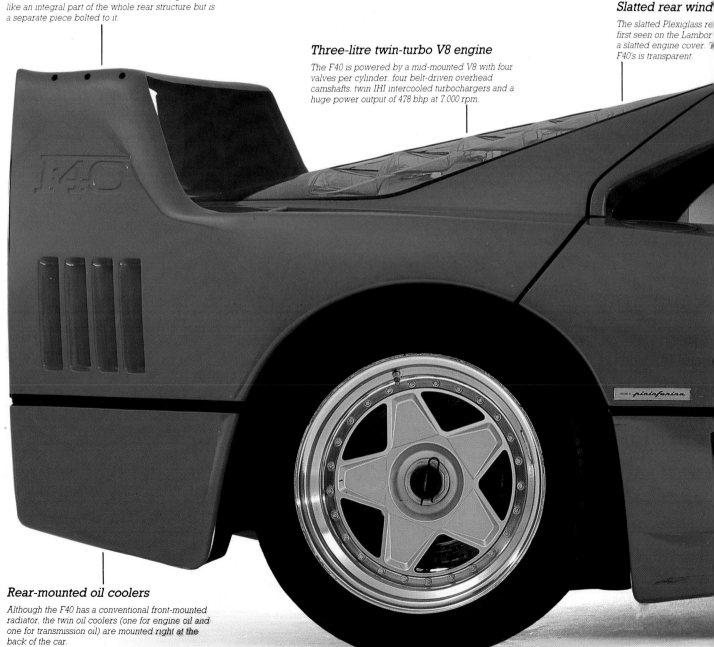

Rear-mounted oil coolers

Although the F40 has a conventional front-mounted radiator, the twin oil coolers (one for engine oil and one for transmission oil) are mounted right at the back of the car.

Above: The overall shape of the F40 mirrors current racing car practice. The basic wedge shape – low at the front, high at the rear – gives good aerodynamic penetration and helps to create downforce for better cornering. The rear wing smooths the airflow around the tail of the car and also generates downforce. The air inlets in the body are designed to take in the maximum amount of air while creating as little turbulence as possible.

Driving the F40: *ultimate road racer*

From the first moment you squeeze yourself into the F40's cockpit, you have no doubt that you are in the ultimate racing car for the road.

The heavy clutch bites sweetly and progressively, and the steering is pleasantly light even at a crawl. The brakes, however, require such a mighty push before the pads and discs reach operating temperature that you wonder for an instant, as the back of the lorry in front looms large, whether they work at all. Designed for three-figure cornering speeds, the suspension's kart-like stiffness gives a jarring ride over urban roads.

Flex your right foot on the throttle, and there's a blur of mind-numbing acceleration. The power is truly explosive, arriving with a ferocity that no other road car can match. The 0-60 mph sprint in 4.5 seconds sounds fine on paper, but the margin in reality is almost unimaginably massive between this figure and the 5-6 second bracket of lesser supercars.

Despite the huge 335/35 rear tyres, the wheels can spin in second, third and even fourth gears on all but the smoothest roads. Serious recalibration of your senses is needed to adjust to this Ferrari street-racer's outrageous performance.

PERFORMANCE & SPECIFICATION COMPARISON	Engine	Displacement	Power	Torque (lb ft)	Max speed	0-60 mph	Length (in/mm)	Wheelbase (in/mm)	Track front/rear	Weight total (lb/kg)	Price
Ferrari F40	V8, quad-cam, 32-valve, twin-turbo	2936 cc	478 bhp 7000 rpm	425 lb ft 4000 rpm	201 mph 323 km/h	4.5 sec	171.6 in 4358 mm	96.5 in 2450 mm	62.8 in 63.2 in	2425 lb 1100 kg	£197,502 (1991)
Aston Martin Virage	V8, quad-cam	5340 cc	330 bhp 6000 rpm	340 lb ft 3700 rpm	157 mph 253 km/h	6.8 sec	184.5 in 4686 mm	100.7 in 2558 mm	55.0 in 56.3 in	4295 lb 1948 kg	£125,000 (1990)
Honda NSX	V6, quad-cam, 24-valve	2977 cc	274 bhp 7000 rpm	210 lb ft 5300 rpm	162 mph 261 km/h	5.2 sec	173.4 in 4405 mm	99.6 in 2530 mm	59.4 in 60.2 in	3020 lb 1370 kg	£55,000 (1991)
Lamborghini Diablo	V12, quad-cam, 48-valve	5729 cc	492 bhp 7000 rpm	428 lb ft 5200 rpm	205 mph 330 km/h	4.2 sec	175.6 in 4460 mm	104.3 in 2650 mm	60.6 in 64.6 in	3474 lb 1576 kg	£158,370 (1991)
Porsche 959	Flat-six, quad-cam, 24-valve, twin-turbo	2851 cc	450 bhp 6500 rpm	370 lb ft 5500 rpm	190 mph 306 km/h	3.6 sec	167.7 in 4260 mm	89.4 in 2272 mm	59.2 in 61.0 in	3197 lb 1450 kg	£160,000 (1987)

Ferrari F40 Data File

T he F40 was inspired by two things: the desire not to be outdone by Porsche in producing the world's fastest roadgoing car (it was stretching things a little to call the Porsche 959 a production car), and the requirement for something really special to celebrate 40 years of Ferrari car production (the 125 had been launched on 12 March 1947). The story has it that Enzo Ferrari wanted something in the mould of one of his favourite older Ferraris – the 250 LM, 'LM' standing for Le Mans. In other words what he wanted was a roadgoing supercar as near to a race car as possible, "a byword for technological excellence and exceptional performance". In the shape of Ferrari's short-lived Group B car, the 288 GTO, and its GTO Evoluzione development, Ferrari had just the foundation for a car to meet both requirements, but with the emphasis more on performance than technology.

Above: Bred on the track, at home on the track. Before its launch, the F40 was speed-tested at circuits in Fiorano, Nardo and Balocco.

Styling

Since much of the F40's development work had been achieved on the GTO Evoluzione, the toughest task in the 12-month timetable between the F40's official go-ahead and launch fell to Pininfarina. By any modern standards, this was a tight schedule for the design of a completely new body style, but one which a generation ago, at the time of spiritual F40 ancestors like the SWB and GTO, would have seemed generous. Years ago, Ferraris used to be created in less than a year.

Pininfarina broke with normal practice by shaping the car directly in model form. The usual procedure would be to clarify the design during sketch work, present a finished set of renderings for Ferrari's approval of the basic shape, make full-scale section drawings, and finally build a full-scale model. The F40, however, was designed in three dimensions on a polyurethane foam model, using only basic sketch work as reference. It was a risky approach, perhaps, but one which Pininfarina's designers, with 30

years' experience, and Ferrari were willing to take.

In a sense, the restrictions in the brief – this job was essentially to give an existing car a smart new suit of clothes – removed many of the choices which take up design time. The GTO Evoluzione was an ugly brute, its wings, cooling apertures and appendages the pragmatic result of three years of testing. A designer had never been near it.

Pininfarina's brief was to design new front and rear sections for the car, but to leave the central passenger cell unaltered. There was room within these constraints to adopt styling cues from Ferraris of the past, such as the three chin-level air intakes at the front (a large central opening for the radiator and smaller ducts on each side to the brakes), echoing the 'face' of countless racing Ferraris of the past. In addition, the full-width wing at the back conjures up the 312P, Ferrari's sports-prototype racer of the early 1970s.

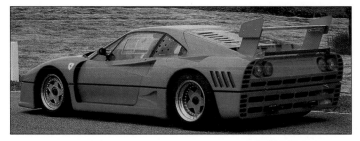

Above: The GTO Evoluzione was a mobile test-bed for the F40, and was never intended for production.

Below: Powerful engines need lots of air to keep them cool, hence the vented cover.

Above: Many mid-engined cars have a vertical rear window and a horizontal engine cover, but Ferrari used a sloping window, slotted for engine cooling, which gives less turbulence.

Left: Hot air from the brakes (and spray from a wet road) flow through the slot in front of the door. Earlier cars had the mirror mounted on the quarter-light.

Below: Yet another air intake – the F40 has 13 altogether. This one is for the gearbox oil cooler.

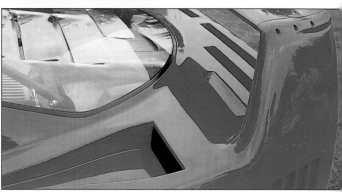

Aerodynamics

Wind-tunnel evaluation on the F40 model proceeded smoothly, most of the effort going into balancing the requirements of drag (a 200 mph top speed demanded a maximum Cd of 0.34) and downforce. One or two radical aerodynamic possibilities were tried, the most distinctive being the fitting of spats to conceal the rear wheels. These would have produced a small increase in top speed, but the practical problems – such as the inhibited flow of cool air to the rear brakes and the difficulty of changing a wheel – dictated their rejection.

The main change, in terms of aerodynamic performance, from the GTO Evoluzione was to give the rear window area a very rounded profile in plan view. Compared with the GTO Evoluzione's flat rear window, the F40's design provides a cleaner airflow over the rear of the car,

allowing the wing to work more efficiently and reducing the extent of aerodynamically undesirable turbulence in the car's wake. Beneath the tail, the tapered profile of the underbody channels on either side of the gearbox provides a small measure of ground effect.

Virtually every aspect of the F40's exterior design is dictated by function. There are 13 intakes to feed air to the intercoolers, to radiators for water, engine oil and gearbox oil, to all four brakes, and into the cabin. Slots on the rear wings, in the rear window and on the flat surface of the rear deck allow hot air to be expelled from the engine compartment, while even the tail panel is a black mesh insert to provide extra cooling. The only external feature with no functional significance is the thin black line running round the car at hip level.

Below: In the wind tunnel, woollen tufts show whether the air is flowing smoothly or whether there is unwanted turbulence.

SPECIFICATION
Ferrari F40

ENGINE

Type:	V8, longitudinally mounted
Construction:	light-alloy block and heads, five main bearings, nickel-coated alloy cylinder liners, dry-sump lubrication
Bore × stroke:	3.23 in × 2.74 in (82.0 mm × 69.5 mm)
Displacement:	2936 cc
Compression ratio:	7.7:1
Valve gear:	four valves per cylinder operated at 46-degree angle by twin belt-driven overhead camshafts per bank of cylinders
Ignition and fuel system:	two Weber-Marelli integral ignition-injection systems (one per bank)
Turbocharging:	two IHI RHB 53LW turbochargers
Maximum boost pressure:	16.1 psi (1.1 bar)
Maximum power:	478 bhp at 7,000 rpm
Maximum torque:	425 lb ft at 4,000 rpm

TRANSMISSION

Type:	five-speed manual with limited-slip differential, mounted in line with engine	
Ratios:	1st	2.769:1
	2nd	1.722:1
	3rd	1.227:1
	4th	0.962:1
	5th	0.766:1
Final drive ratio:	2.727:1	
Clutch:	Borg & Beck dry double-plate, hydraulically actuated	

BODY/CHASSIS

Type:	separate steel tube chassis frame with bonded structural composite panels in carbonfibre/Nomex/Kevlar honeycomb; composite coupé body in carbonfibre/glassfibre/Kevlar

RUNNING GEAR

Steering:	rack and pinion
Suspension:	front: independent with double wishbones, coil spring/damper units and anti-roll bar rear: independent with double wishbones, coil spring/damper units and anti-roll bar
Brakes:	ventilated cast-iron/aluminium discs front and rear, without servo-assistance, 12.9-in (330-mm) diameter
Wheels:	light-alloy Speedline split-rims, 8 in × 17 in front, 13 in × 17 in rear
Tyres:	Pirelli P Zero, 245/40 ZR17 front, 335/35 ZR17 rear

DIMENSIONS AND WEIGHT

Length:	171.6 in (4358 mm)
Width:	77.6 in (1970 mm)
Height:	44.3 in (1124 mm)
Wheelbase:	96.5 in (2450 mm)
Track:	62.8 in (1594 mm) front, 63.2 in (1606 mm) rear
Turning circle:	38.1 ft (11.6 m)
Kerb weight:	2,425 lb (1100 kg)

PERFORMANCE

Acceleration:	0-30 mph 2.2 sec
	0-40 mph 2.7 sec
	0-50 mph 3.3 sec
	0-60 mph 4.5 sec
	0-70 mph 5.3 sec
	0-80 mph 6.1 sec
	0-90 mph 7.2 sec
	0-100 mph 8.8 sec
	0-110 mph 10.0 sec
	0-120 mph 11.5 sec
	0-130 mph 13.6 sec
	0-140 mph 16.0 sec
	0-150 mph 18.5 sec
Standing km:	20.9 sec
Maximum speed:	201 mph (323 km/h)
Fuel consumption:	15.35 mpg (urban), 32.85 mpg (56 mph), 27.43 mpg (75 mph)
Price (1991):	£197,502

Performance figures from ROAD & TRACK

Ferrari F40 kindly supplied by Ten Tenths

Triple exhaust pipes

Given that the F40 is a V8-engined car, the presence of three exhausts is a little confusing. The mystery is cleared up when it is learned that the centre exhaust is for the excess turbo boost which is bled off through the wastegates.

Triple air intakes

The main, wide front air intake is for the front-mounted water radiator, while the two smaller outboard ducts are provided to feed air to the massive ventilated front disc brakes.

ntral steel cage

er the ultra-lightweight composite body panels
e is a central steel frame or cage which
des a rigid structure for passenger protection.
milar to the traditional spaceframe approach
pt that the F40 uses various lower internal
osite body panels firmly bonded to the steel, to
de extra stiffness.

Wind-up windows

It might seem obvious that a car the price of an F40 would have electric windows, but in fact they are just the conventional wind-up variety. Even that is an — improvement over the original design, which featured sliding Perspex windows.

Twelve-piece body

The F40's non-load-bearing body is made up of 12 sections (made from Kevlar, carbonfibre and glassfibre, depending on the strength required). The bonnet and engine covers are the two largest, followed by the roof, doors, sills and rear-three-quarter bodywork.

Single rear damper units

Unlike some other ultra-high-performance cars, the F40's rear suspension features just a single coil spring/damper unit on each side, rather than the pairs of similar units used on rivals such as the Countach and Diablo.

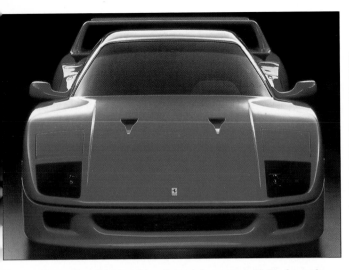

Above: Pop-up headlight pods each contain separate lights for main and dipped beams. The panels below the pods contain turn indicators, side lights, and lights for flashing when the main pods are down.

Suspension and brakes

Apart from the usual experimentation with spring, damper and anti-roll bar rates, the suspension of the F40 went ahead to production unaltered from the GTO Evoluzione's classical layout of double wishbones front and rear, with the rear spring/damper struts mounted above the upper wishbones. Koni coil-and-damper units are used, operating directly between the uprights and the chassis brackets without any intermediate levers or rockers. Each front unit runs from the base of the upright to meet the chassis between the arms of the upper wishbone, but the rears are attached at the top of the uprights and locate to the frame well above the height of the wheel rims.

Developing a braking system (in conjunction with Brembo) strong enough to handle 200-mph performance turned out to be a lengthy process. A great deal of work went into lowering pad and disc

temperatures and eliminating vibration, while an early casualty of the development process was the removal of servo-assistance. The non-servo brakes, in the end, were reckoned to give acceptable pedal effort together with the bonus of superior feel. Ferrari claims that the 92.6-lb pedal weight required to produce 1 g deceleration is comparable with the performance of some cars with servo-assistance.

The discs with which Ferrari finished up are huge, complex and expensive to manufacture. To avoid their size creating too much unsprung weight, the 12.9-in discs follow pre-carbonfibre Formula 1 practice in having an aluminium core with cast-iron friction surfaces, together with generous lateral passages and cross-drillings for cooling. Brembo four-piston aluminium calipers are fitted to the trailing edge of the front discs and the leading edge of the rears.

Below: Front suspension is by double wishbones, with coil spring/damper units and an anti-roll bar.

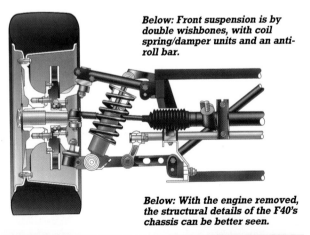

Below: With the engine removed, the structural details of the F40's chassis can be better seen.

Engine

The design basics of the production F40 engine follow familiar Ferrari practice. The V8's cylinder banks are angled at 90 degrees. The block, crankcase and heads are made of aluminium/silicon alloy (Silumin) cast in Maranello's foundry. Shrink-fitted aluminium cylinder liners are hardened with nickel/silicon alloy (Nikasil). Two overhead camshafts per bank, driven by toothed rubber belts, operate four valves per cylinder. With a cylinder diameter of 82 mm and a stroke of 69.5 mm, the V8 is over-square and displaces 2936 cc. The low compression ratio of 7.7:1 is explained by the presence of twin IHI turbochargers blowing at a maximum

of 16 psi, which helps give the impressive output of 478 bhp at 7,000 rpm.

The engine's detail features differ somewhat from those used in the GTO. The oil system, still dry-sump with a rear-mounted cooler and tank, was refined with enlarged lubrication passages in the crankshaft and cooling jets directed onto the piston crowns. The larger IHI turbochargers are water-cooled and supplied via larger Behr intercoolers. The wider cylinder bore allows larger valves, the exhaust ones having hollow stems. A multi-butterfly inlet system adds to the sophistication of the Weber-Marelli ignition-injection installation.

Below: Ferrari used aluminium/silicon alloy for the F40's block, crankcase and cylinder heads. Note the two overhead camshafts, each with five bearings, already installed in the cylinder head.

Below: The sla[t] rear window le[ts] cooling air into engine bay an[d] allows some rearward visio[n]

Below right: The large ribbed unit on top of the engine is one of the turbocharger intercoolers.

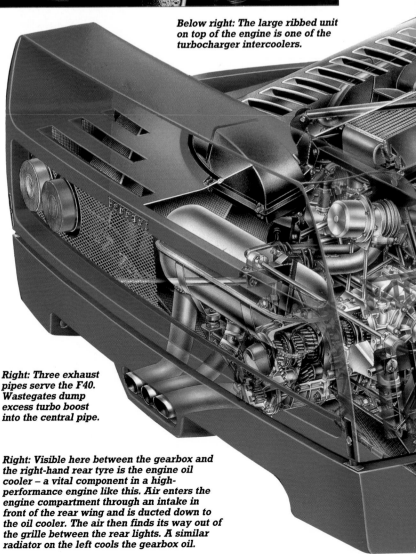

Right: Three exhaust pipes serve the F40. Wastegates dump excess turbo boost into the central pipe.

Right: Visible here between the gearbox and the right-hand rear tyre is the engine oil cooler – a vital component in a high-performance engine like this. Air enters the engine compartment through an intake in front of the rear wing and is ducted down to the oil cooler. The air then finds its way out of the grille between the rear lights. A similar radiator on the left cools the gearbox oil.

Above: Each F40 engine was built by hand by skilled Ferrari craftsmen. The completed engine was then run on the bench for four hours and thoroughly tested before it was ready to be fitted into the car.

Left: Each of the four camshafts drives eight valves. Valve clearances are adjusted by changing the shim between the cam lobe and the tappet. The exhaust valves have hollow stems which are filled with sodium to help to disperse the heat.

Below: This is a completed engine, ready to be fitted into an F40. Red cylinder heads are familiar to Ferrari owners. 'Testa Rossa', the name of two famous Ferraris, is Italian for red head.

Below: Some F40s have no spare wheel but carry a compressed tyre sealer to deal with punctures. The spare wheel well can then be used for luggage.

Above: The outer panels and floor are made of woven Kevlar and carbonfibre, which gives them great strength and lightness.

Right: The whole tail section hinges up to give access to the engine for checking routine items like engine oil level and drivebelt tension. Note the asymmetric tread of the 335/35 ZR17 rear tyres, and the two oil coolers (for engine and gearbox lubricants) on either side of the silencer.

Lamborghini
Countach

Marcello Gandini's Countach is a 20-year-old design, but the Lamborghini still has the power to shock and, thanks to its 5.2-litre 455-bhp quad-cam V12, leaves most of the opposition in its 180-mph wake.

Above: The long, Testarossa-like strakes (for brake cooling) in the skirts show that this is the Anniversary model, the final variation on the Countach theme. Inset: Ferrucio Lamborghini is a Taurean, hence the bull badge, transformed by Lamborghini into a fighting bull.

When Ferrucio Lamborghini went into the car business in 1963 he adopted his birth sign, the Taurean bull, as his badge, and when he started giving his cars names, he named them mostly in connection with fighting bulls. There was one major exception. In the early 1970s, Lamborghini's second great mid-engined supercar (following in the wheeltracks of the legendary Miura) was taking shape at Lamborghini's Sant'Agata factory near Bologna, and in Nuccio Bertone's styling studios in Turin. At first, it was simply known as project number 112 and later as the LP500, for *Longitudinale Posteriore* (the Italian for its inline rear-engine layout) and the five litres of the engine in the prototype.

And then one day the first completed prototype was wheeled out of the styling shops. Bertone himself saw it in the flesh and spontaneously let out a low exclamation: "*Countach!*".

The word is from local Piedmontese dialect, with no literal translation (or no printable one!) but if you say it in the same way that Bertone said it the first time he saw the stunning new Lamborghini, you'll know what it means – and why it stuck.

. . . the fastest car in the world . . .

The Countach had a hard act to follow in the Miura, but with it Lamborghini wanted to carry his challenge to Ferrari one stage further – to take the whole concept of the Miura as state-of-the-art roadgoing supercar and to refine it even more. He wanted the new car to be more usable than the Miura, which was staggeringly fast and still unique among the most powerful supercars in its transverse mid-engine layout, but which did have something of a reputation for being hard to drive near its limits. Now he wanted to combine this near-racing performance with the less demanding nature of a true grand touring car, to make it the sort of car that any wealthy buyer with taste but not necessarily racing driver skills could properly enjoy over long distances, at high speeds, in comfort and safety.

Most of all, he wanted it to be the fastest and best car in the world, which really meant it had to outperform any Ferrari.

Lamborghini's attitude to Ferrari was antagonistic, and it was Ferrari's attitude to Lamborghini that had turned him into a car-builder in the first place. Ferrucio had always been interested in cars and had raced, but his main business was building tractors and air-conditioning equipment. He was wealthy and he owned many fine cars, including Ferraris. Once he had cause

Top: Late in 1987 the Countach was given a neater sill treatment, which made it the most attractive version since the original Countach. The Anniversary model of 1988 can be distinguished by its five-spoke alloy wheels.

Above: The Lamborghini's stiff suspension means that the Countach can have the minimum of ground clearance between the Anniversary's front air dam and the road.

Driving the Countach: an awesome heavyweight

The Countach experience begins even before you turn the ignition key: first you have to get into the car, and that isn't as straightforward as with some! The doors open easily on their counterbalancing struts, and open high, but you still have to negotiate the wide sills, and the Countach stands only 3 ft 6 in tall. Once you're in, though, it is a superb environment. Forward visibility is superb, sideways is OK, rearwards is non-existent, especially with the optional wing. The massive engine needs care: let the pumps tick, dab the throttle a couple of times, then turn the key, and once it bursts into life, give it time to warm up. Then it will be

untemperamental, easy to live with. The gear change is less friendly, with a racing-pattern 'dog-leg' first; the clutch is enormously heavy and sensitive. Everything about the Countach feels heavyweight and intimidating at first, but it gets better. It needs a positive attitude, plus respect and some mechanical sympathy, but driven well the Countach is awesome. It has the precise and solid feel of a racing car, massive and flexible power, phenomenal grip and superb brakes. It communicates everything that it is doing, but it would take a good driver to find its true limits – and that is the ultimate compliment.

PERFORMANCE & SPECIFICATION COMPARISON	Engine	Displacement	Power	Torque (lb ft)	Max speed	0-60 mph	Length (in/mm)	Wheelbase (in/mm)	Track front/rear	Weight total (lb/kg)	Price
Lamborghini Countach Quattrovalvole	V12, quad-cam, 48-valve	5167 cc	455 bhp 7000 rpm	369 lb ft 5200 rpm	178 mph 286 km/h	4.9 sec	162.9 in 4138 mm	96.5 in 2451 mm	58.7 in 63.2 in	3188 lb 1446 kg	£116,432 (1991)
Ferrari Testarossa	Flat-12, quad-cam, 48-valve	4942 cc	390 bhp 6300 rpm	362 lb ft 4500 rpm	174 mph 280 km/h	5.2 sec	176.6 in 4485 mm	100.4 in 2550 mm	59.8 in 65.4 in	3675 lb 1667 kg	£115,500 (1991)
Lotus Esprit Turbo SE	Inline-four, turbo, 16-valve	2174 cc	264 bhp 6500 rpm	261 lb ft 3900 rpm	161 mph 259 km/h	4.9 sec	171.0 in 4343 mm	96.0 in 2438 mm	60.0 in 61.2 in	2650 lb 1202 kg	£46,300 (1991)
Aston Martin V8 Vantage	V8, quad-cam	5340 cc	406 bhp 6200 rpm	390 lb ft 5000 rpm	170 mph 274 km/h	5.4 sec	181.3 in 4605 mm	102.8 in 2611 mm	59.3 in 59.0 in	4001 lb 1815 kg	£110,000 (1989)
Porsche 928 S4 SE	V8, quad-cam, 32-valve	4957 cc	310 bhp 5900 rpm	295 lb ft 4100 rpm	160 mph 257 km/h	5.5 sec	177.9 in 4518 mm	98.1 in 2492 mm	61.1 in 60.9 in	3488 lb 1582 kg	£64,496 (1991)

Pop-up headlights

Four headlights are the least required by a car capable of 180 mph. They are concealed beneath the flap behind the glass-covered indicator and side lights. The spotlights on the nose were also used instead of headlight-flashing.

NACA cooling ducts

The Countach's side ducts are borrowed from aircraft practice, but they alone were not enough to feed sufficient cooling air into the side radiators and had to be supplemented by the extra ducts on top of the car.

Split-rim alloy wheels

The Countach runs on 15-in diameter split-rim alloy wheels, but there's an enormous difference between front and rear. Fronts are 8.5 in wide, while the rears are a full 12 inches. The wheels shown here on the Anniversary model, introduced in 1988, are the third distinctive style fitted.

Separate tubular steel chassis

The original Countach used a monocoque sheet steel construction. That was changed in production to an immensely complicated welded tubular steel separate chassis, designed by Marchesi of Modena.

Pirelli P Zero tyres

The first Countachs ran on Michelin XWX radials, but Lamborghini decided that superior tyres were needed to get the best from the car and re-engineered it to suit the new low-profile Pirelli P7s in 1978. Tyre size is a massive 225/50 VR15 front and 345/35 ZR15 rear. The last of the line shown here used Pirelli P Zero.

Testarossa influence

On the Anniversary model Lar these skirts with Testarossa-li covering a duct for brake coo.

to complain to Ferrari about a recurring fault on one of his cars; Ferrari told him the fault was his and not the car's, that a tractor-maker could hardly understand a true thoroughbred. And so Lamborghini went off to prove him wrong.

He showed his first car in Turin in 1963, launched the Miura in 1966, and in 1971 unveiled the Countach prototype to a stunned audience at the Geneva Show. It had been styled at Bertone by the young Marcello Gandini (who had also created the Lamborghini Miura); it had an astonishingly futuristic shape with geometrically sharp lines, an openly aggressive stance, and amazing doors that opened vertically like an insect's wings.

This prototype wasn't just a pretty face, though. Under the stunning body, the Countach was already largely complete.

The prototype had a five-litre engine, but for production a four-litre was chosen – and was more than adequate. The new engine and transmission layout, with longitudinal engine and the gearbox ahead of the block for compactness and weight distribution, was a touch of genius from chassis designer and Lamborghini chief engineer Paolo Stanzani. At a stroke, that overcame several of the Miura's thornier problems; it made the Countach a better-balanced car, it separated the engine and gearbox lubrication in a way the early Miuras hadn't been able to do, and it eliminated the troublesome gear linkage that had always plagued the Miura.

It even allowed the Countach to be shorter in both length and wheelbase than its transverse-engined predecessor!

Gandini's original styling changed a little as the car was finalised, mainly in being obliged to sprout more cooling ducts (notably the scoops behind the side windows) but if anything the changes only made the car look more spectacular and aggressively unique. It obviously wouldn't have great rearward visibility, and the early prototype even had a periscope rear view mirror.

Below: If you really intended to exploit all of your Countach's 180-mph performance, Lamborghini claimed that the optional rear wing would be a sensible investment to increase its grip, albeit a rather expensive one at £1,600.

Gradually, Stanzini and chief test driver Bob Wallace, a highly talented New Zealander, made what was under the skin work, doing thousands of miles of high-speed testing, hundreds of hours of re-engineering, and finally getting the car right. By the time the car appeared at Geneva 1973 (still almost a year from production) it was very close to being finalised; in March 1974 it was launched as the LP400 Countach.

It had the 375-bhp four-litre V12, a five-speed gearbox, and an often-quoted but never proven top speed of "over 190 mph".

And from there, the Countach got better and better. First (with some assistance from Grand Prix team owner Walter Wolf) it changed onto the new lower-profile Pirelli P7 tyres, rejigged its

Power jumped to a Ferrari-beating 455 bhp

entire suspension and became even meaner looking as the LP400S, from 1978. Next, in the face of new competition from Ferrari's Boxer, it grew to 4.8 litres in the LP500S, and took the power – recently compromised by making the car more driveable – back to a quoted 375 bhp. The decline in sales which had started with the LP400S was stopped by the new '500'.

Even cars like the Countach have to stay on their toes, though, and when Ferrari launched the superb Testarossa in 1984, Lamborghini were already on their way to the next-generation Countach. That was launched at Geneva in 1985, in the guise of the heavily re-engineered *quattrovalvole*, with its capacity increased to almost 5.2 litres, and with four valves per cylinder. The power output jumped instantly to a Ferrari-beating 455 bhp, yet with cleaner emissions and better flexibility, and the Countach was once again on top.

That was the end of the major mechanical changes, even though the Countach never stood still in the area of chassis development as new tyre equipment became available. Late in 1987, the bodywork was updated with new side sills (with functional brake scoops), and late in 1988 the bodywork was more dramatically updated, with more rounded scoops and neater front and rear treatment. There were new wheels and better interior equipment, too, but the Anniversary model, as it was dubbed, was to be the end of the Countach. The Diablo was waiting in the wings.

Above: A Countach 500S in action. The 500S was powered by the five-litre 375-bhp version of the V12. The extra 825 cc over the 400S gave the Countach more torque, at over 300 lb ft.

Mid-rear mounted engine

Behind the driver it's all engine and transmission. Despite the fact that the engine is a big V12, it is all between the driver and the rear axle line, with the transmission mounted ahead of the engine.

The Countach was introduced on the stylist Bertone's (rather than Lamborghini's) stand at the 1971 Geneva Show, designed by Marcello Gandini and called the LP500. LP stood for *Longitudinale Posteriore* – in other words, it had its five-litre engine mounted inline behind the seats.

The Countach entered production in 1974, but with the smaller four-litre quad-cam V12 from the Lamborghini Miura, mounted longitudinally rather than transversely as in the Miura.

In 1978 the LP400S was introduced, with Pirelli P7 tyres, flared wheel arches, a deeper nose spoiler and the boot-mounted rear wing. The next significant change came three years later, in 1981, with the LP500S, when the engine size was increased to five litres.

In 1985 the capacity of the V12 was increased again, this time up to 5167 cc, by increasing the stroke, and four valves per cylinder were fitted to produce the *Quattrovalvole*, with power increasing from 375 bhp to 455 bhp.

...borghini added ...e side strakes ...g.

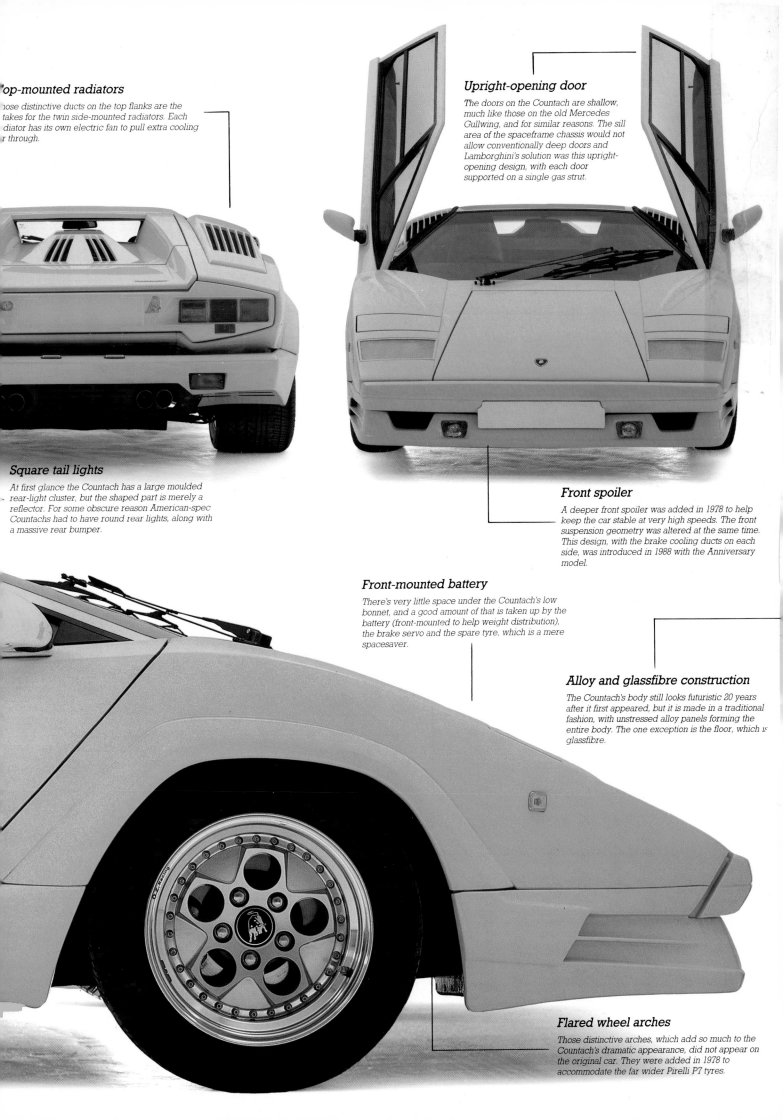

Top-mounted radiators

Those distinctive ducts on the top flanks are the intakes for the twin side-mounted radiators. Each radiator has its own electric fan to pull extra cooling air through.

Upright-opening door

The doors on the Countach are shallow, much like those on the old Mercedes Gullwing, and for similar reasons. The sill area of the spaceframe chassis would not allow conventionally deep doors and Lamborghini's solution was this upright-opening design, with each door supported on a single gas strut.

Square tail lights

At first glance the Countach has a large moulded rear-light cluster, but the shaped part is merely a reflector. For some obscure reason American-spec Countachs had to have round rear lights, along with a massive rear bumper.

Front spoiler

A deeper front spoiler was added in 1978 to help keep the car stable at very high speeds. The front suspension geometry was altered at the same time. This design, with the brake cooling ducts on each side, was introduced in 1988 with the Anniversary model.

Front-mounted battery

There's very little space under the Countach's low bonnet, and a good amount of that is taken up by the battery (front-mounted to help weight distribution), the brake servo and the spare tyre, which is a mere spacesaver.

Alloy and glassfibre construction

The Countach's body still looks futuristic 20 years after it first appeared, but it is made in a traditional fashion, with unstressed alloy panels forming the entire body. The one exception is the floor, which is glassfibre.

Flared wheel arches

Those distinctive arches, which add so much to the Countach's dramatic appearance, did not appear on the original car. They were added in 1978 to accommodate the far wider Pirelli P7 tyres.

Chassis and body

The Countach chassis is a true spaceframe, a complicated lattice of straight tubes welded together in geometrically complex patterns to give immense strength for minimum weight – with much more 'space' than 'frame'. Each tube, so far as is possible, acts only in a straight line, feeding only compression or tension loads (rather than bending loads, which are harder to deal with) into its neighbours. The main elements of the Countach chassis are a large central tunnel (widening out to accept the gearbox from the centre) and two massive side sills. There are two more large side-member structures behind the cockpit to embrace the engine and to carry the rear suspension pickups, a box-like front assembly to support the front suspension, and internal panels which form the transverse bulkheads. On top of the

Above: The first Countach had a monocoque chassis but the production cars had this complicated tubular steel spaceframe, shown here from the front.

main chassis there is a lighter tubular structure which forms the basis for the bodywork, which is virtually entirely hand-formed from aluminium except for some glassfibre panels which line the floor, much of the engine bay and the front 'boot'. On late models, the additional styling panels were also in glassfibre. The hand-shaped alloy panels were then welded, rivetted or bonded on, and the car took shape. The most complex operation of all was fitting the distinctive, upward-hinging doors, no two of which were exactly identical, and that could take many hours of skilled work.

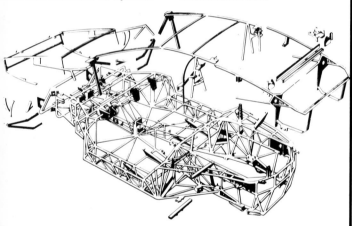

Above: The main chassis had a far lighter tubular steel superstructure, which formed the foundation for the bodywork.

Transmission

While the Miura used type numbers prefaced by TP, the Countachs are prefaced by LP – for Transversale Posteriore and Longitudinale Posteriore respectively. That is the big difference between the two cars – in English, the transverse rear-engined layout of the Miura against the longitudinal rear-engined layout of the Countach (although both are strictly mid-engined, with engine ahead of rear axle line). The Countach solution to fitting such a big engine so far forward in an acceptably compact car is brilliant. The engine and five-speed gearbox assembly are mounted apparently 'back-to-front' with the gearbox ahead of the engine and virtually between driver and

passenger, with the gear change far forward on a short extension. The drive from the engine is taken through a conventional clutch directly into the gearbox, the output from the gearbox is brought back to the engine end, taken down through a simple set of gears and to a driveshaft which passes back through a special, sealed tube in the engine's sump, below the crankshaft. At the far end of the engine, in a casing integral with the sump unit, is the final drive, from which the short driveshafts emerge to the hubs. It is marginally heavier than a conventional arrangement and the centre of gravity is very slightly higher, but overall it gives the most compact layout and best possible weight distribution.

Engine

Over the years, the Countach engine underwent enormous changes from the first two-valve-per-cylinder four-litre unit which launched the car with 375 bhp in 1974, to the 5.2-litre four-valve 455 bhp of the final 'Anniversary' models – yet fundamentally it was the same engine. It was based on the V12 that one-time Ferrari engineer Bizzarrini had designed back in 1963, and one of the finest engines in the world. Its dozen cylinders are set in a narrow, 60-degree vee, it has a light-alloy block and light-alloy cylinder heads, an immensely strong steel crankshaft with seven main bearings, and its four overhead camshafts are driven by chains. In the later quattrovalvole versions there are four valves per cylinder and a choice of fuel systems – six twin-choke downdraught Weber carburettors for European-spec cars, or Bosch K-Jetronic injection for the more environmentally sensitive American market. The inlet tracts are in the middle of the vee and very straight, and the exhausts on the outside are like two nests of snakes. It is a very free-breathing, free-revving and efficient engine, giving an impressive 88 bhp per litre in European form. It is also immensely strong and reliable, and very refined – all characteristics, of course, that Lamborghini had insisted on in the original concept of the Countach as a supercar without vices.

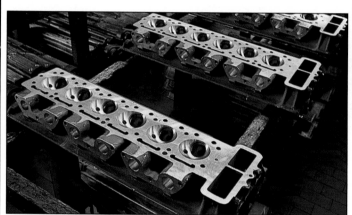

Above: Alloy cylinder heads. Note the enormous valve area, later made even bigger by fitting four valves.

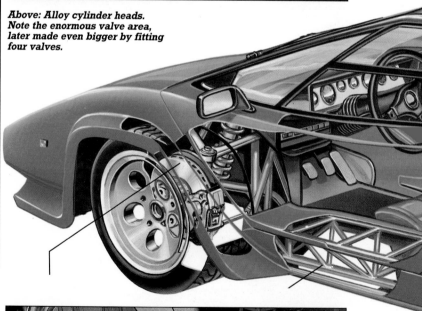

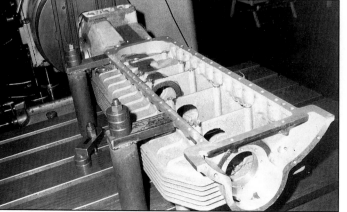

Left: To allow the gearbox to be in front of the engine and close to the driver, making for an excellent gear change, the output from the gearbox is dropped down and then fed back through a special sealed tube in the sump.

SPECIFICATION
1990 Lamborghini Countach Quattrovalvole Anniversary

ENGINE

Type:	V12 (60-degree), longitudinal mid-mounted; alloy block and head with wet cylinder liners; seven main bearings
Bore×stroke:	85.5 mm×75 mm
Displacement:	5167 cc
Compression ratio:	9.5:1
Valve gear:	four valves per cylinder operated by twin chain-driven overhead cams per bank of cylinders
Fuel supply:	six downdraught Weber 44DCNF carburettors
Ignition:	Marelli electronic
Maximum power:	455 bhp (DIN) at 7,000 rpm
Maximum torque:	369 lb ft (DIN) at 5,200 rpm

TRANSMISSION

Type:	five-speed manual transmission mounted in front of engine; hypoid bevel final drive with ZF limited slip differential	
Ratios:	1st	2.232:1
	2nd	1.625:1
	3rd	1.088:1
	4th	0.858:1
	5th	0.707:1
Final drive ratio:	4.09:1	

BODY/CHASSIS

Type:	separate multi-tube steel chassis with glassfibre floor, alloy and Kevlar body panels

RUNNING GEAR

Steering:	rack and pinion
Suspension:	front: independent with double wishbones, coil springs, telescopic dampers and anti-roll bar rear: independent with wishbones, trailing arms, anti-roll bar and twin co-axial coil spring/damper units per side
Brakes:	discs front and rear: 11.81 in diameter front and 11.02 in diameter rear; dual circuit, servo-assisted
Wheels:	split-rim alloys: 8.5 in×15 in front and 12 in×15 in rear
Tyres:	Pirelli P Zero 225/50 VR15 front and 345/35 VR15 rear

DIMENSIONS AND WEIGHT

Length:	162.9 in (4138 mm)
Width:	78.7 in (2000 mm)
Height:	42.1 in (1069 mm)
Wheelbase:	96.5 in (2451 mm)
Track:	58.7 in (1491 mm) front, 63.2 in (1606 mm) rear
Kerb weight:	3,188 lb (1446 kg)

PERFORMANCE

Acceleration:	0-30 mph 2.1 sec
	0-40 mph 2.7 sec
	0-50 mph 3.5 sec
	0-60 mph 4.9 sec
	0-70 mph 6.0 sec
	0-80 mph 7.2 sec
	0-90 mph 9.0 sec
	0-100 mph 10.6 sec
	0-110 mph 12.3 sec
	0-120 mph 15.5 sec
	0-130 mph 18.5 sec
	0-140 mph 21.1 sec
	0-150 mph 25.1 sec
	0-160 mph 32.1 sec
	0-170 mph 44.7 sec
Standing ¼ mile:	13.0 sec
Standing km:	23.3 sec

Acceleration in gear:	mph	fifth	fourth	third
	30-50	5.8	4.5	3.6
	40-60	5.8	4.5	3.4
	50-70	5.8	4.4	2.8
	70-90	5.7	4.1	2.8
	80-100	5.7	3.8	3.0

Maximum speed:	178 mph (286 km/h)
Overall fuel consumption:	13.7 mpg
Price:	£116,432 (1991)

Performance figures from AUTOCAR

Lamborghini Countach kindly supplied by Portman Lamborghini Limited

Lamborghini Countach Data File

The founder of Lamborghini was Ferrucio Lamborghini, a tractor manufacturer who decided to enter car production to outshine Enzo Ferrari after a personal argument. That's one account; another is that Ferrucio simply wanted to build the best supercar in the world, having found faults with all those he owned, including his Ferraris.

The first Lamborghini to emerge from Lamborghini's Sant'Agata plant near Bologna was the 350 GT of 1964, powered by the Bizzarini-designed 3.5-litre V12. First year's production was just 13 cars. The 350 GT was followed by the similar-looking 400 GT with an enlarged version of the quad-cam V12. That four-litre powerplant produced 320 bhp, enough to give a maximum speed approaching 160 mph. Combined production of 350 and 400 GT models was 393 between 1964 and 1968.

Next model was the Miura, which made its debut alongside the 400, in 1966. This marked Lamborghini's switch from front-engined cars to mid-engined, using the same V12 but mounted transversely behind the driver. Styled by Bertone, it was far more elegant than the earlier cars. By the time Miura development had ended in the early 1970s the SV model was producing 385 bhp from its 3929-cc V12, to give a top speed in the 170-mph bracket. Total Miura production was 765 between 1966 and 1973.

To transcend the Miura, Lamborghini needed something dramatic – the Countach, the car which provided Lamborghini with continuity from the days when Ferrucio Lamborghini himself controlled the company, through the takeovers by the Swiss Mimram family in 1980 and Chrysler in 1987.

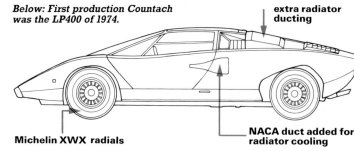

Below: First production Countach was the LP400 of 1974.

extra radiator ducting

Michelin XWX radials

NACA duct added for radiator cooling

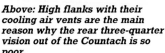

Below: Major visual change came with the LP400S of 1978.

rear wing for extra downforce

glassfibre spoiler

different-style wheels and Pirelli P7 tyres

glassfibre wheel-arch extensions

Top: The first Countach was shown at the 1971 Geneva Show. Designed by Marcello Gandini at Bertone, the untested prototype was finished so late that it had to be driven overnight from Sant'Agata to Geneva.

Above: By the time the Countach had reached production in 1974 it had gained those distinctive NACA ducts on the side and the top-mounted cooling scoops. The scoops meant that two small rear-side windows could be fitted.

Above: High flanks with their cooling air vents are the main reason why the rear three-quarter vision out of the Countach is so poor.

Above: The rear wing may look like the wildest of styling gimmicks but it was actually a functional option, adding rear downforce at high speed.

Above: Although the engine is mid-mounted, the 'transmission tunnel', which is part of the chassis, continues under the leather-trimmed fascia.

Below: Battery and spare spacesaver tyre live under the front hatch, and there is a tiny boot in the rear behind the engine hatch.

Styling

The Lamborghini Countach was designed by one of the great Italian styling houses, Bertone. In particular it was the work of Marcello Gandini (who became well known to British TV audiences in 1990 through the ads for another car he designed years later, the Citroën BX).

The origins of the Countach's styling can be found in a Bertone show car from as early as 1968. That was the Alfa Romeo-based Carabo. The most obvious similarity was the front-hinged doors, which opened vertically from one pivot. Another Carabo element continued into the new design was the very shallow windscreen angle, the windscreen forming a continuation of the bonnet line.

The first Countach, which appeared at the Geneva Show in March 1971, was a much 'cleaner' design than the Countachs we're now

familiar with. There was none of the complicated detail which makes the car visually so interesting. There was no NACA duct cut into the side, no extra cooling scoops on the top, and just a clean line around the wheel arches rather than the add-on extensions that appeared with the LP400S in 1978. It was a pure-looking design, but it certainly lacked the dramatic appeal added by all the extra bits and pieces.

One of the more daring features, apart from those doors, was the shape of the rear wheel arch. It was a total contrast to the pure round arch at the front. One of the few drawbacks of the LP400S was how the glassfibre wheel-arch extensions masked that line. The final styling touch was the rear wing, which is actually functional as well as flamboyant. It's only an option, but the Countach would not be complete without it!

Left: The alloy block and sump of the Countach V12. Note the final-drive casing at the end of the sump, which also houses the shaft taking drive from the gearbox mounted ahead of the engine. The driveshaft flanges can be seen on the side of the final drive. The Lamborghini engine is a 60-degree V12 with twin chain-driven overhead camshafts for each bank of cylinders. At the top right of the engine are the sprockets which will drive the duplex cam chains.

Below: The Countach has always been powered by a V12 but the displacement has changed over the years, from 4.0 to 4.8 and then 5.2 litres. This is an engine from the LP500, with six sidedraught Weber carburettors. Later cars had downdraught Webers or, in North America, Bosch K-Jetronic fuel injection.

radiator cooling ducts

radiator fan

Below: Getting air to the flank-mounted radiators required NACA ducts on the side of the car and the air scoops, shown above the fans.

alloy sump and transmission shaft housing

Above: Engine and transmission are ahead of the rear axle line, making the Countach a genuine mid-engined car. Rear suspension is the expected double-wishbone system, but in keeping with other supercars from the E-type up to the Testarossa, the Countach has double coil spring and damper units on each side.

Lamborghini Diablo

Yet again, Lamborghini and Gandini redefine the essence of the supercar. Where the Countach was hard-edged, uncompromising, almost confrontational, the Diablo's form is soft and subtly seductive – but it's even faster.

Above: Marcello Gandini dumbfounded the motoring world – and many an innocent bystander – with the Miura in the 1960s and the Countach in the 1970s and 1980s, and has left us speechless again in the 1990s with the Diablo. Again, too, it's the Lamborghini fighting bull emblem (inset) that adorns his creation.

When Lamborghini unveiled the Diablo in Monte Carlo in January 1990, they knew it had to be something special to satisfy all those owners and commentators who had been saying for years that the Countach would be an impossible act to follow. They now had another audience to impress, too, in the top brass at the Chrysler Corporation in America, which since 1987 had owned Lamborghini virtually lock-stock-and-barrel.

When the razzmatazz died down after the festivities of a three-day unveiling party, they must have breathed a sigh of relief; the world liked the Diablo, and Chrysler seemed well pleased with their investment in Lamborghini.

They had bought the project with the company. It had been initiated as long ago as mid-1985, when Lamborghini president Emile Novaro simply asked his design and engineering teams to build a Countach successor. It was taken as read that it had to be one of the fastest cars in

the world (and preferably *the* fastest), but it had to go beyond even the Countach in offering world-beating performance in a package that was also user-friendly and with all the creature comforts that the modern supercar owner demands – less of a raw, pseudo-racing car, and more of a practical and hassle-free masterpiece.

The most complete Lamborghini to date . . .

Like most Lamborghinis (with the notable exception of the Countach) the Diablo is named after a fighting bull – because the bull was the birth sign of company founder Ferruccio Lamborghini. Diablo (which also happens to be Spanish for 'devil') was the bull that fought El Chicorro in 1869, "with speed, courage and fierceness". Thanks to the mixture of Lamborghini's

Latin flair for building supercars and Chrysler's ability to refine (and pay for) production detailing, its namesake is the most 'complete' Lamborghini to date – for performance, for finish and comfort, even in the fact that it is 'environmentally friendly' and acceptable from the start in all world markets.

Just before the Diablo project started, in the early 1980s, Sant'Agata's technical staff comprised just 14 people; by the time the Diablo was launched there were nine engineers, 18 draughtsmen, 26 prototype builders, 35 test engineers and three people working on certification. The company had survived desperate times through the 1970s, but with the backing of the Swiss-based Mimran family and the engineering and management skills of Giulio Alfieri it survived long enough for Chrysler to take over in 1987.

At the head of Chrysler was Lee Iacocca, who was not only of Italian descent, but was also the man who had created Ford's 'Total Perform-

ance' programme in the early 1960s, backed both the GT40 and the Cobra, and put a sporty feel back into Chrysler.

He knew what Chrysler expected from Lamborghini: "We want to create in Sant'Agata our most advanced laboratory for top-end automotive engineering, taking advantage of Lamborghini's experience within the supercar market. . . No change of emphasis will be made to Lamborghini's general technical and philosophical approach. . .".

So the Diablo project, type P132 in the factory, fell into good hands, and although Chrysler had their own financial crises to contend with, they backed it to the hilt.

Performance figures better than Ferrari's F40

As Lamborghini technical director Luigi Marmiroli explained, the Diablo had to bring a philosophy up to date: "The days of the Miura and the Countach were an age of few regulations, when imagination was the main limiting factor. Now, safety and environmental requirements are far more restrictive – and that affects everything, particularly body design. . .

"Now we have this fine balance between technology and craftsmanship. We use the best computers, but it isn't a car designed by computers; we use the best wind tunnels, but it isn't designed by the wind tunnels; it's designed by men, for men, using electronics where they're appropriate, but not forgetting the romance. . .".

As for Chrysler, they demanded romance with quality, and invested heavily in it for the Diablo production process. Everyone in the company, from the president down to the workers, who now have quality-control supervision at every major workstation, was involved; and right through the design programme, Chrysler resources helped to take Lamborghini engineering and add the refinements that only a bigger organisation can offer – most conspicuously in detailing Marcello Gandini's body design, in creating a cabin with virtually no parts-bin compromises, and in making sure every component was the best available for the job.

Yet at the end of it, the first supercar to be launched in the 1990s principally had to be the fastest production car in the world – with no additional qualifications. So the car has the classic basic layout of the Countach, but takes everything one stage further. It is a bit bigger and heavier, but even more powerful with no less

Below: With the line of its forward-extended cabin swooping down past the driver's feet to a vestigial nose, the Diablo echoes modern racetrack trends, but it's a more civilised and sophisticated package than its predecessor. The design is far more refined and integrated, with no need for ugly tacked-on scoops.

Above: Chrysler facilities and expertise had considerable influence in refining the Diablo design, but by no means made it bland – it's still every millimetre an exotic thoroughbred.

Top right: There's no mistaking the Diablo's mid-engined layout. With a minimal nose, it is the antithesis of 1930s, 1950s and 1960s sports cars with long, forward-thrusting bonnets, but the impact is just as great.

than 492 bhp, and much more aerodynamic.

When Lamborghini unveiled it, they quoted a maximum speed of 202.1 mph, acceleration to 100 km/h (62 mph) in 4.09 seconds, and a standing kilometre time of 20.7 seconds. It was lost on no-one that all those figures were just marginally better than Ferrari's strictly limited-edition F40 – previously regarded as 'the fastest car in the world'. They are not the sort of figures that many people will ever verify, but they had been independently certified at the Nardo test-track, and although 202 mph was easily achieved, the Diablo was said to have reached 210 mph on at least one occasion. Lamborghini also promised a four-wheel-drive version for the near future (to be known as the VT), the option of a semi-automatic transmission, and possibly even 'semi-active' electronically-controlled suspension damping, all in a car which is now as comfortable and well-equipped as even the most demanding customer could ever wish – and which is a true production model, not a limited-edition car like its rivals.

Lamborghini Diablo

Lamborghini had greater problems creating the Diablo than their rival supercar manufacturers had in making 200-mph-plus cars, in that the last of the Countach line, the Anniversary, was such an outstanding machine. It limited Lamborghini's options in producing its replacement. The V12 engine was already in the logical place, longitudinally mid-mounted, the suspension design was adequate for the performance, and the looks were still as spectacular as any of its rivals. Consequently, it took Lamborghini over five years to come up with a worthy successor. It was much the same mixture as before, but with improvements all round, a larger chassis, and more power.

Alloy, composite and steel body

The Diablo's body shell is made from a mixture of materials. Steel is used for the roof; wings are alloy, as are the doors; and a new composite material is used for the nose, engine cover, sills and bumpers.

Engine-cooling air vents

The air used to cool the V12's twin radiators is exhausted from the back of the engine bay via large vents on either side of the car.

Three-way catalytic convertor

Despite its extraordinary performance, the D[
goes some way towards having a 'green' ima[
having a three-way catalytic convertor to rec[
exhaust emissions, thus equipping the car fo[
stringent North American market.

Extremely low-profile tyres

The Diablo is equipped with some of the lowest-
profile tyres found on any production car, with
245/40-section fronts and 335/35 rears.

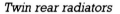

Side-mounted oil coolers

The vents on the lower side panels are not, as you
might assume, for brake cooling but to feed air to
the oil coolers, which are mounted directly ahead of
the rear wheels.

Twin rear radiators

One area in which the Diablo differs from the
Countach is in having its twin radiators mounted
right at the rear of the engine bay, each assisted by
a large electric fan.

Multi-piece alloy wheels

The Diablo, like the Countach Anniversary before it,
has split-rim alloy wheels.

Above: Bigger, heavier and thirstier than the Countach, the Diablo is also faster; outperforming any Ferrari, it's a prime contender for 'world's fastest' status. Power comes from a new 5.7-litre, fuel-injected version of Lamborghini's 48-valve V12, which is more powerful, torquier and more tractable than ever. Early tests indicate a 0-60 mph time just over four seconds and maximum speed comfortably over 200 mph. The Diablo is also more environmentally friendly, with three-way catalytic converters behind the engine.

Driving the Diablo: *fastest of all?*

The Diablo is even wider than a Countach, and feels it. The driving position is excellent and the seats give superb lateral support, but there is minimal room for the feet because the cockpit is so far forward that the front arches intrude deep into the footwells. The trim is luxurious but the instrument binnacle is odd, with the big dials well separated and often obscured by hands on the thick-rimmed wheel. Controls, even the clutch, are reasonably light, and for a car with close to 500 bhp it feels almost docile at low speeds. Massive power is available from almost any speed; between 3,500 and 7,500 rpm it is truly ferocious in both noise

and delivery; a Diablo will hit 60 mph in 4.2 seconds – in first gear – on its way to a standing kilometre in 20.7 seconds and a maximum of 205 mph. In each case, the car is claimed to be quicker than Ferrari's fearsome F40. It can feel quite nervous, with ultra-responsive steering and a darting feel from the big tyres and firm suspension. The grip in corners is awesome, but you must always remember how much car is behind you, and how much power. The Diablo is not a forgiving car – that weight and power in the tail are ever ready to take charge. The Diablo certainly demands skill, but it rewards it too.

PERFORMANCE & SPECIFICATION COMPARISON	Engine	Displacement	Power	Torque (lb ft)	Max speed	0-60 mph	Length (in/mm)	Wheelbase (in/mm)	Track front/rear	Weight total (lb/kg)	Price
Lamborghini Diablo	V12, quad-cam, 48-valve	5729 cc	492 bhp 7000 rpm	428 lb ft 5200 rpm	205 mph 330 km/h	4.2 sec	175.6 in 4460 mm	104.3 in 2650 mm	60.6 in 64.6 in	3474 lb 1576 kg	£158,370 (1991)
Ferrari F40	V8, quad-cam, 32-valve, twin-turbo	2936 cc	478 bhp 7000 rpm	425 lb ft 4000 rpm	201 mph 323 km/h	4.5 sec	171.6 in 4358 mm	96.5 in 2450 mm	62.8 in 63.2 in	2425 lb 1100 kg	£193,299 (1990)
Porsche 959	Flat-six, quad-cam, 24-valve, twin-turbo	2851 cc	450 bhp 6500 rpm	370 lb ft 5500 rpm	190 mph 306 km/h	3.6 sec	167.7 in 4260 mm	89.4 in 2272 mm	59.2 in 61.0 in	3197 lb 1450 kg	£160,000 (1987)
Aston Martin Virage	V8, quad-cam	5340 cc	330 bhp 6000 rpm	340 lb ft 3700 rpm	157 mph 253 km/h	6.8 sec	184.5 in 4686 mm	100.7 in 2558 mm	55.0 in 56.3 in	4295 lb 1948 kg	£125,000 (1990)
Lamborghini Countach 5000S Quattrovalvole	V12, quad-cam, 48-valve	5167 cc	455 bhp 7000 rpm	369 lb ft 5200 rpm	178 mph 286 km/h	4.9 sec	163.0 in 4140 mm	96.5 in 2450 mm	58.7 in 63.2 in	3188 lb 1446 kg	£116,432 (1991)

Vertical doors

One thing that just had to be carried over from the Countach was the door arrangement. Apart from the length of the doors, there was no reason why they could not have opened in the conventional fashion. Opening upward on one hinge did improve access and avoided the danger of damaging the edges of the doors but, more importantly, it helped to recreate the impact of the original Gullwing Mercedes but without the difficult sealing problems created by gullwing doors.

Above: Lamborghini's unique up-and-forward door opening is used again. The Diablo's bodywork follows the top of the wheel arch so closely that it is hard to see how suspension movement is possible.

Chassis and suspension

The Diablo owes its layout to the Countach, but with major changes from end to end. A multi-tubular spaceframe is used but the tubes are square rather than round, which speeds production (because square tubes are easier to weld) and also makes it simpler to add the component mounting points. Different grades of steel are used in different areas – high strength around the cockpit, and standard at front and rear to produce crumple zones. The welded-in roof is made of steel as before, so are the door shut-panels, but there are other materials in the mix. Wings and doors are in a light alloy but harder than the Countach's vulnerable skin; the removable centre tunnel is of carbonfibre; nose and engine covers, bumpers and sills are moulded in a new and ultra-light composite called Autoclave. The mid-engine layout remains, with the gearbox ahead of the engine, the final drive behind it and a driveshaft running through the sump. The suspension layout is also familiar, with double wishbones, coil springs and telescopic dampers all round – single spring/damper units on each front corner, twin ones at the rear. There are hefty anti-roll bars at each end, and anti-squat and anti-dive geometry is built in. Where the Countach suspension was rigidly mounted, the Diablo uses firm rubber bushes at the pick-up points to reduce harshness without sacrificing precise control. Steering is by rack and pinion, without assistance, and the brakes are massive, ventilated discs (bigger even than the Countach's at the front), with racing-type calipers but no ABS, to maintain feel. ABS may be added later, and the chassis was designed from the start to accept four-wheel-drive components and electronically-controlled damping.

Below: The Diablo's rear suspension, like that of the Countach, uses fabricated unequal-length wishbones with twin coil spring/damper units. Huge ventilated disc brakes are fitted on all four wheels.

Engine

Although the Diablo's all-alloy V12 is derived from the final Countach engine (and so can trace its ancestry back to the first Lamborghini V12, designed by Giotto Bizzarrini in 1963), it is virtually a new engine. The basic architecture of 12 cylinders in a 60-degree 'V', seven main bearings, four chain-driven camshafts and four valves per cylinder remains, but almost every detail is different. The block is stronger, the heads are new, with better combustion chamber shapes, the ancillary layout is more compact, and the engine is even lighter, with fewer components. Capacity has gone up a stage further, from 5167 cc to 5729 cc, by increases in both bore and stroke, from 85.5 mm×75.0 mm to 87.0 mm×80.0 mm. Compression ratio is increased from 9.5:1 to 10.0:1, largely made possible by a new management system. European Countach engines used six twin-choke Weber carbs, US-spec cars had Bosch K-Jetronic injection, and both used Marelli electronic ignition; all Diablos have a new sequential multipoint-injection system, its electronic management developed by Lamborghini, and known as Lamborghini Iniezione Elettronica. Each cylinder bank has its own electronic control unit, mapped to engine speed, crank position, atmospheric pressure, air and water temperatures, throttle position, and a lambda probe in the emission system – which has full catalyst equipment and means the Diablo runs on unleaded fuel! The LIE includes a fault-diagnosis capability with an onboard display. All these changes take power up from 455 bhp at 7,000 rpm to no less than 492 bhp at the same revs, and peak torque from 369 lb ft to 428 lb ft, both at 5,200 rpm.

Below: Lamborghini developed the Diablo's electronically-managed sequential multipoint fuel-injection system in-house.

Below: With its abbreviated front and upswept rear, the Diablo has very little overhang at either end.

Above: Front suspension, like the rear, is by unequal-length wishbones but with single coil-over-damper units, not pairs.

Above: Although overall construction and layout superficially similar, the Diablo is significantly different from the Countach in many details. For start, it's larger in all dimensions (nearly six inc. longer in wheelbase), and its spaceframe chassi fabricated from square- rather than round-sectio steel tubing, for the sake of ease and speed of welding and simplicity of mounting ancillary components. Various new materials are used: do and wing skins are made from a more durable li alloy of aluminium, while other body panels are carbonfibre and other ultra-light composites.

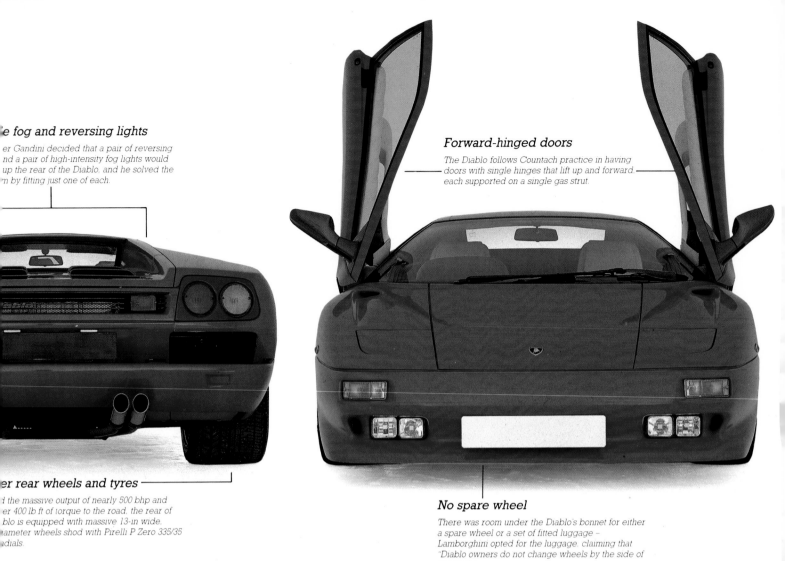

e fog and reversing lights

er Gandini decided that a pair of reversing
nd a pair of high-intensity fog lights would
up the rear of the Diablo, and he solved the
n by fitting just one of each.

r rear wheels and tyres

d the massive output of nearly 500 bhp and
er 400 lb ft of torque to the road, the rear of
blo is equipped with massive 13-in wide,
ameter wheels shod with Pirelli P Zero 335/35
idials.

Forward-hinged doors

The Diablo follows Countach practice in having
doors with single hinges that lift up and forward,
each supported on a single gas strut.

No spare wheel

There was room under the Diablo's bonnet for either
a spare wheel or a set of fitted luggage –
Lamborghini opted for the luggage, claiming that
"Diablo owners do not change wheels by the side of
the road."

Ventilation scoops

Cabin ventilation is provided by the two small
scoops just in front of the windscreen. The Diablo, at
Chrysler's insistence, is also air-conditioned.

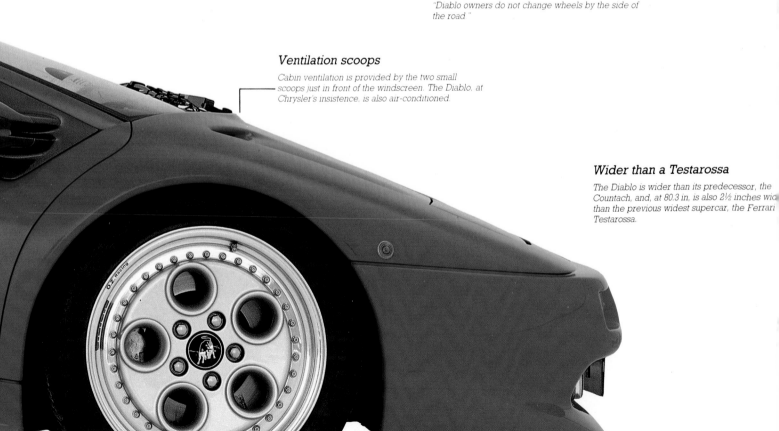

Wider than a Testarossa

The Diablo is wider than its predecessor, the
Countach, and, at 80.3 in, is also 2½ inches wid
than the previous widest supercar, the Ferrari
Testarossa.

SPECIFICATION

1991 Lamborghini Diablo

ENGINE

Type:	60-degree V12, quad-cam, longitudinally mid-mounted
Construction:	light-alloy cylinder block and heads with Nikasil-lined steel liners
Bore×stroke:	87 mm×80 mm
Displacement:	5729 cc
Compression ratio:	10.0:1
Valve gear:	four valves per cylinder operated by twin chain-driven overhead camshafts per bank of cylinders
Fuel system:	Lamborghini LIE electronic sequential multipoint injection
Ignition:	electronic
Maximum power:	492 bhp at 7,000 rpm
Maximum torque:	428 lb ft at 5,200 rpm

TRANSMISSION

Type:	five-speed manual	
Ratios:	1st	2.31:1
	2nd	1.52:1
	3rd	1.12:1
	4th	0.88:1
	5th	0.68:1
Final drive ratio:	2.41:1	

BODY/CHASSIS

Type:	high-strength steel and carbonfibre chassis with aluminium-alloy and composite body panels

RUNNING GEAR

Steering:	rack and pinion
Suspension:	front: independent with unequal-length wishbones and coaxial coil spring/damper units mounted on top of the hub; anti-dive geometry rear: independent with double unequal-length wishbones, twin coil spring/damper units and anti-roll bar; anti-squat geometry
Brakes:	ventilated discs all round, 330-mm diameter and 32-mm thickness front, 284 mm×22 mm rear
Wheels:	multi-piece alloy, 8.5 in×17 in front, 13 in×17 in rear
Tyres:	Pirelli P Zero, 245/40 ZR17 front, 335/35 ZR17 rear

DIMENSIONS AND WEIGHT

Length:	175.6 in (4460 mm)
Width:	80.3 in (2040 mm)
Height:	43.5 in (1105 mm)
Wheelbase:	104.3 in (2650 mm)
Track:	60.6 in (1540 mm) front, 64.6 in (1640 mm) rear
Dry weight:	3,474 lb (1576 kg)

PERFORMANCE

Acceleration:	0-30 mph 2.1 sec
	0-40 mph 2.9 sec
	0-50 mph 3.5 sec
	0-60 mph 4.2 sec
	0-70 mph 5.2 sec
	0-80 mph 6.1 sec
	0-90 mph 7.1 sec
	0-100 mph 8.5 sec
	0-110 mph 9.8 sec
	0-120 mph 11.3 sec
	0-130 mph 13.6 sec
	0-140 mph 15.8 sec
	0-150 mph 18.4 sec
	0-160 mph 23.8 sec
	0-170 mph 33.7 sec
Standing ¼ mile:	12.3 sec
Maximum speed:	205 mph (330 km/h)
Average fuel consumption:	15.3 mpg
Price (1991):	£158,370

Lamborghini Diablo kindly supplied by Portman Lamborghini

Lamborghini Diablo Data File

The Countach was first shown as a prototype in 1971, went into production in 1974 and survived for over 15 years. In that time it went from four litres to 5.2, gained four-valve cylinder heads and climbed from 375 bhp to 455 bhp. It started on tall and relatively narrow tyres, gained ever wider and lower ones, and its looks became steadily more aggressive. When Lamborghini first planned its successor in 1985 they had no reason to change the brilliant layout devised by Paolo Stanzani, with the engine mounted 'back-to-front', the gearbox between driver and passenger, and power taken via a shaft through the sump back to a rear final-drive unit. The Diablo would just have more of everything. In 1985, Lamborghini started testing a 'super-Countach', the *Evoluzione*, which had lightweight composite body panels and a 600-bhp development of the V12 engine. It was used to test not just the engine and composites, but also many other ideas for the Diablo – including a sophisticated four-wheel-drive system – before it was used for crash-testing. The Anniversary Countach (celebrating 25 years of Lamborghini car production in 1988) helped try out some of the comfort options, but the Diablo proper would be almost all new. Its square-tube spaceframe chassis gained almost six inches in the wheelbase (partly for cabin space, partly for ride comfort and more forgiving handling) and the car is over 10 inches longer, an inch and a half wider and taller, and 400 lb heavier. A rumoured six-litre engine didn't materialise, but the heavily revised 5.7 litres and almost 500 bhp is enough – especially as the new shape brings drag down from a barn-like 0.41 to 0.31 Cd.

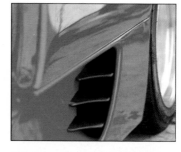

Above: Rear intakes echo other supercars' overdone strakes; pop-up headlights (right) are backed by driving lamps.

disegno *Marcello Gandini*

Above: Gandini styled earlier Lamborghinis while at Bertone.

Left: Big, round rear lights were a Chrysler touch.

Right: Diablo wheels feature large, round holes, picking up the theme of the rear lights and big-bore quadruple exhausts.

Above: Cleaner and more slippery as well as more lovely, the Diablo has a 0.31 drag coefficient, far superior to that of the Countach.

Styling

Other stylists, including Giugiaro, were asked to submit ideas for the Diablo, but the name on the car is that of Marcello Gandini – the man who styled both the Miura and Countach for Bertone and now as an independent is the most in-demand supercar stylist of all. The mechanical layout is much as on the Countach, so the Diablo has a clear family resemblance, but Gandini gave it a character of its own. This design was not Gandini's first; that was produced in mid-1986 and went as far as a full-sized model, but in early 1987 Lamborghini's new owner, Chrysler, asked for a rethink. Gandini's second submission was rejected; his next, with further input from Chrysler, became the Diablo. Changes weren't necessarily critical of Gandini's work, but Chrysler's massive technical resources meant details to improve aspects like aerodynamics and cooling could be refined far more than had previously been possible.

The Diablo is bigger than the Countach, but smoother and tidier. It has more glass, with the waistline dropping dramatically at the front, almost to the purely rounded wheel arch. The overhangs are even shorter than before, but most noticeably, all the details are much more integrated; the cooling scoops for engine bay and rear brakes are sculpted into the body rather than stuck onto it; the inlets above the front wings for cockpit ventilation are so neat. Even the bumpers no longer seem an afterthought, and the drag factor is an impressive 0.31 Cd. The interior was entirely done by Chrysler, and mainly by Bill Dayton. It is roomier and lighter than that of the Countach, and again it looks more integrated, less dependent on the parts bin.

Below: Chrysler designed the interior. It's comfortable and mostly functions well, although the wheel obscures some dials.

Lamborghini Countach

cooling ducts for engine

Testarossa-influenced styling strakes on Anniversary model

Lamborghini Diablo

tidier styling all round

driver sits further forward

wheelbase 6 in longer than Countach

Below: By mid-engined supercar standards, the Diablo's rearward visibility is not bad. The engine cover has large cooling louvres.

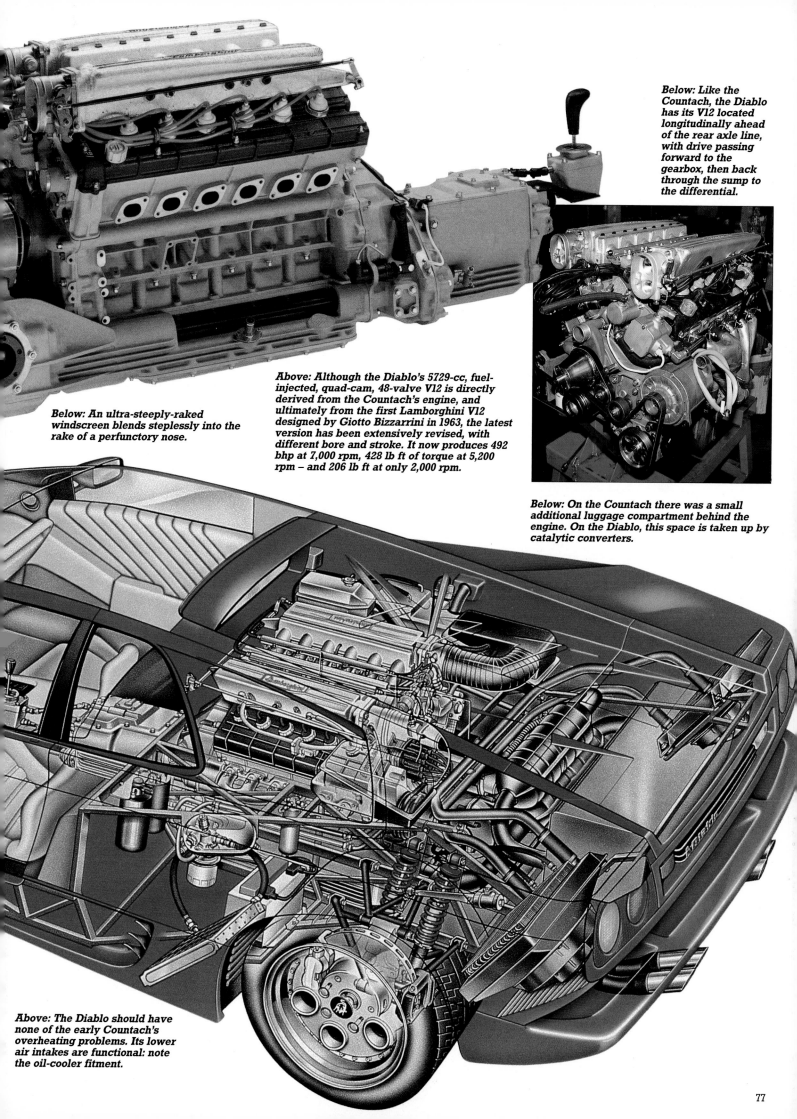

Below: Like the Countach, the Diablo has its V12 located longitudinally ahead of the rear axle line, with drive passing forward to the gearbox, then back through the sump to the differential.

Below: An ultra-steeply-raked windscreen blends steplessly into the rake of a perfunctory nose.

Above: Although the Diablo's 5729-cc, fuel-injected, quad-cam, 48-valve V12 is directly derived from the Countach's engine, and ultimately from the first Lamborghini V12 designed by Giotto Bizzarrini in 1963, the latest version has been extensively revised, with different bore and stroke. It now produces 492 bhp at 7,000 rpm, 428 lb ft of torque at 5,200 rpm – and 206 lb ft at only 2,000 rpm.

Below: On the Countach there was a small additional luggage compartment behind the engine. On the Diablo, this space is taken up by catalytic converters.

Above: The Diablo should have none of the early Countach's overheating problems. Its lower air intakes are functional: note the oil-cooler fitment.

Maserati Bora

Maserati's answer to the success of mid-engined supercars from rivals Lamborghini and Ferrari was one of Giugiaro's first styling jobs when he set up Ital Design. With quad-cam 4.7- or 4.9-litre V8 power, the Bora had 160-mph capability.

aserati's first road cars did not appear until relatively recently, in 1958. By that time the company had developed an enormous reputation in motor racing, having produced one of the all-time greats in the shape of the Maserati 250F, which the likes of Stirling Moss and Juan Manuel Fangio drove so effectively. Even before the 250F had made a mark, Maserati had enjoyed success in the unlikely arena of Indianapolis as winners of the Indy 500 in 1939 and 1940.

With such a pedigree, it was a surprise that Maserati did not cash in earlier and start a road-building programme as well as producing their effective sports racers after the war. When road cars were finally developed they were strictly conventional front-engined rear-drive models and most of them sold well, building a reputation for practical and reliable high performance with a distinctive character. They kept Maserati well up among the supercar ranks, but by the mid-1960s a new era was starting, as first Lamborghini with the Miura and then Ferrari with the Dino moved the mid-engine layout from race track to production.

Innately conservative, Maserati couldn't respond immediately, and their image suffered for it. By the late 1960s they were slipping towards the fringes of Italy's supercar hierarchy, overshadowed by the glamour of old rivals Ferrari and the technical adventure of relative newcomers Lamborghini. Even Ford would have a mid-engined production model by 1970, in the De Tomaso Pantera.

In isolation, there was very little wrong with Maserati's cars; they still combined very high performance with a reputation for long-distance comfort and solid reliability that was second to none, but, without a mid-engined model, Maserati knew they would soon lack credibility.

Fortunately, they at least had a sound financial base to work from. In January 1968 they had signed an agreement with Citroën to co-operate on future designs and production – and especially to develop a new V6 engine for Citroën's planned high-performance luxury saloon, the SM. By March 1968, Citroën were the majority shareholder in Maserati, and they stayed that way until 1975, when the company was taken over by Alessandro De Tomaso.

By then, Maserati were ailing, but in 1968 they had had their best-ever year, building some 675 cars.

Making the very best of proven principles

On top of that and the Citroën backing, Maserati undoubtedly had the technical ability to join the new ranks of the mid-engined carmakers. Their long-time chief engineer Giulio Alfieri (who later did a brilliant job in helping to save Lamborghini) was one of the most respected people in the business, whose apparent conservatism was more a case of making the very best of proven principles. By late 1968 he had Citroën's full backing to build a mid-engined Maserati – or, more properly, two closely related mid-engined Maseratis, the first with the existing V8 engine and the second a basically similar car with the projected V6 engine from the SM, and a much lower price tag.

The V6-engined car would be launched in 1972, as the Merak, but the V8 came first, as the Bora – named, like many Maseratis, after a famous wind. Although the engine was amidships, the Bora followed familiar Maserati practice in many respects, in insisting on practicality and comfort even at the expense of weight and sophistication. *Tipo*

117, as it was known at the factory, was necessarily quite a big car, even though it was definitely only a two-seater. Most of the bulk, however, was within the wheelbase, which was a couple of inches longer than the capacious Ghibli's. That was unavoidable, because Alfieri's budget had still only allowed him to take the straightforward route of mounting the engine (the long-serving V8 virtually unchanged from the Ghibli and Mexico) and ZF gearbox longitudinally and in line, rather than starting with a clever but expensive concept like the Miura's transverse engine and gearbox-in-sump layout.

The main chassis was a massively strong steel unitary shell, with a square-section steel tube subframe to carry the engine, transmission and rear suspension – all mounted to the rear of the body at four points, each with careful attention to sound and vibration insulation. The large single radiator was in the nose of the car, with two big electric fans. Suspension was by conventional wishbones and coil springs all round, and steering was rack and

Below: By the time Citroën took control of the company in 1968, Maserati had already been upstaged in bringing the mid-engine configuration from the track to the road by supercar rivals Lamborghini (pioneering with the sensational Miura in 1966) and Ferrari. The Bora entered production in 1971.

Left and far left: The Bora is one of those exceptional designs that look beautifully balanced from almost any angle. Its stylist, Giorgetto Giugiaro, had already created perhaps the all-time classic Maserati, the Ghibli, during his time at Ghia, but the Bora/Merak project was one of the first assignments for his own studio, Ital Design. Echoes of the Ghibli can still be detected at the front and in the side-window upsweep.

pinion. The large, ventilated disc brakes were one of the few really innovative aspects of the car, borrowing their high-pressure, servo-operated hydraulic system from the latest Citroën saloons – and generating mixed reactions to their combination of extraordinary stopping power but sometimes undesirable over-sensitivity.

The Citroën hydraulics had other uses too. The seats of the Bora didn't move fore and aft, but the pedals did – hydraulically, and at the touch of a button. The seat also pivoted along its front edge to give hydraulic height adjustment, and the steering column could be raised and lowered manually, and moved in and out for reach. Very few people ever complained about not being able to find a decent driving position in the Bora . . .

The car was clothed by Giorgetto Giugiaro, as one of the first projects undertaken by his new styling house, Ital Design. He did a fine job not only in giving the Bora a handsome and distinctive look, but also in making the whole package more compact and accommodating than it really had any

right to be. In spite of that two-inch longer wheelbase, the Bora finally came out some nine inches shorter overall than the Ghibli and almost three inches narrower, yet still with ample passenger space and even quite generous luggage space under the front 'bonnet'.

Muscular enough to give thundering performance

Nor did Maserati stint on the trimmings, tackling the problem of potentially high noise levels with the mid-engine layout by building-in plenty of soundproofing as well as those carefully-cushioned subframe mountings. The interior was fully trimmed in leather and had good quality carpeting, with electric windows and air conditioning both on offer. It even had a clever additional luggage space built in behind the seats and running back alongside the engine bay, which was ideal for

taking a small briefcase or the other odds and ends which most other mid-engined cars couldn't accommodate in the cabin.

That really typified the Bora's determination to be a usable, comfortable, long-distance GT car in the proper sense rather than just a flamboyant mid-engined pseudo-racer, and on that basis it was very successful. The first prototype was running during 1970 and the car was unveiled at the Geneva Motor Show in March 1971, with few changes and genuinely ready for production. The strong engineering and many luxury touches made it a very heavy car for a two-seater, but the 4.7-litre V8 (launched with 310 bhp) was muscular enough to give it thundering, near-160 mph performance – if rather less outright acceleration than some of its lighter competitors. More to the point, it was truly refined, with low noise levels, tireless cruising ability and a fine blend of comfortable ride and sporty roadholding. It was expensive and thirsty, but to the typical Maserati customer it was a more than acceptable step into the modern world.

The Bora went on sale in America in 1974 once Maserati had confronted new safety and emissions requirements, and at the inevitable expense of some power. In 1975, a 4.9-litre version of the V8 (with a slightly longer stroke) was offered, not so much for more power as for even more flexibility, and that was standardised for Europe too by 1977. By then though, Maserati under De Tomaso had financial problems and the energy crisis had knocked a big hole in exotic car sales. Without any further significant changes, the Bora survived until 1980, by which time around 570 cars had been built, but by then Maserati were looking to smaller, more efficient cars for their salvation.

Maserati Bora

The Maserati Bora was in some ways a link from one era to another; in others it was a dinosaur. The link is between the old and thirsty heavyweight supercars like the Ferrari Daytona and the newer breed of mid-engined exotics, while its dinosaur nature is shown in a fuel consumption that would, on a good day, average 12 mpg. That clearly reveals the car as a design pre-dating the fuel crisis of the early 1970s, which brought about the extinction of exotics like the Bora and in fact prompted the creation of the Bora's lookalike smaller brother, the V6 Merak.

Double-glazed interior window

Separating the driver from the V8 just behind his seat was a rear window, double-glazed for extra sound protection.

Quad-cam V8

The sting in the Bora's tail came from an all-alloy quad-cam V8 with the conventional two valves per cylinder. With four Weber downdraught carburettors pumping in fuel the engine produced 310 bhp from its 4.7 litres.

'Overdriven' but uneconomical

The Bora's transmission had the novelty that both fourth and fifth gear ratios were less than 1:1, at 0.85:1 and 0.74:1 respectively, giving a relaxed 28 mph per 1,000 rpm in top gear. Despite this, and the car's excellent aerodynamics, the Bora was still extremely thirsty.

Ventilated discs

The combination of the Bora's substantial weight and high top speed led to vented discs being specified for both front and rear brakes.

Glassed-in rear engine cover

To provide access to the mid-mounted V8 engine, the Bora was fitted with a very large engine cover that incorporated top and side windows.

Normal-profile tyres

Today, cars capable of the Bora's 160-mph performance have low-profile tyres as an aid to handling and roadholding. In contrast, the Bora ran on ordinary 70-section tyres, 215/70 front and rear.

Above: Unlike many other supercars, the Bora underwent few styling alterations in what was quite a lengthy period in production, other than accommodating protruding bumpers to meet US regulations. Under the skin, the only significant change was an increase in engine displacement from 4.7 to 4.9 litres (by means of a longer stroke) to compensate for American exhaust emission restrictions. This alteration came in 1975 on US-spec cars and in 1977 on others.

Driving the Bora: *predictable power*

The Bora was one of the most successful of the first-generation mid-engined cars; even the visibility is better all round than in many competitors. The sound and feel of the four-cam V8 falls somewhere between that of a big US V8 and an exotic V12 – with the deep rumble of the first overlain by the lighter feel of the second, though without the typical mechanical clatterings. The power is impressive more for its slogging willingness than for any high-revving hysteria – after all, the red-line starts at only 5,500 rpm. You are always aware that the Bora is a heavy car, yet an impressively quick one, capable of 0-60 mph

acceleration in around 6½ seconds and 0-100 mph in less than 15 seconds. Although its tyres are relatively modest for so much weight and power, the car has lots of grip, plenty of traction and a very forgiving nature. It corners with little roll, and its handling is pleasantly responsive to both steering and throttle inputs. There's enough power to provoke oversteer, and caution is advisable in wet conditions, but that's true of any very powerful rear-drive car. It has its faults: the ride is hard enough to upset the line over bumps and the brakes are ferocious, but the Bora is one of the safest and most enjoyable cars of its type.

PERFORMANCE & SPECIFICATION COMPARISON	Engine	Displacement	Power	Torque (lb ft)	Max speed	0-60 mph	Length (in/mm)	Wheelbase (in/mm)	Track front/rear	Weight total (lb/kg)	Price
Maserati Bora	V8, quad-cam	4719 cc	310 bhp 6000 rpm	339 lb ft 4200 rpm	160 mph 257 km/h	6.5 sec	171.0 in 4343 mm	102.5 in 2604 mm	57.8 in 57.0 in	3342 lb 1516 kg	£10,345 (1973)
Alfa Romeo Montreal	V8, quad-cam	2593 cc	200 bhp 6500 rpm	173 lb ft 4750 rpm	137 mph 220 km/h	8.1 sec	166.0 in 4216 mm	92.5 in 2350 mm	54.3 in 52.5 in	2811 lb 1275 kg	£4,999 (1973)
De Tomaso Pantera	V8, overhead-valve	5763 cc	350 bhp 6000 rpm	333 lb ft 3800 rpm	162 mph 261 km/h	5.4 sec	168.1 in 4270 mm	99.0 in 2515 mm	59.5 in 62.1 in	3131 lb 1420 kg	£6,696 (1973)
Jaguar E-type V12	V12, overhead-cam	5343 cc	272 bhp 6000 rpm	304 lb ft 3600 rpm	142 mph 229 km/h	6.8 sec	184.5 in 4686 mm	105.0 in 2667 mm	53.0 in 53.0 in	3230 lb 1465 kg	£3,367 (1973)
Lamborghini Jarama	V12, quad-cam	3929 cc	350 bhp 7500 rpm	289 lb ft 5500 rpm	162 mph 261 km/h	6.8 sec	175.0 in 4445 mm	93.5 in 2375 mm	55.1 in 55.1 in	3472 lb 1575 kg	£9,172 (1973)

Maserati Bora Data File

Although they had been famous as racing car manufacturers since the mid-1920s, as Indianapolis winners in 1939 and 1940, and as World Champion Grand Prix constructors in 1957, until the late 1950s Maserati, rather like Ferrari, had only ever dabbled with building road cars. They didn't start a serious production programme until 1958, with the six-cylinder 3500 GT, and that was after they had pulled out of racing because of pressing financial problems. Once they did make the move into production, however, they made quite a success of it. The 3500 GT took annual Maserati output into three figures for the first time in its first year of production, and they followed it up with six- and eight-cylinder models like the 5000 GT, the *Quattroporte* (literally, four-door), the Mistral, Sebring, Ghibli and Mexico.

The Bora, and its smaller-engined brother, the V6 Merak, were Maserati's first venture into the realm of the mid-engined supercar. It was a move virtually forced on the company by the clearly more exotic products from Ferrari and Lamborghini. The V8 Bora appeared first, at the 1971 Geneva Motor Show, followed a year later by the V6 Merak.

Above: The Bora's nose, with its trident-adorned split grille and hidden headlamps, evoked that of the Ghibli. American safety rules later foisted on it a projecting bumper in place of the distinctive grille.

Above: Engineered by Giulio Alfieri, the Bora was the first mid-engined Maserati to enter production. It was unveiled at the Geneva Motor Show in 1971 and hardly modified at all before being put on sale.

Styling

It was only logical that Maserati should turn to Giorgetto Giugiaro to clothe their exciting new project, as he had produced brilliant work for them before. In 1966, while working as head of design at Ghia, he had been in inspired form, creating not only the De Tomaso Mangusta but also what many would rate as one of the most flawless and timeless shapes ever: the Maserati Ghibli. Now running his own show at Ital Design, he was the obvious choice for the Bora/Merak commission. In common with other Maseratis, the Bora was to be a robust, dependable and practical Grand Tourer, not a fragile and temperamental exotic, and it was hugely to Giugiaro's credit that the car's styling managed to contribute to this element of its character at the same time as having great visual impact and excitement. The end result looked powerful, dynamic and eager, as muscular and purposeful as any competitor, yet was considerably more convenient to live with (in the modern idiom, more 'user-friendly') than others of its ilk. For a mid-engined sports car it provided reasonable all-round visibility, well thought-out luggage space, and a comfortable, nicely-trimmed interior without needless ostentation. It's a testament to Giugiaro's skill that he managed to package a large V8 never intended for mid-engined location to such good effect. In all, it was a solid, compact, well-packaged and effective design.

Above: Giugiaro had every reason to be proud to put his name on the Bora, which not only looked fine but was also a very easy kind of supercar to live with.

Left: Details like this extra cubbyhole, accessible from the engine compartment, added to the Bora's useability.

Left: The corresponding door to the right-hand side of the engine bay gave access to the remotely-located coolant header tank. The single, large radiator was mounted in the nose, and air was drawn through it by twin electric fans.

Above: The Bora's interior was as pleasing as its exterior. Unlike some other models (including early Meraks, which borrowed the dash of the Maserati-engined Citroën SM), it had a traditional and comprehensive instrument array. Trim and furnishings were comfortable and high-class without being ostentatious; upholstery was leather. Visibility from the cabin was better than that in most mid-engined cars.

Left: Later-model Boras gained a Bosch electronic ignition pack, as part of the process of cleaning up the engine to comply with increasingly stringent American emission-control regulations. The Bora entered the US market in 1974; the year after, the V8 was enlarged from 4.7 to 4.9 litres.

SPECIFICATION
1973 Maserati Bora

ENGINE

Type:	V8, quad-cam
Construction:	light-alloy block and heads, five main bearings
Bore×stroke:	93.9 mm×85 mm
Displacement:	4719 cc
Compression ratio:	8.5:1
Valve gear:	two valves per cylinder operated by twin overhead camshafts per bank of cylinders
Fuel system:	four Weber DCNF/14 downdraught carburettors
Ignition:	mechanical by coil and distributor
Maximum power:	310 bhp (DIN) at 6,000 rpm
Maximum torque:	339 lb ft at 4,200 rpm

TRANSMISSION

Type:	ZF five-speed manual	
Ratios:	1st	2.58:1
	2nd	1.52:1
	3rd	1.04:1
	4th	0.846:1
	5th	0.74:1
Final drive ratio:	3.77:1	

BODY/CHASSIS

Type:	unitary body/chassis assembly with subframes front and rear for suspension

RUNNING GEAR

Steering:	rack and pinion, with hydraulic damper
Suspension:	front: independent with upper and lower wishbones, coil springs, telescopic dampers and anti-roll bar rear: independent with upper and lower wishbones, coil springs, telescopic dampers and anti-roll bar
Brakes:	Girling ventilated discs front and rear with Citroën high-pressure hydraulic actuation
Wheels:	light alloy, 7½×15 in
Tyres:	Michelin 215/70 VR15 front and rear

DIMENSIONS AND WEIGHT

Length:	171.0 in (4343 mm)
Width:	70.5 in (1791 mm)
Height:	43.0 in (1092 mm)
Wheelbase:	102.5 in (2604 mm)
Track:	57.8 in (1468 mm) front, 57.0 in (1448 mm) rear
Kerb weight:	3,342 lb (1516 kg)

PERFORMANCE

Acceleration:	0-30 mph 2.5 sec		
	0-40 mph 3.3 sec		
	0-50 mph 5.1 sec		
	0-60 mph 6.5 sec		
	0-70 mph 8.0 sec		
	0-80 mph 9.9 sec		
	0-90 mph 12.4 sec		
	0-100 mph 14.7 sec		
	0-110 mph 17.9 sec		
	0-120 mph 23.0 sec		
Standing ¼ mile:	14.6 sec		
Standing km:	26.2 sec		
Acceleration in gear:	mph	fifth	fourth
	30-50	7.7	6.7
	40-60	7.7	6.2
	50-70	7.5	6.0
Maximum speed:	160 mph (257 km/h)		
Overall fuel consumption:	10.9 mpg		
Price (1973):	£10,345		

Performance figures from AUTOCAR

Maserati Bora kindly supplied by Geoffrey Addison

Five-speed ZF gearbox

The transmission was mounted behind the engine, further to the rear of the car, and Maserati used a tough ZF five-speed unit rather than one of their own design.

Aerodynamics by eye

The Bora was styled by the young Giugiaro before he had access to the wind tunnels that shape today's designs. Even so, the end result was an impressive Cd of only 0.30, which helps account for the Bora's impressive top speed of 160 mph.

Front-mounted radiator

The Bora pre-dated the trend of fitting radiators on the car's flanks, nearer the engine. The usual front-mounted radiator was retained, with long pipes leading back to the engine, cooled by twin electric fans.

Double-wishbone suspension

Classic double-wishbone suspension was the norm for performance cars in the early 1970s, and the Bora followed that fashion.

High-pressure brake hydraulics

Maserati was under Citroën control when the Bora was built, but the only obvious Citroën feature was the very high-pressure brake hydraulic system in which the brake pedal acted more like a switch than a lever.

Early alloy bodies

The very first Boras had hand-crafted aluminium-alloy bodies, but by the time production was fully under way the alloy had been changed to steel, even though output was still very low.

Monocoque construction

Unlike the famous 'Birdcage' Maserati sports car, with its extremely complex spaceframe chassis, the Bora used welded sheet-steel construction forming a very stiff monocoque.

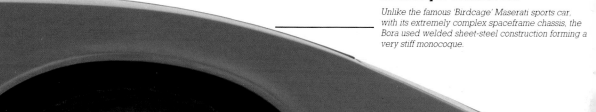
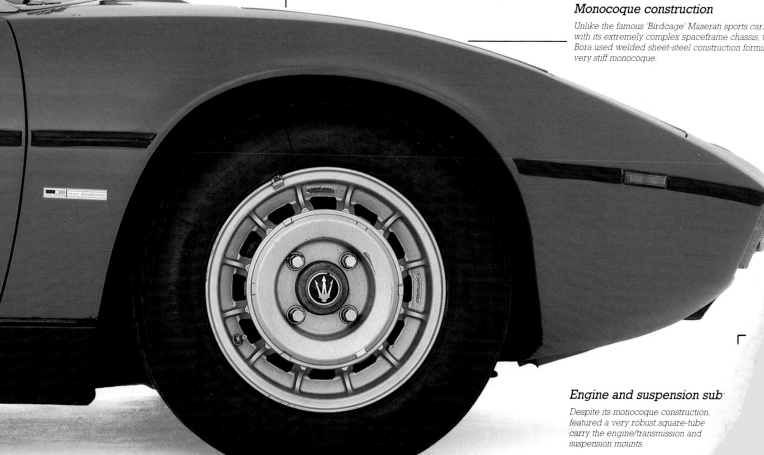

Engine and suspension sub·

Despite its monocoque construction, featured a very robust square-tube carry the engine/transmission and suspension mounts.

Below: The Merak was conceived alongside the Bora to use the V6 engine created for the Citroën SM. It was easy to distinguish the Merak by its flat rear deck with 'flying buttresses'.

Maserati Merak

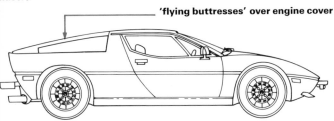

'flying buttresses' over engine cover

Below: Both models had a very similar profile but the Bora's fastback was enclosed by large expanses of glass, while the Merak's consisted merely of struts and thin air. The two outlines here depict the obtrusive bumpers added to US-market cars for crash protection.

Maserati Bora

lift-up engine cover

glassed-in rear section

fuel filler cap

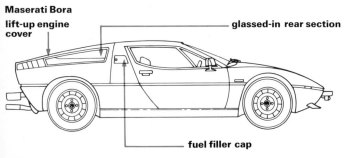

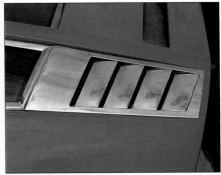

Left: Extractor louvres neatly integrated with the rear side-window line were another noteworthy Bora styling detail. On some cars they appeared in bright metal; on others they were matt black.

Chassis/body

One surprising thing about the Bora is that, aside from the fact that it pioneered the mid-engine layout for Maserati and had some interesting hydraulic innovations courtesy of Citroën, it was really a very conventional piece of engineering. The chassis was a combination of square-section steel tubes and pressed-steel panels, forming a unitary front and centre shell with a strong but simple rear subframe carrying the whole engine, transmission and suspension assembly. The entire rear end of the car could be detached for major maintenance in just a couple of hours. By, say, Miura standards, the shape of the virtually all-steel outer body is quite conservative, but that was Giugiaro's contribution to the theme of practical GT car rather than flashy exotic. The long wheelbase is compensated for visually by short front and rear overhangs; the bluff nose (with proper radiator grilles), although not particularly low, has the inevitable pop-up headlights, and the main styling feature is in the flip-up curve of the door windows and the neat rear window treatment – the biggest visual difference between the Bora and its baby brother Merak. The whole rear deck, with its acres of glass, tilts backwards for everyday engine access. In spite of a fairly square-cut tail, Kamm-style, the Bora isn't a particularly slippery car aerodynamically, but that's another compromise for practicality, and at least it has no nasty vices at high speed and no need for tacky add-on spoilers. It just looks very good.

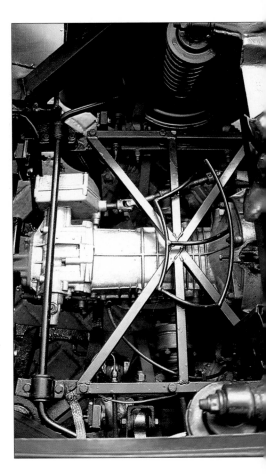

Suspension/running gear

Maserati's new association with Citroën in theory gave Alfieri access to some very interesting and generally highly acclaimed technology. Citroën were especially renowned for their oleo-pneumatic suspension (giving a supple ride with outstanding damping control) and their high-pressure braking systems, but in the end Alfieri was content to take only the powerful brakes – and those with a conventional pedal rather than the earlier Citroën floor-mounted button. Even that wasn't entirely popular, with many people admiring the power of the system but complaining that the strictly 'on-off' feel was very difficult to adapt to in a sports car. One area in which Alfieri resisted the Citroën parts-bin was in the Bora's suspension, which was strictly conventional, with the familiar layout of unequal-length upper and lower wishbones all round, controlled by coil-spring/damper units and anti-roll bars. Amazingly, that made the Bora the first production Maserati with independent rear suspension. Nor did Alfieri adopt Citroën's quirky power-assisted steering, preferring instead to use a more sports-car-like geared rack-and-pinion system with about three turns from lock to lock. As usually for a mid-engined car, with inevitable rear weight bias (the Bora was approximately 42/58 per cent front to rear), the Bora had similarly-sized wheels front and rear – 7½-in × 15-in Campagnolo alloys, usually with 215/70 × 15-in Michelin XWX radials – but little else about it was out of the ordinary.

Above: The hefty top-frame mount of the coil/damper unit (top of picture) was a key point of the Bora rear suspension.

Engine

While others saw V12s as a basic requirement for supercar status in the early 1970s, Maserati, even with the financial cushion of their alliance with Citroën, were content to stick with their 90-degree V8. It was an old engine but a good one, with a fine pedigree. It had originated in the late 1950s, as a racing design for the 450S sports racer; by the mid-1960s it had evolved into production form, in front-engined models like the Indy, Ghibli, Mexico and the Quattroporte. What it lacked in cylinders, it compensated for with good old-fashioned capacity,

at a hefty 4.7 litres. It was acceptably light thanks to its all-alloy construction, comfortably oversquare, and strong, with a five-main-bearing crankshaft. Two overhead camshafts per bank were conventionally driven by chains and operated two inclined valves per cylinder in hemispherical combustion chambers, with notably less mechanical fuss than some of its V12 rivals. Again in contrast to its V12 counterparts, it was quite a low-revving engine, with maximum power delivered at only 6,000 rpm – and even that was 500 rpm beyond the

sustainable red-line. With four twin-choke downdraught Weber carburettors it produced 310 bhp, but even more usefully, torque peaked at some 339 lb ft, with a formidable spread. It was uncomplicated, strong and reliable, at the expense of a fairly prodigious thirst. In 1975, a year after the Bora had made its belated entry to the US market, Maserati offered a 4.9-litre version, in partial compensation for the power-sapping emissions controls it had had to adopt. In European tune, this gave 320 bhp with even more torque.

Left: Access to the engine was convenient, thanks to the large, backward-hinged aft cabin section. The entire subframe assembly could be detached in an hour or two for major maintenance.

Left: Longitudinally mounted behind the engine, a five-speed ZX transaxle sat between the rear wheels. The Bora was constructed with a unitary front and centre shell on which was hung a fabricated rear subframe bearing the complete driveline and rear suspension. Note the anti-roll bar location above the frame rails.

Above: Maserati's V8 engine was a tough and reliable 90-degree four-cam V8 descended from the power units of their 1950s sports racers. Unlike most of its exotic European rivals, it was not a rev-happy screamer but had masses of low-down torque. The 4.9-litre version gave 320 bhp at 6,000 rpm and 339 lb ft at 4,200 rpm.

Above left: The engine, transaxle and rear suspension were all carried by a subframe fabricated from heavy, square-section tube, and the whole assembly was bolted to the body structure on four vibration-damped mounts.

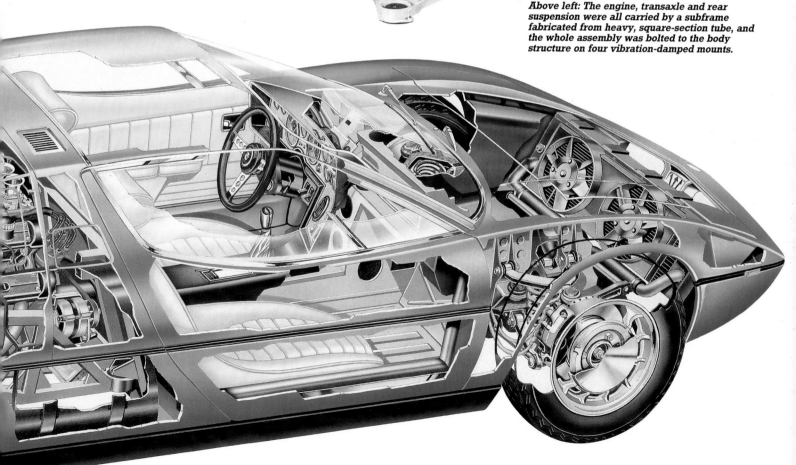

Above: The Bora, although of heavier build than some of its rivals, was still very much a racing chassis developed to be civilised on the road. Its mid-engine configuration with all-independent suspension by unequal-length wishbones and coil-spring/damper units with anti-roll bars at each end was typical of sports racers of its day. The quad-cam V8 breathed through four twin-choke Weber carburettors.

Nissan 300ZX

Nissan built the archetypal sports cars of the 1970s – the satisfying but simple 'Z-cars'. When they created their 1990s flagship, the 300ZX, Nissan made a sophisticated supercar capable of 155 mph and 0-60 mph in 5.6 seconds.

Above: A deeper front dam and a rear spoiler distinguish the Turbo models. In Europe only the 2+2 Turbo version has been offered.

Right: A 300ZX hallmark is the steeply raked windscreen. The hiked-up tail is intended to evoke contemporary sports racers.

I n the 1970s the Datsun 240Z and its successors became the best-selling sports cars of all time. This was the first Japanese car to make inroads into a part of the market that belonged traditionally to the British. As a response to its main audience in the United States, the 'Z-car' became less of a pure sports car and more of a boulevard cruiser as the years went by. It evolved into the 280ZX and then the 300ZX. When the time came to plan a replacement, Nissan decided to go back to first principles.

That was in 1984. A wind of change was soon to blow through the Nissan Technical Centre at Atsugi, an hour's drive from Tokyo. Nissan Motor Corporation's new president, Yutaka Kume, instituted 'Programme 901'. That indicated a corporate aim: to become number one in automotive technology in the 1990s. The new-generation 300ZX was to be the flagship for this advanced technology.

The engineers of Product Planning Group No. 4 wanted to get back to the idea that had made the 240Z such a sensation 15 years before. But it was far from easy to translate those values into 1990s terms. They had a good starting point in that President Kume had decreed that future Nissans should, above all, provide driving pleasure. Katsuo

Yamada, project leader at the time, says that the engineers had concluded that the idea for a true sports car should start with high performance.

A logical result of these basic principles might have been to produce a two-seater with the mid-engined layout of a racing car. Honda were to adopt such a configuration for the NSX, and, indeed, Nissan had built and exhibited mid-engined Mid-4 prototypes.

But it did not take long for the project team to discard the mid-engined idea for the new 300ZX. Shigeyuki Yamaoka, Yamada's successor as head of the project, says: "A high-performance car with a mid-ship engine is appreciated by those who have higher driving skills. We wanted the 300ZX to be enjoyed by a wide spectrum of customers all over the world." There were other considerations too: the previous models had shown that a high proportion of customers demanded 2+2 seating and generous luggage space, neither of which could be provided in a mid-engined car of reasonable dimensions.

So the new car was to be front-engined with rear drive. After studying various alternatives it was decided to continue with a three-litre V6 engine based on the VG30 unit that powered the

previous ZX, though by the time its development was complete there was hardly any of the original engine left.

Four cams, four valves per cylinder, electronic fuel injection, variable valve timing, and an ignition coil for each cylinder (direct ignition) were all incorporated. In normally-aspirated form the new engine produces 222 bhp. The later version with twin turbochargers and intercoolers – the only type to be sold in Europe – is boosted to between 280 and 300 bhp. The dual intake and exhaust systems for the Turbo are particularly complicated; a mass of pipework takes up every bit of available space under the bonnet.

Four-cam, 24-valve V6 with twin turbos

Although, for reasons of weight and bonnet height, it was decided not to adopt four-wheel drive, the new 300ZX benefits from most other aspects of Nissan's 'new deal' technology. In the interests of tenacious roadholding, sharp but predictable handling and reasonable ride comfort, the

car was given sophisticated multi-link suspension at front and rear. The power steering is a novel twin-orifice system for more consistent response. There is electronic anti-lock braking and a viscous-coupling limited-slip differential. And it has the Super HICAS rear-wheel steering system. The latter is unlike other rear-steer systems in that the computer responds to chassis sensors that indicate high-speed cornering by providing a twitch of counter-steer before settling with all four wheels pointing in the same direction. Though the rear-wheel movements are subtle – usually no more than 0.5 degrees – the effect is rather like the rally drivers' technique of flicking the steering onto opposite lock before turning into a corner.

Packaging all this equipment within a modern but unusual compact coupé body was quite a triumph for Nissan's design studio. By using a 'cab forward' stance, they managed to achieve almost a mid-engined appearance. A long wheelbase (5 in greater than that of the old 300ZX) and short overhangs front and rear produced a car that was shorter overall but more spacious inside. Cleverly, although the 2+2 version is 8 in longer than the two-seater, at a glance the two are virtually indistinguishable. The windscreen is among the steepest-angled of any production car and, in conjunction with flush side glass (which uses a track system not unlike the Audi 100's), this helps keep the drag coefficient down to 0.31. As in the previous 300ZX, a

T-bar system provides the opportunity to take out one or both smoked-glass roof panels for open-air motoring.

Each feature of the new car was the result of careful research into the likes and demands of the sports car buyer. In this, Nissan were remarkably thorough. They even produced a scientific paper on the precision and ease of movement of sports car gearshifts... with the result that the new 300ZX was given double-cone synchronisers on second and third gears, a new lever linkage, and (on the Turbo) servo-assistance for the clutch.

As their 'target' for performance and handling Nissan took the Porsche 944 Turbo, and the new 300ZX became the first Nissan to have an extensive overseas test programme, which included road and track driving in Europe and North America in company with rival cars. The European-specification 2+2 Turbo had extensive testing at high speed on German autobahns and on the old 14-mile Nürburgring road circuit, where Nissan's testers lapped faster than Porsche's could manage with a 928 GT. Performance figures compare well with the Porsche 944 Turbo's: 155 mph maximum, 0-60 mph in 5.6 seconds, and 0-100 mph in 15.

"The best damn sports car in the world"

The new 300ZX was launched first, in normally-aspirated form, onto the US market. The 2+2 and Turbo (which is available only as a two-seater in the USA) followed later in the year. Normally-aspirated cars for Australia and all versions for the Japanese home market came next and then, from April 1990, the special 2+2 Turbos for Europe.

In recognition of their 155-mph potential on the autobahn, the cars for Europe undergo a special test procedure at the end of the production line at Nissan Shatai in Hiratsuka City, the Z-car factory. Each spends 50 minutes on a high-speed rolling road dynamometer, a period which includes con-

Left: You can spot that this pearl-yellow example is a two-seater by the fuel filler opening ahead of the rear left wheel arch, and you can tell it's an American-market car by its unbadged nose. Nissan build the 300ZX in turbocharged and normally-aspirated, two-seater and 2+2 forms. This one is unblown but a turbocharged version of the two-seater is available in the US.

Above: British and other European 300ZXs carry the Nissan logo (inset picture, top) between their headlamps; on Japanese home-market cars this is replaced by a large 'Z' badge. All the Turbo cars have Nissan's development of four-wheel steering, which they call Super HICAS.

Nissan 300ZX

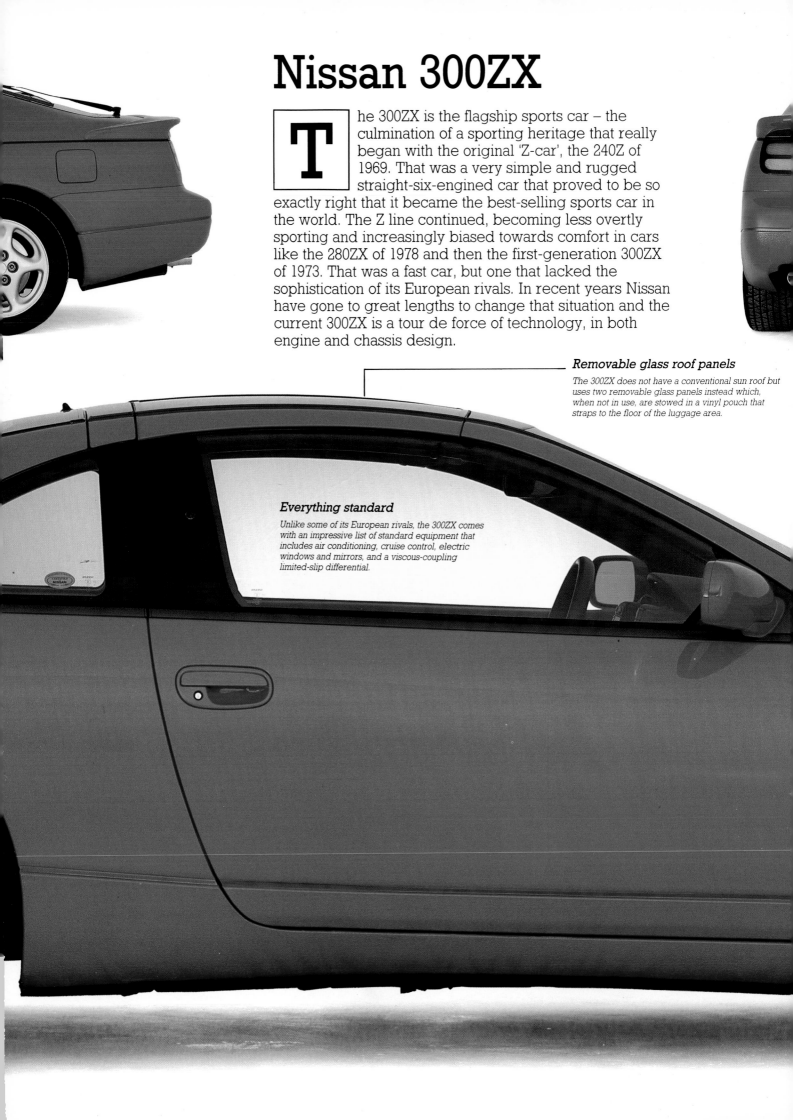

T he 300ZX is the flagship sports car – the culmination of a sporting heritage that really began with the original 'Z-car', the 240Z of 1969. That was a very simple and rugged straight-six-engined car that proved to be so exactly right that it became the best-selling sports car in the world. The Z line continued, becoming less overtly sporting and increasingly biased towards comfort in cars like the 280ZX of 1978 and then the first-generation 300ZX of 1973. That was a fast car, but one that lacked the sophistication of its European rivals. In recent years Nissan have gone to great lengths to change that situation and the current 300ZX is a tour de force of technology, in both engine and chassis design.

Removable glass roof panels

The 300ZX does not have a conventional sun roof but uses two removable glass panels instead which, when not in use, are stowed in a vinyl pouch that straps to the floor of the luggage area.

Everything standard

Unlike some of its European rivals, the 300ZX comes with an impressive list of standard equipment that includes air conditioning, cruise control, electric windows and mirrors, and a viscous-coupling limited-slip differential.

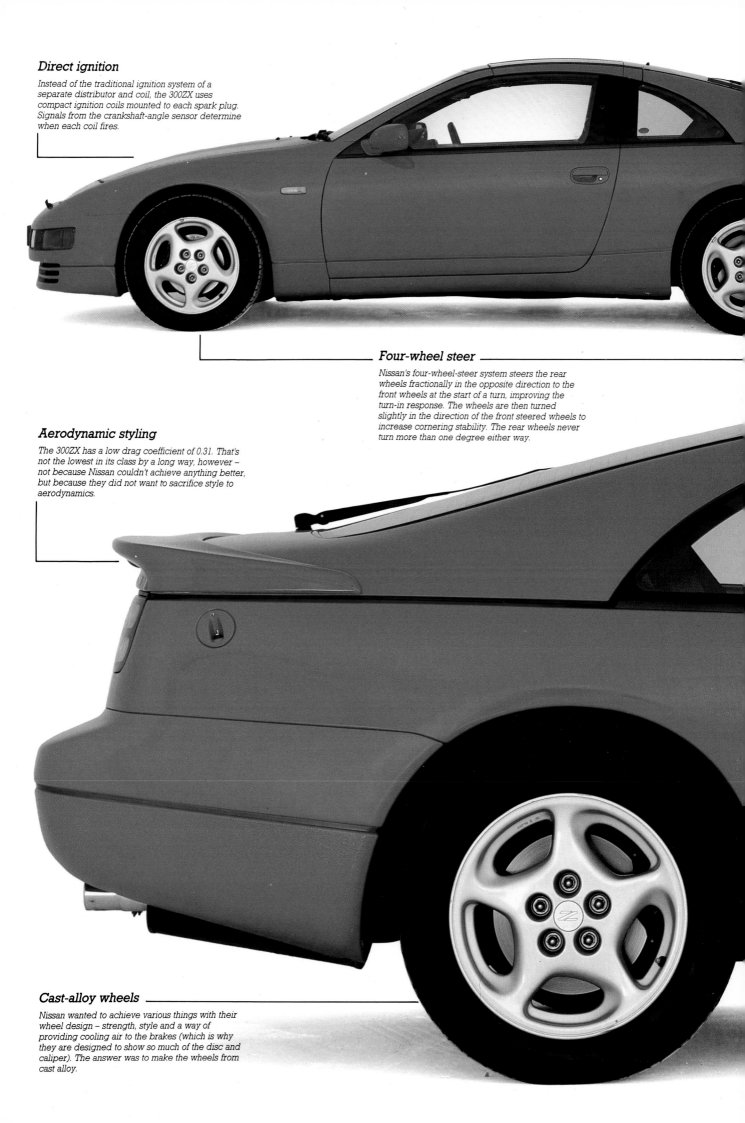

Direct ignition

Instead of the traditional ignition system of a separate distributor and coil, the 300ZX uses compact ignition coils mounted to each spark plug. Signals from the crankshaft-angle sensor determine when each coil fires.

Four-wheel steer

Nissan's four-wheel-steer system steers the rear wheels fractionally in the opposite direction to the front wheels at the start of a turn, improving the turn-in response. The wheels are then turned slightly in the direction of the front steered wheels to increase cornering stability. The rear wheels never turn more than one degree either way.

Aerodynamic styling

The 300ZX has a low drag coefficient of 0.31. That's not the lowest in its class by a long way, however – not because Nissan couldn't achieve anything better, but because they did not want to sacrifice style to aerodynamics.

Cast-alloy wheels

Nissan wanted to achieve various things with their wheel design – strength, style and a way of providing cooling air to the brakes (which is why they are designed to show so much of the disc and caliper). The answer was to make the wheels from cast alloy.

tinuous running at maximum speed.

The initial response to the new 300ZX was terrific. In America, it immediately went to the top of the class. In Japan, it sold better than any previous Z-car. In Britain, it had the distinction, pre-Honda NSX, of being the most expensive Japanese car ever offered, starting at £34,500, though the price has since been reduced to £30,650.

The new model, despite a significantly higher price than its predecessor in all markets, was given an enthusiastic welcome by car magazines. It was a different order of Z-car, which bore comparison with even more expensive machinery from other manufacturers. In naming it their 1990 Import Car of the Year, *Motor Trend* said: "Dollar for dollar, this is the best damn sports car in the world."

Above: The Super HICAS system enhances high-speed handling on Turbos. It senses speed, steering angle and driver input, and first applies a tiny twitch of counter-steer, then turns the rear wheels (by under one degree) in the same direction as the fronts.

Driving the 300ZX: Porsche class

The 300ZX is a car that envelops you with its sweeping facia and side trim, and places everything – wheel, pedals, gear lever, instruments – in an ideal position.

The controls work with precision, and the engine sounds and feels sweet and strong. Hustled through a series of bends the car reassures the driver with its well-balanced handling. There is little body roll, dip or squat. The ride is firm but not unreasonably so. And the 300ZX *goes* – thrusting to a regulated 155 mph.

The value of four-wheel steering is notoriously difficult to assess. Suffice it to say that the normally-aspirated 300ZX that is sold in America feels good enough without it, but that Nissan's engineers thought it an important addition for the Turbo. At speed, Super HICAS certainly makes the car eager to turn into a corner; the steering is, in any case, high-geared.

Like any powerful car, the 300ZX Turbo demands caution on slippery roads. Though there is power aplenty at low revs, there is a definite further push beyond 2,700 rpm, when the turbochargers are developing full boost. On Britain's roads, just about the only disadvantage of the 300ZX is its considerable girth – an inch under six feet.

PERFORMANCE & SPECIFICATION COMPARISON	Engine	Displacement	Power	Torque (lb ft)	Max speed	0-60 mph	Length (in/mm)	Wheelbase (in/mm)	Track front/rear	Weight total (lb/kg)	Price
Nissan 300ZX	V6, twin-cam, 24-valve, turbo	2960 cc	280 bhp 6400 rpm	274 lb ft 3600 rpm	155 mph 249 km/h	5.6 sec	178.1 in 4525 mm	101.2 in 2570 mm	58.9 in 60.4 in	3485 lb 1581 kg	£30,650 (1991)
Ferrari 348 tb	V8, quad-cam, 32-valve	3405 cc	300 bhp 7000 rpm	224 lb ft 4000 rpm	153 mph 246 km/h	5.6 sec	166.5 in 4229 mm	97.8 in 2484 mm	59.0 in 62.2 in	3300 lb 1497 kg	£74,587 (1991)
Honda NSX	V6, quad-cam, 24-valve	2977 cc	274 bhp 7000 rpm	210 lb ft 5300 rpm	162 mph 261 km/h	5.2 sec	173.4 in 4405 mm	99.6 in 2530 mm	59.4 in 60.2 in	3020 lb 1370 kg	£55,000 (1991)
Lotus Esprit Turbo SE	Inline-four, 16-valve, turbo	2174 cc	264 bhp 6500 rpm	261 lb ft 3900 rpm	161 mph 259 km/h	4.9 sec	171.0 in 4343 mm	96.0 in 2438 mm	60.0 in 61.2 in	2650 lb 1202 kg	£47,310 (1991)
Porsche 944 Turbo	Inline-four, turbo	2479 cc	250 bhp 6000 rpm	258 lb ft 4000 rpm	154 mph 248 km/h	5.7 sec	165.4 in 4200 mm	94.5 in 2400 mm	58.2 in 57.1 in	2698 lb 1224 kg	£43,648 (1991)

Nissan 300ZX Data File

Number two among Japan's carmakers – behind Toyota – Nissan did not become a major player on the world stage until the mid-1960s when they started to export in volume to the United States.

They were active in rallying and racing with their Datsun Bluebird saloons but their first real sports car was a roadster which looked rather like (though in fact preceded) the MGB. It was called the Fairlady – because Nissan's president at the time had enthused about the musical *My Fair Lady*. The name is still used today for the Japanese-market 300ZX.

The roadster's engine grew from 1.5 and 1.6 to two litres – the latter 2000 Sports becoming the mainstay of the official Datsun racing programme in the USA. By 1969 Nissan had the confidence to introduce a sports car specially for the US market. They were to use a 2.4-litre straight-six overhead-cam engine. With the style of a Jaguar E-type, the size of a Porsche 911, the performance of an Austin-Healey 3000, and the price of an MGB GT (in America), the new car would be an instant success. Fairlady Z sounded too sissy a name for America, so the project number was adopted instead: 240Z.

As exhaust-emission regulations became more severe, a bigger engine and fuel injection became necessary to maintain the Z-car's performance. Over the years, the 240Z became the 260Z and – for the US only – the 280Z.

The Z-cars' success prompted Nissan's US company to ask for their successor to be 'up-scale', more luxurious, and more elaborately equipped. The 280ZX was the result. By 1982 all Datsun cars had adopted the corporate name 'Nissan'. A year later a new V6 three-litre engine was announced, which was to turn the Nissan 280ZX into the 300ZX.

The original 300ZX had a five-year run. In its final version, sold only in Japan, it had a four-cam, 24-valve engine. That, in basis, was virtually the only thing carried over to the new Z-car – apart, of course, from the name.

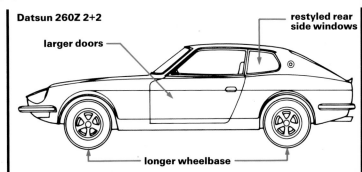

Datsun 260Z 2+2
larger doors — restyled rear side windows — longer wheelbase

Above: By 1981 you could buy a turbocharged two-seater 280ZX in the US. For 1982, both two- and four-seaters had the turbo option in left-hand-drive markets.

Below: Though its lines echoed the original 'Z-car' theme, the 280ZX was a new car, with a semi-trailing-arm rear end and a T-bar roof option.

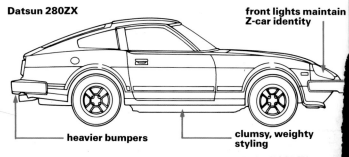

Datsun 280ZX
heavier bumpers — front lights maintain Z-car identity — clumsy, weighty styling

Below: The first 300ZX came in 1983, equipped with the VG30 V6 engine, producing 170 bhp or 228 bhp with turbo. Although based on the 280 floorpan, its body was all new and much better aerodynamically.

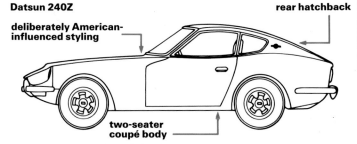

Above and outline below: The original Z-car, the 1969 Datsun 240Z, was an immediate success. With a 2.4-litre straight-six and strut suspension all round, it offered "the looks of an E-type and the performance of a Porsche, for the price of an MGB". Conceived for the USA, it didn't reach the UK until 1971.

Datsun 240Z
deliberately American-influenced styling — rear hatchback — two-seater coupé body

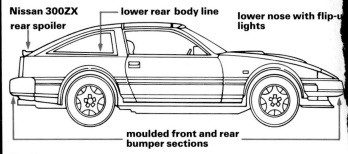

Nissan 300ZX
rear spoiler — lower rear body line — lower nose with flip-up lights — moulded front and rear bumper sections

Above: Successor to the 240Z was the 2.6-litre 260Z, introduced in 1974. The increase in capacity was a response to US Federal emissions and safety stipulations and didn't bring any improvements in performance (in fact the 240Z was faster).

Top of next column: With the 260Z came a 2+2 option; after 1976 few two-seaters were sold in Europe. In America by 1975 ever-tightening emission regulations necessitated fuel injection and a further stretch in capacity to 2.8 litres.

Styling

In contrast to the original 240Z, which was based on designs by a German, Albrecht Goertz, and the final facelift of the old 300ZX, done by Nissan Design International in California, the new 300ZX was designed entirely in Japan. Nissan's design team see it as indicating a maturity in Japanese car design. Yoshio Maezawa, deputy general manager of the Nissan Design Centre and the co-ordinator of the project, says: "I want people to regard it first as good, and then secondly as Japanese." Group C sports-racing cars were the inspiration for the 'cab forward' stance and the high tail, which exposes four exhaust pipes and some of the rear suspension. Faced with a variety of ideas for the new car, the management took the unusually bold step of choosing the most radical design, by Isao Sono. He explains its key features: "We wanted to place the driver at the centre of the car to achieve a visual balance. We made the side windows very characteristic, and the steeply raked windscreen and unusual headlamps add to its personality." Although aerodynamic stability and a low drag factor were important requirements, Nissan's designers did not let the wind tunnel dictate the shape of the 300ZX. They were happy to achieve a Cd of 0.31 and a lift coefficient close to zero, front and rear. The normally-aspirated car is the 'pure' design, but the higher performance of the Turbo demanded a deeper front apron and tail spoiler to ensure stability.

SPECIFICATION
1991 Nissan 300ZX

ENGINE

Type:	V6, twin-cam
Construction:	cast-iron block, light-alloy heads
Bore×stroke:	87 mm×83 mm
Displacement:	2960 cc
Compression ratio:	8.5:1
Valve gear:	four valves per cylinder operated by twin belt-driven camshafts per bank of cylinders
Fuel system:	Nissan electronic fuel injection with twin Garrett T2/2.5 turbochargers and air-to-air intercoolers
Ignition:	Nissan Direct Ignition System
Maximum power:	280 bhp (PS-DIN) at 6,400 rpm
Maximum torque:	274 lb ft at 3,600 rpm

TRANSMISSION

Type:	five-speed manual gearbox	
Ratios:	1st	3.21:1
	2nd	1.93:1
	3rd	1.30:1
	4th	1.00:1
	5th	0.75:1
Final drive ratio:	3.69:1 (limited-slip differential)	

BODY/CHASSIS

Type:	unitary-construction body/chassis with two-seater coupé body

RUNNING GEAR

Steering:	rack and pinion, power-assisted, with HICAS four-wheel steer
Suspension:	front: independent multi-link system with lower wishbones, telescopic dampers and anti-roll bar rear: independent multi-link system with coil springs, telescopic dampers and anti-roll bar
Brakes:	11-in (279-mm) diameter ventilated discs front, 11.7-in (297-mm) diameter ventilated discs rear; servo-assisted with electronic ABS
Wheels:	cast alloy, 16-in diameter
Tyres:	Michelin MXX, 225/50 ZR16 front, 245/45 ZR16 rear

DIMENSIONS AND WEIGHT

Length:	178.1 in (4525 mm)
Width:	70.9 in (1800 mm)
Height:	49.4 in (1255 mm)
Wheelbase:	101.2 in (2570 mm)
Track:	58.9 in (1495 mm) front, 60.4 in (1535 mm) rear
Kerb weight:	3,485 lb (1581 kg)

PERFORMANCE

Acceleration:	0-30 mph 2.3 sec
	0-40 mph 3.2 sec
	0-50 mph 4.3 sec
	0-60 mph 5.6 sec
	0-70 mph 7.6 sec
	0-80 mph 9.4 sec
	0-90 mph 11.6 sec
	0-100 mph 14.5 sec
	0-110 mph 17.6 sec
	0-120 mph 21.3 sec
	0-130 mph 26.7 sec
Standing ¼ mile:	14.4 sec
Standing km:	25.6 sec

Acceleration in gear:	mph	fifth	fourth	third
	30-50	9.3	5.6	3.9
	40-60	8.3	5.1	3.7
	50-70	7.8	5.0	3.7

Maximum speed:	155 mph (249 km/h)
Overall fuel consumption:	17 mpg
Price (1991):	£30,650

Performance figures from AUTOCAR

Nissan 300ZX kindly supplied by Ancaster Nissan

DARS multi-link rear suspension

Standing for Diagonal A-arm Rear Suspension, the Nissan multi-link rear system is designed to provide the most precise wheel control possible and to give a slight measure of toe-in under both braking and acceleration to aid stability.

Unique headlights

To achieve the desired nose profile, Nissan introduced a new headlight assembly produced by their suppliers, Ichiko Kogyo, who developed a new glass-pressing process.

Quad-cam V6

The V6 used in the current 300ZX is a total redesign of the previous V6 engine. It's a 60-degree V6 with a cast-iron block and alloy heads, four valves per cylinder, electronic fuel injection and a power output of 280 bhp at 6,400 rpm, giving an impressive ratio of 95 bhp per litre.

Twin turbos

The Nissan 300ZX's V6 engine is equipped with a turbocharger and intercooler for each bank. Turbo lag is decreased (and thus engine response improved) with two smaller turbos, rather than one large one.

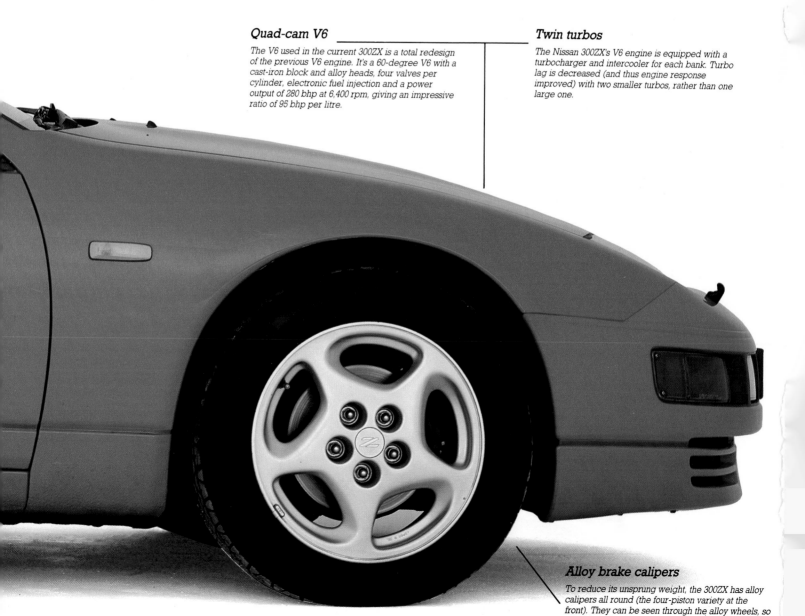

Alloy brake calipers

To reduce its unsprung weight, the 300ZX has alloy calipers all round (the four-piston variety at the front). They can be seen through the alloy wheels, so considerable effort was made to make them attractive.

Two-seater and 2+2 versions were designed together, and are hard to tell apart, though there is five inches difference in wheelbase. The small rear seats of the 2+2 mean that the fuel tank is moved back behind the axle line, so that the filler is behind the left-hand rear wheel rather than in front of it – a quick identification point.

Right: This is the unadorned nose of a non-turbocharged, two-seater, American model. In a reversal of what we've become accustomed to, Nissan have given their US-spec cars stiffer damping and quicker steering than those intended for Europe. According to the company's market research, those American drivers who buy sports cars value responsiveness above all else, while European buyers can make more use of high-speed stability.

Above: The 300ZX's interior was designed to echo its external curvatures with twin, wrap-around cockpits. Instrumentation is straightforward analogue-type – gimmicky electronic displays were eschewed in an effort to make the car as functionally effective as possible from the driver's viewpoint.

Left: Most of the switchgear is almost, but not quite, at the driver's fingertips. The left-hand pod, here, carries controls for air conditioning and wash-wipe; lighting, rear-screen heater and cruise-control master switch are on its right-hand counterpart.

Below: The normally-aspirated car has smoother lines from the rear, thanks to the absence of the Turbo's tailgate spoiler.

Body/chassis

Compared with the previous 300ZX, the unitary hull of the new car is at least 20 per cent more rigid. The complete body is 55 lb heavier than that of the old car. Reinforced box-sections form a kind of supplementary under-floor frame. Corrosion-resistant zinc-nickel-plated Dura Steel is used for most of the outer body panels, though the bonnet and bumper armatures are of aluminium alloy, and plastics are used for the front apron and the front and rear bumper outer shells. The rigid structure was essential to get full benefit from the multi-link suspension that the 300ZX has both front and rear. This system, expensively devised with the aid of Nissan's two Cray super-computers, is now used on a number of their high-performance cars. Based on a double-wishbone layout, additional links achieve geometry that is closer to ideal and avoids unwelcome toe-angle changes. The 300ZX Turbo purposely provokes changes of angle at the rear wheels with its Super HICAS rear-wheel steering system.

This is computer-controlled, responding to sensors that detect the car's speed, turning angle and steering-wheel movement. If these exceed pre-determined values, the computer directs a hydraulic actuator to steer the rear wheels very slightly, thus aiding cornering, particularly at high speed. In fact, it is a double action, for Super HICAS first introduces a touch of counter-steer before turning the rear wheels in the same phase as the front ones. Unlike some other types of four-wheel steering, the 300ZX system is intended only to improve high-speed swerve response; it provides no advantage for parking. The front-wheel steering is power-assisted, with a computer controlling the degree of assistance, depending on the car's speed; this is made more consistent by an unusual twin-valve arrangement in the hydraulic circuit. The 300ZX's brakes are racing-style with aluminium calipers (four-piston type at the front) on show through the spoked alloy wheels, like those of a Porsche 959.

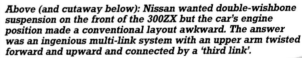

Above (and cutaway below): Nissan wanted double-wishbone suspension on the front of the 300ZX but the car's engine position made a conventional layout awkward. The answer was an ingenious multi-link system with an upper arm twisted forward and upward and connected by a 'third link'.

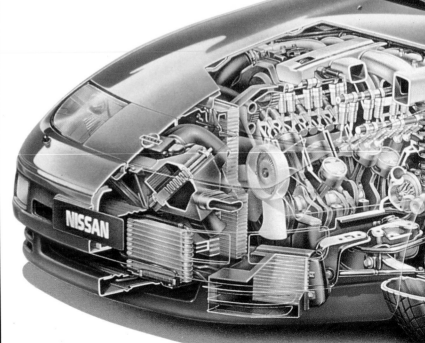

Engine

Nissan's aim for the engine of the 300ZX was 250-300 bhp, but with ample torque in the low- and medium-speed range, and excellent throttle response and smoothness. That was a tall order, best achieved, they concluded, by a three-litre V6 engine equipped with twin turbochargers. They started with the V6 engine used in the previous ZX – a 60-degree unit with an iron block and aluminium heads – but it would need to rev higher than before to achieve the required output. Four valves per cylinder would be needed, operated by two camshafts per bank. To give the engines the flexibility they desired, variable valve timing was introduced. NVCS (Nissan Valve Timing Control System) uses electronic control and hydraulic actuation of a spring-loaded helical gear at the inlet camshaft pulleys to reduce valve 'overlap' at low speeds and light loads. The 300ZX engine produces 222 bhp normally-aspirated or 300 bhp (280 bhp in European spec) turbocharged at 6,400 rpm. At these outputs, without NVCS, the car's low-speed running would not have been acceptable. ECCS, standing for Electronic Concentrated Control System, is the engine-management computer that controls the valve timing, along with the fuel injection and NDIS direct ignition system, which provides a separate coil atop each spark plug. The two turbochargers, mounted on cast-iron exhaust manifolds either side of the engine, are Garrett T2/T25 hybrids. The boosted charge air passes through intercoolers mounted in the nose. The pipe runs are fiendishly complicated, as inlet air has to go back from the air cleaner to the turbos, forward to the intercoolers and back again to the inlet manifolds. Inlet and exhaust systems are dual throughout, though incoming air feeds the opposite cylinder bank through what Nissan call a cross-ram manifold. Arranging all this pipework to fit in the confined under-bonnet space of the 300ZX is a considerable feat!

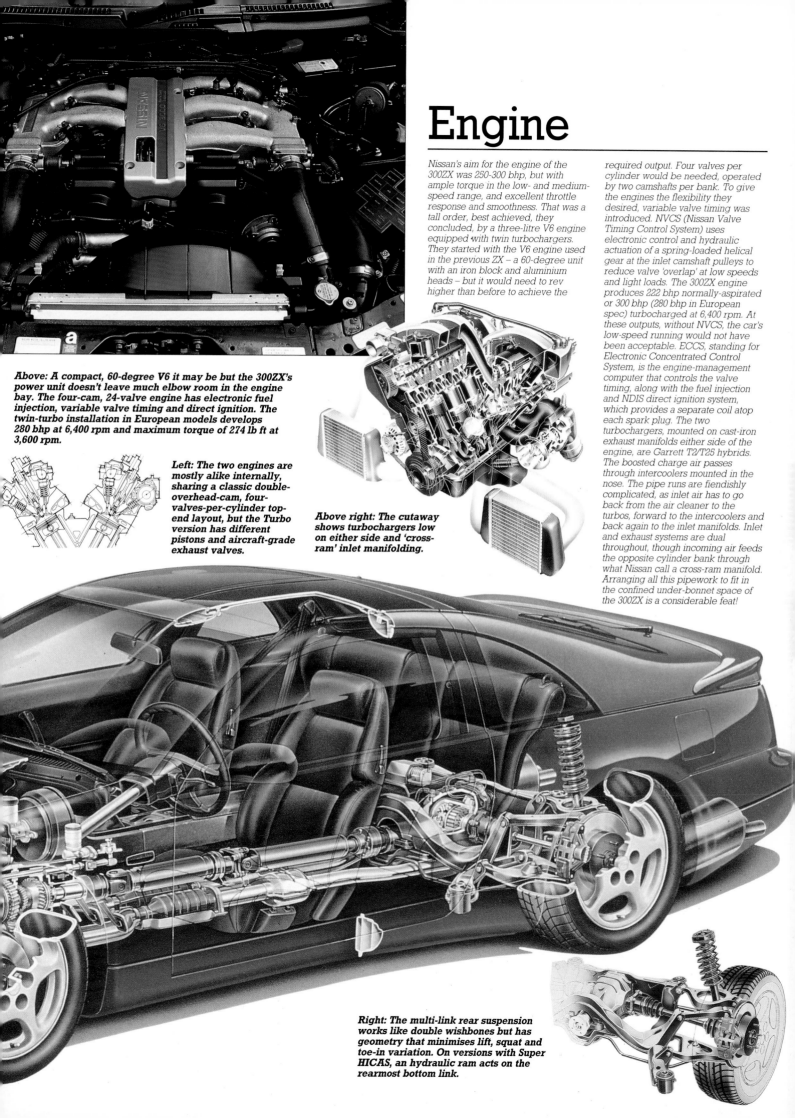

Above: A compact, 60-degree V6 it may be but the 300ZX's power unit doesn't leave much elbow room in the engine bay. The four-cam, 24-valve engine has electronic fuel injection, variable valve timing and direct ignition. The twin-turbo installation in European models develops 280 bhp at 6,400 rpm and maximum torque of 274 lb ft at 3,600 rpm.

Left: The two engines are mostly alike internally, sharing a classic double-overhead-cam, four-valves-per-cylinder top-end layout, but the Turbo version has different pistons and aircraft-grade exhaust valves.

Above right: The cutaway shows turbochargers low on either side and 'cross-ram' inlet manifolding.

Right: The multi-link rear suspension works like double wishbones but has geometry that minimises lift, squat and toe-in variation. On versions with Super HICAS, an hydraulic ram acts on the rearmost bottom link.

Aston Martin V8 and Vantage

Born over 20 years ago, the Aston Martin V8 survived and flourished. By the 1980s there were Vantage and Volante Vantage versions, with over 400 bhp from quad-cam V8s and a top speed in Lamborghini Countach territory.

Above: An Aston Martin V8 in full flight. The perfect proportions of William Towns' design tend to mask the V8's sheer size; it's longer, taller and heavier than all its exotic rivals, and Aston Martin classified it as a four-seater.

As the 1960s wore on, Aston Martin realised they would lose their position as pre-eminent builders of supercars unless they could come up with more power. Rivals, notably Ferrari and Maserati, had steadily increased power outputs, and it was clear that for all its virtues the Aston twin-cam six was soon going to look pretty tame compared with the likes of the 4.4-litre V12 in the Ferrari Daytona.

Tadek Marek, Aston's gifted Polish-born engineer, who had designed the six-cylinder engine, set to work. If he ever thought of following Ferrari down the V12 route there's no evidence of it, and the appeal of a V8 layout was obvious – it was compact and smooth enough to give Aston-style levels of refinement. Marek's initial approach was to use as much of the old twin-cam six as possible, and the cylinder head layout was carried across intact. Thus the earliest V8 consisted of two four-cylinder adaptations of the straight-six top end allied to a 90-degree V8 crankcase. A bore of 96 mm and stroke of 83 mm gave a displacement of 4.8 litres.

Unfortunately, this simple solution didn't really work, and by the time teething problems had been overcome and the engine had gone into production in 1969, displacement had risen to 5340 cc. The car it was to power, the DBS V8, was introduced in September that year, distinguished from its six-cylinder predecessor by the power bulge in the bonnet and by being no less than 21 mph faster in absolute top speed, while that massive V8 engine could power the bulky Aston to 60 mph in an amazing six seconds.

The definitive look to the V8 came in 1972, when the original fussy four-headlamp treatment was scrapped in favour of two large lights. Unfortunately, a fast, powerful and very thirsty car (you were lucky to return 15 mpg overall) like the Aston V8 was just what the world did not need during the energy crisis of the early 1970s, and

the car was lucky to survive at all. But late in the 1970s, when the world had recovered its appetite for high performance, Aston Martin set about turning the V8 into one of the world's most potent supercars.

... to 60 mph in a lightning six seconds

By this time the company had, in a curious reversal of the usual practice of the time, switched back from the original and troublesome Bosch fuel injection to four Weber IDF downdraught carburettors. Those carbs were just one of the things changed to form the tuned Vantage version in 1977, when the main choke size went up to 48 mm from 42 mm. The idea was to make the big V8 breathe better and the camshaft profiles were changed, larger valves fitted and

more valve overlap introduced. The changes were extremely effective; power output rocketed from 306 bhp to 360 bhp at 5,800 rpm and eventually up to 406 bhp at 6,200 rpm.

That extra power and torque required some chassis changes even to as able a car as the V8, and the rear track was widened, different Koni dampers fitted and stiffer rear springs introduced. A deep spoiler was added at the front, along with that distinctive Vantage hallmark, the blanked-off radiator grille; cooling air was now fed in through the spoiler vents.

Despite topping 4,000 lb the Vantage was extraordinarily quick; a rear brake pipe fractured on *Autocar*'s top speed test run, but by then the Vantage had already reached 167 mph, while it took a mere 5.4 seconds to reach 60 mph.

The British heavyweight was never regarded as the most sophisticated of cars; where the exotic continental opposition had mid-mounted engines, the Aston's was in the traditional place – right at the front. The car did not even have fully independent rear suspension, but supporters of its de Dion system would argue that it was just as good – the rear wheels were connected by a solid beam that curved back around the differential, which was fixed to the chassis along with the inboard rear brake calipers. The net result was that each rear wheel stayed upright at all times and yet there wasn't the heavy penalty in unsprung weight that goes along with a live rear axle.

Keeping a truly high-performance car on the

... the Vantage had reached 167 mph

road is mostly down to the tyres and, in 1983, the Vantage was given flared wheel arches to allow for even larger Pirelli P7s, of 275/55 VR15 size. Everything about the Vantage was massive. In that, it followed the philosophy of the great pre-war Le Mans-winning Bentleys. These may have been criticised by Ettore Bugatti as the fastest trucks in the world, but they were fast, strong and very successful. The Aston maintained that British brute-force approach; it was longer and higher than Ferrari's massive Testarossa, and just as quick, while it dwarfed Lamborghini's Countach. It went to prove that there is more than one way of building a supercar. Who's to say which is right?

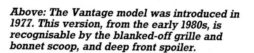

Above: The Vantage model was introduced in 1977. This version, from the early 1980s, is recognisable by the blanked-off grille and bonnet scoop, and deep front spoiler.

Above: In 1983 the Vantage was improved and given larger 275/55 VR15 Pirelli P7 tyres. The switch required wider wheel arches to accommodate the extra rubber.

Above and left: Aston Martin introduced the convertible Volante model as early as 1977, but it was almost 10 years before you could buy a Volante with Vantage power. In addition to the usual Vantage features of front and rear spoilers, the Vantage Volante had skirts joining front and rear wheel arches.

Aston Martin V8 Vantage Volante

Aston Martin have produced tuned, Vantage, versions of their cars since the DB2 of the early 1950s. Vantage versions were usually offered only on the coupé models as Aston felt the more flexible convertible chassis were less well equipped to handle the extra power. That was the situation with the V8 Volante which was introduced in 1977. Almost 10 years later, in 1986, Aston relented, changed their policy and offered the Volante in Vantage form to combine maximum performance with the delights of open-air motoring. The Vantage Volante was the culmination of the V8 line introduced as far back as 1969, and it's a tribute to the original design that it could still be in demand two decades later.

seater

...d-head V8 is described by Aston as a four-...nd where that rear-seat space would have ...t by some manufacturers in making the car a ...ble, the Volante still has four seats.

Rear-mounted CD player

The Vantage Volante has the luxury of a multi-sta... CD player. The player is actually mounted in the... boot but controlled from the driver's seat.

Hood up for more performance

The only way to get the Volante near to its 170 mph top end is to have the roof in place; convertible cars with the top down generate a enormous amount of extra wind resistance.

Alloy bodywork

Aston Martins have had hand-crafted aluminium alloy bodies since the earliest days, and the Volante is no exception.

Chrome bumpers

A sign of the age of the Aston's design is the traditional chrome bumpers where other manufacturers have plastic-covered and colour-coded deformable devices.

Power-operated hood

The lined convertible top is power-operated. It can only be raised or lowered when the ignition is on and the handbrake set.

de Dion rear axle

The Aston is the fastest performance car in the world not to have independent rear suspension. It uses a de Dion rear axle which connects the two rear wheel hubs with a light beam, while the differential is chassis-mounted rather than incorporated into the axle.

Fo[r]

The
seat
been
conv

Above: Astons in action. The V8 is an old design, markedly narrow and upright compared with today's supercars. Although the Aston has a virtually neutral weight distribution front to rear (despite its big front-mounted engine), its high centre of gravity does take some counteracting. The V8's de Dion axle does a good job of keeping the rear wheels as near perpendicular to the road as possible, but the Aston cannot match its more modern and exotic mid-engined rivals in terms of its ultimate grip.

Driving a Vantage: *sheer performance*

At first you might think that over 400 bhp in such an old design is a recipe for disaster, that the enormously powerful V8 is only good for straight-line speed, and that it can only be driven by a strong and courageous driver.

You would be very surprised, and pleasantly so. The Vantage may be rather tall and upright compared with exotic rivals like the Countach or Testarossa, and that does have a penalty in absolute cornering power. It leans enough to negate the grip of its massive low-profile Pirelli P7s, which like to be kept as near perpendicular to the road as possible. But if cornering limits are not quite in the mid-engined Lamborghini class the Vantage makes up for that with superb handling, courtesy of its perfect weight distribution and just the right degree of assistance to the power steering.

That, and some of the most powerful brakes fitted to any car, gives you the confidence to exploit the performance, and that's prodigious. In only 13 seconds you can be travelling at 100 mph, having passed 60 mph in a mere 5.4 seconds. The stability and ease of control even at 150 mph means the determined *autobahn* driver can go on to 170 mph!

PERFORMANCE & SPECIFICATION COMPARISON	Engine	Displacement	Power	Torque (lb ft)	Max speed	0-60 mph	Length (in/mm)	Wheelbase (in/mm)	Track front/rear	Weight total (lb/kg)	Price (1988)
Aston Martin V8 Vantage	V8, quad-cam	5340 cc	406 bhp 6200 rpm	390 lb ft 5000 rpm	170 mph 274 km/h	5.4 sec	181.3 in 4605 mm	102.8 in 2611 mm	59.3 in 59.0 in	4001 lb 1815 kg	£87,000
De Tomaso Pantera GT5S	V8, overhead-valve	5763 cc	350 bhp 5500 rpm	N/A	160 mph 257 km/h	5.4 sec	168.1 in 4269 mm	99.0 in 2514 mm	59.5 in 62.1 in	3219 lb 1460 kg	£47,621
Ferrari Testarossa	Flat-12, quad-cam, 48-valve	4942 cc	390 bhp 6300 rpm	362 lb ft 4500 rpm	171 mph 275 km/h	5.2 sec	176.6 in 4485 mm	100.4 in 2550 mm	59.8 in 65.4 in	3675 lb 1667 kg	£91,195
Lamborghini Countach Quattrovalvole	V12, quad-cam, 48-valve	5167 cc	455 bhp 7000 rpm	369 lb ft 5200 rpm	178 mph 286 km/h	4.9 sec	162.9 in 4138 mm	96.5 in 2451 mm	58.7 in 63.2 in	3188 lb 1446 kg	£86,077
Porsche 911 Turbo	Flat-six, overhead-cam, turbo	3229 cc	300 bhp 5500 rpm	317 lb ft 4000 rpm	160 mph 257 km/h	4.9 sec	168.9 in 4290 mm	89.5 in 2273 mm	56.4 in 59.1 in	3051 lb 1384 kg	£57,852

V8, Vantage and Volante Data File

Aston Martin have been producing sports cars since the company founders Lionel Martin and Robert Bamford joined forces in 1914. The first car was a modified Isotta-Fraschini, but the first Aston Martin (the 'Aston' part of the name coming from the Aston Clinton hill climb) appeared in 1919.

The company did not last long in its first incarnation. By 1925, just after the Motor Show, the company was wound up. It was then bought by £6,000 by W.S. Renwick and moved to Feltham in Middlesex.

The best and most famous early Aston Martin model was the 11.9HP International that was produced from 1926 to 1935. It was powered by a four-cylinder overhead-cam engine with dry-sump lubrication, and proved a very successful sports racer. The first post-war model was soon overtaken by events when the company was taken over by David Brown. Brown had also acquired Lagonda, and with it an engine designed by the great W.O. Bentley. The Bentley-designed 2.6-litre six-cylinder twin-cam engine powered the early DB series of cars: the DB2, DB2/4, DB3, DB3S. In 1959 Aston Martin won the Le Mans 24 Hours (with the DBR1) , after many years competing in the French classic, and the World Sports Car Championship along the way.

A totally new production model, the DB4, was introduced in 1960, and that evolved steadily, into the DB5 of James Bond *Goldfinger* fame and the 2+2 DB6. The end of that line was the differently styled DBS, which evolved into the V8 series shown here.

David Brown had sold out to Company Developments in 1972 and the DB tag was consequently dropped. Over the past few years Aston Martin has had a difficult time, but some real security was brought to the company with the Ford takeover of 1987, and the way was clear for new models like the V8 Virage.

Styling

Where the DB4 had a very sophisticated look thanks to the work of the Italian styling house, Touring of Milan, Aston Martin turned to a young British designer for the DBS in 1967. William Towns had originally been hired to design only seats, but his coupé shape was an instant success. Towns had essentially stretched the DB6's wheelbase by just one inch and widened the track front and rear by 4.5 inches. It was a more angular design than the DB6 it replaced, with more sharply defined lines to the tops of the wings and rectangular rear lights.

In retrospect, the DBS looks like an interim design between the DB6 and the V8; the redesign that changed it into the V8 improved the look considerably, making it appear far more substantial and every inch a British muscle car.

In 1977 Aston Martin followed their usual practice in building a Volante convertible version of the V8 which, top down, looked even more elegant. Although the purity of the V8 Volante's lines were spoiled somewhat by some added-on skirts and boot-lid spoiler in the Vantage version, William Towns' design was still a classic when the V8 finally went out of production in 1988 after nearly 20 years.

Above: In 1972 the DBS V8 was restyled at the front and the changed model became known simply as the Aston Martin V8.

Right: One of the main changes between the DBS V8 and the V8 that followed it was the switch from four small headlights to larger single lights on each side.

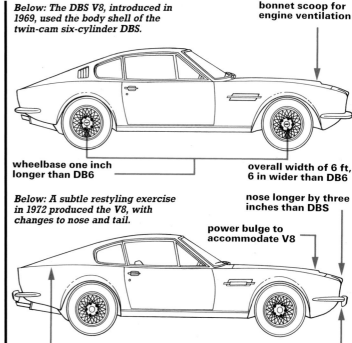

Below: The DBS V8, introduced in 1969, used the body shell of the twin-cam six-cylinder DBS.

bonnet scoop for engine ventilation

wheelbase one inch longer than DB6

overall width of 6 ft, 6 in wider than DB6

Below: A subtle restyling exercise in 1972 produced the V8, with changes to nose and tail.

nose longer by three inches than DBS

power bulge to accommodate V8

higher rear wing line

two rather than four headlights

Below: The Vantage model featured spoilers front and rear.

front nose spoiler

boot-lid spoiler

larger Pirelli P7 tyres from 1983

Above: The boot-lip spoiler identifies this as the rear of the tuned Vantage version rather than the ordinary V8.

Left: Aston Martin have long concentrated on their image of producing luxurious high-performance cars. The Connolly leather interiors can be ordered in a number of different colour schemes, each with the obligatory walnut dashboard and door capping.

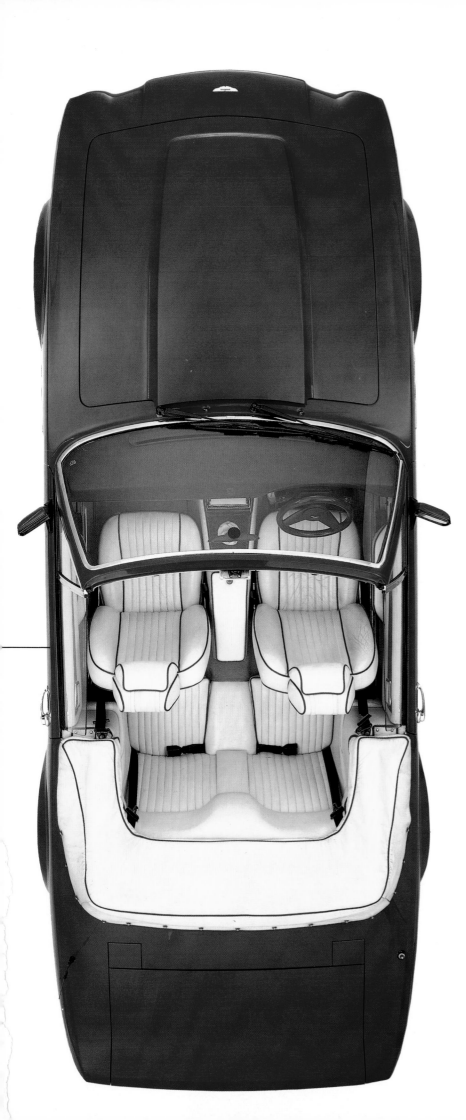

SPECIFICATION

1988 Aston Martin V8 Vantage

ENGINE

Type:	V8, quad-cam
Construction:	light alloy cylinder block and heads, 'wet' cylinder liners and five main bearings
Bore×stroke:	100 mm×85 mm
Displacement:	5340 cc
Compression ratio:	9.0:1
Valve gear:	two valves per cylinder operated by twin chain-driven overhead camshafts per bank of cylinders
Fuel system:	four Weber 48 IDF downdraught carburettors
Ignition:	electronic
Maximum power:	406 bhp at 6,200 rpm
Maximum torque:	390 lb ft at 5,000 rpm

TRANSMISSION

Type:	five-speed ZF manual gearbox	
Ratios:	1st	2.90:1
	2nd	1.78:1
	3rd	1.22:1
	4th	1.00:1
	5th	0.85:1
Final drive:	Hypoid bevel with limited slip differential	
Ratio:	3.54:1	

BODY/CHASSIS

Type:	welded steel section floorpan chassis with alloy two-door coupé bodywork

RUNNING GEAR

Steering:	rack and pinion, power-assisted
Suspension:	front: independent with double wishbone, coil springs and telescopic Koni dampers rear: non-independent with de Dion axle with twin trailing arms per side and Watts linkage with coil springs and Koni telescopic dampers
Brakes:	discs front and rear; fronts 11.5-in diameter and ventilated, rears 10.4-in diameter and mounted inboard next to differential
Wheels:	cast aluminium alloy, 8 in×15 in
Tyres:	275/55 VR15 Pirelli P7s

DIMENSIONS AND WEIGHT

Length:	181.3 in (4605 mm)
Width:	72.0 in (1829 mm)
Height:	52.0 in (1321 mm)
Wheelbase:	102.8 in (2611 mm)
Track:	59.3 in (1506 mm) front, 59.0 in (1499 mm) rear
Kerb weight:	4,001 lb (1815 kg)

PERFORMANCE

Acceleration:	0-30 mph 2.2 sec 0-40 mph 2.8 sec 0-50 mph 3.8 sec 0-60 mph 5.4 sec 0-70 mph 6.9 sec 0-80 mph 8.5 sec 0-90 mph 10.8 sec 0-100 mph 13.0 sec 0-110 mph 15.8 sec 0-120 mph 20.7 sec 0-130 mph 26.0 sec
Standing ¼ mile:	13.7 sec

Acceleration in gear:	mph	fifth	fourth	third
	30-50	7.2	5.7	4.4
	40-60	6.9	5.2	3.9
	50-70	6.8	5.1	4.0
	60-80	6.8	5.4	4.0
	70-90	7.1	5.5	4.2

Maximum speed:	170 mph (274 km/h)
Overall fuel consumption:	13.5 mpg
Price (1988):	£87,000

Performance figures courtesy of AUTOCAR

Aston Martin V8 Vantage Volante kindly supplied by Douglas Trevor Jones of Woodlift Joinery

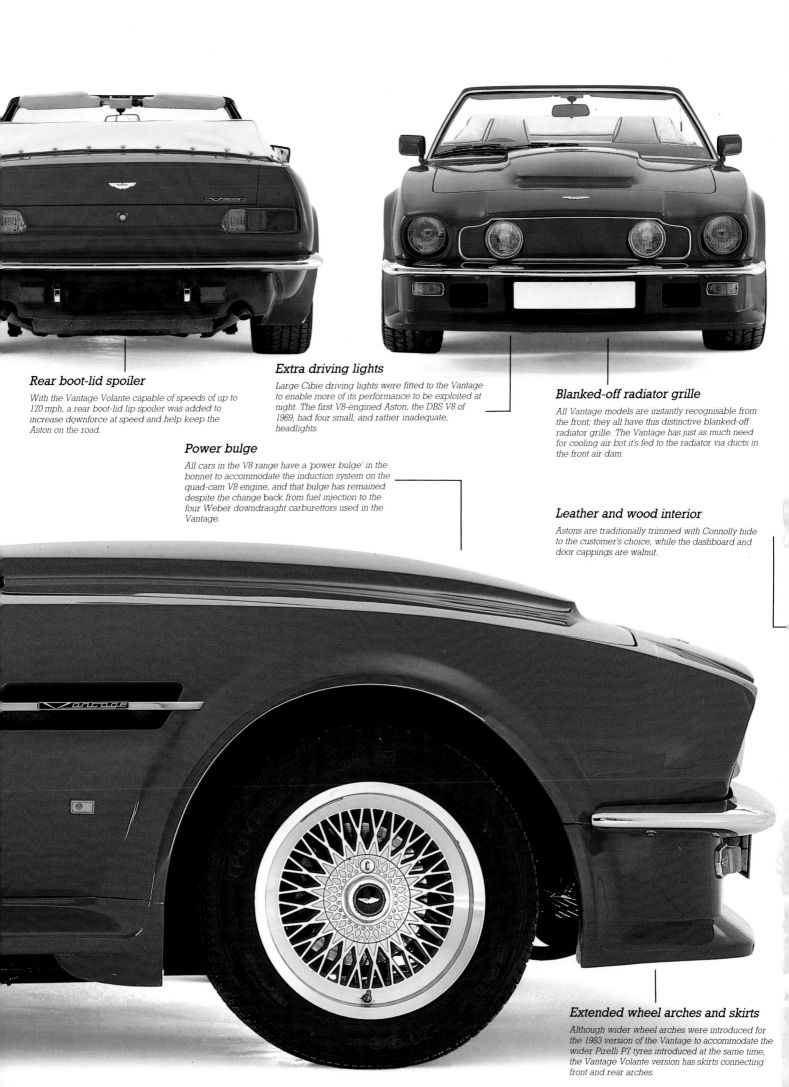

Rear boot-lid spoiler

With the Vantage Volante capable of speeds of up to 170 mph, a rear boot-lid lip spoiler was added to increase downforce at speed and help keep the Aston on the road.

Extra driving lights

Large Cibie driving lights were fitted to the Vantage to enable more of its performance to be exploited at night. The first V8-engined Aston, the DBS V8 of 1969, had four small, and rather inadequate, headlights.

Power bulge

All cars in the V8 range have a 'power bulge' in the bonnet to accommodate the induction system on the quad-cam V8 engine, and that bulge has remained despite the change back from fuel injection to the four Weber downdraught carburettors used in the Vantage.

Blanked-off radiator grille

All Vantage models are instantly recognisable from the front; they all have this distinctive blanked-off radiator grille. The Vantage has just as much need for cooling air but it's fed to the radiator via ducts in the front air dam.

Leather and wood interior

Astons are traditionally trimmed with Connolly hide to the customer's choice, while the dashboard and door cappings are walnut.

Extended wheel arches and skirts

Although wider wheel arches were introduced for the 1983 version of the Vantage to accommodate the wider Pirelli P7 tyres introduced at the same time, the Vantage Volante version has skirts connecting front and rear arches.

Engine

Aston Martin engine designer Tadek Marek's original intention in designing the Aston Martin V8 was to use as much as possible of the existing six-cylinder twin-cam. It was a nice idea, but it didn't work quite as conveniently in practice. The angle between inlet and exhaust valves on the twin-cam heads had to be narrowed for space reasons, and the original block design proved to be insufficiently rigid. That problem was solved with a stiffer crankcase, longer cylinder head studs, bigger main bearing caps and an enlarged displacement, up to 5340 cc, from the original 4.8 litres.

Originally fuel was supplied via Bosch mechanical fuel injection but problems of difficult starting, poor idling and poor drive-away characteristics if the engine was not warm led to the switch to a quartet of Weber 48 IDF downdraught carburettors.

The Vantage version of the engine, with 360 bhp rather than 306 bhp, appeared in 1977, with revised cam timing, larger valves and larger, 48-mm choke Weber IDF downdraught carburettors.

In 1986 Aston returned to fuel injection, although the Vantage continued with its quartet of Weber carbs. By the time the Vantage went out of production in the late 1980s its output was 406 bhp at 6,200 rpm.

The Volante

There have been Volante, or convertible, versions of Aston Martin coupés since the DB2 of 1950. Converting coupé to convertible was in most cases simple, as the cars had separate chassis rather than being of monocoque construction, where the roof is an integral part of the car's structure.

The V8 Volante appeared in 1977 and in its case the conversion wasn't quite as simple as it should have been, given the Aston's very substantial box-section steel chassis, but in fact the first car did suffer scuttle shake until extra strengthening was welded in to secure the windscreen footings more firmly to the centre bulkhead and

Above: The ultimate development of the V8 line, the Vantage Volante, combined the performance of the most highly-tuned model with the top-down appeal of the convertible, or Volante, version.

front of the transmission tunnel.

Originally, only an 'ordinary' version of the Volante was offered, on the grounds that the extra power of the Vantage would be too much for the open car. In 1986, however, Aston Martin decided that the open car could cope with over 400 bhp, and the Vantage Volante was born.

Below: The most notable feature at the rear of the V8 is the use of a de Dion rear axle. A de Dion axle is essentially a tube that rigidly connects both wheel hubs and is curved to clear the differential unit, which is mounted to the chassis. It's an improvement over the old-fashioned live axle because it is far lighter; the springs no longer have to carry the unsprung weight of the differential and brakes, which in this case are inboard discs. Both wheels are kept upright and parallel to each other during cornering, which is not always the case with an independent system. The main drawback is that both rear wheels have to react even when only one hits a bump.

Above: The V8 Volante was introduced in 1977. It's the most attractive version of William Towns' original design, not burdened by the add-on skirts and spoilers added to the Vantage cars.

Right: There was little fundamental change to the interiors over the years, the two-spoke steering wheel being the most obvious on this left-hand-drive automatic.

Below: In 1986 extra power and convertible motoring was combined to form the Vantage Volante.

Volante produced in both V8 and Vantage form

Right: The de Dion axle is located by twin trailing links, coil springs and Koni dampers.

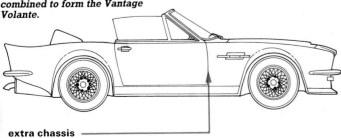

extra chassis strengthening

Inside the V8 Vantage

The Aston Martin is a very traditional design, with a front-mounted engine driving the rear wheels. Engine block and heads are aluminium alloy so the car is not unduly front-heavy. In fact its weight distribution is surprisingly neutral; at 50.6 front to 49.4 rear, it would be hard to improve. The quad-cam engine requires a power bulge to accommodate it, even though the proposed angle between the inlet and exhaust valves was reduced to make the engine lower.

Power is fed from the engine to a fixed rear limited slip differential, while rear suspension is a de Dion system and the brakes are mounted inboard.

The chassis is a very strong assembly of welded steel sections and it must account for a considerable percentage of the Aston's great weight of over 4,000 lb, as the body panels as well as the engine are alloy.

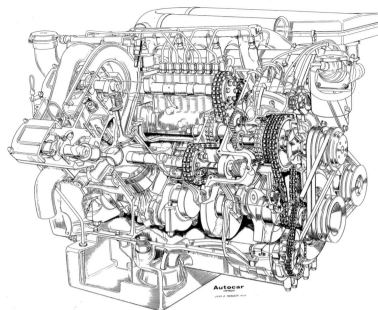

Below: The Aston's body is aluminium alloy, the car's main structural strength coming from the steel platform chassis.

Above: The Aston Martin V8 engine combines the American approach of a large displacement, in this case 5.3 litres, with the more European tradition of twin overhead camshafts for each bank of cylinders, and aluminium alloy construction. Each engine is meticulously assembled by one man.

Above: The cutaway of an early Aston Martin V8 shows the chain drive to the overhead camshafts and the two valves per cylinder operating in hemispherical combustion chambers. The fuel injector pipes can be seen at the top.

Left: The V8's block is aluminium alloy and the cylinders run in so-called 'wet' liners. They are sleeves that are located in the block, to form cylinder walls. The coolant flows around the sleeves, hence 'wet' liners.

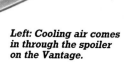

Left: Cooling air comes in through the spoiler on the Vantage.

Jaguar E-type

Jaguar's proud boast was that they provided grace and pace. In 1961 they backed up that boast with the E-type. Supremely beautiful and capable of 150 mph, it was the perfect combination of looks and performance.

'Sensational' has become a devalued word. But the launch of the E-type in 1961 caused a very real sensation.

Exciting, fast and sensually stylish, the E-type became an integral part of the Swinging Sixties along with the Beatles, long hair and mini-skirts. It stood for automotive escapism, but with a ridiculously low price brought that escapism within the grasp of a far wider audience than before. This was no hyper-priced Italian exotic, a plaything for the seriously wealthy. However, it matched the exotics' performance, more than matched their styling and was certainly more practical. It was hardly surprising that the Jaguar E-type was a winner.

At the beginning of the 1960s Jaguar needed a quantum leap, for the XK series, which had itself caused such a sensation in 1948, was now approaching senility. Improvements such as disc brakes and a styling facelift had helped to rejuvenate the ageing hero, but there was no disguising its great age.

Meanwhile, Jaguar had made its name internationally by emphatic victories on the race-tracks of the world, in particular at the most important, Le Mans, in the famous 24-hour race. When the decision was taken back in 1950 to build a sports racing car, Jaguar had appointed aerodynamicist Malcolm Sayer.

Sayer was a fascinating man who was vastly ahead of his time. From a background in the aircraft industry, he had taught himself the principles of aerodynamics and fully understood their importance. Having designed the body of the successful C-type, which had to retain a family

Automotive escapism at a ridiculously low price

resemblance to the XK120, he was given a freer hand to create its successor.

In 1953 Sayer designed a prototype that was strikingly similar to the E-type of eight years hence. Working closely with his boss, engineering director Bill Heynes, Sayer built a car of monocoque construction, influenced by the Alfa Romeo Disco Volante (flying saucer).

From this prototype evolved the legendary D-type. The 'D' succeeded against the more powerful, larger-engined Ferraris, due in part to its superbly efficient, slippery shape.

But racing was becoming prohibitively expensive, and following a horrific accident at Le Mans in 1955 it was believed that cars would be restricted to three litres in future. Jaguar decided to build a smaller car that could, in different versions, be a Le Mans contender and very high performance road car. Once Sayer began to design the E-type, however, it became clear that combining a road and race design was impossible and that the E-type would be a road car only.

By 1960, chief test driver Norman Dewis was rushing around in a couple of prototype roadsters. It had been intended originally to produce only an open version, but Bob Blake, a brilliant American sheet metal craftsman who worked closely with Sayer, had other ideas.

He took some welding rods and mocked up a 'fastback' superstructure on one of the open cars. Chairman Sir William Lyons happened to walk into the experimental shop at that moment. He looked at it in silence for some time. Finally he announced, "It's good. We'll make it."

The E-type was launched in March 1961 at the Geneva Motor Show and the reaction was

Left: The E-type's performance, great even today but incredible in the 1960s, owed much to the aerodynamic shape created by Malcolm Sayer. Series I roadsters like this can exceed 140 mph, but with the hood up.

Right: The E-type heralded a new age – the 1960s. Its looks suggested speed, freedom and confidence – a complete contrast to the dull world of the 1950s.

amazing. Film stars flew in to place their orders. Outside, the two press cars, the Roadster 77 RW and the Fixed Head 9600 HP, were giving demonstration runs and petrifying the potential customers, who even took to forging invitations to get a ride.

In Britain the aura was fuelled by road tests of both cars, 9600 HP just managing the magic 150 mph. Normally blasé motoring journalists raved about the car's attributes.

The performance was breathtaking but, in true Jaguar tradition, this was blended with remarkable docility. With a completely new independent rear suspension, designed by Bob Knight, the car had excellent road-holding and a level of ride and comfort that was unheard-of for a performance car. The shape was stunning and the price unbelievable. It was around half that of an Aston Martin and a third of the price of contemporary Ferraris.

However, with its monocoque construction it was far more advanced. The only disappointing features were the brakes, which were barely adequate for the prodigious performance, the archaic manual gearbox, and the surprisingly uncomfortable seats.

In April four examples appeared on the Jaguar stand at the New York Show. The reaction

Below: The exposed front lights show that this is a Series II car with the larger, 4.2-litre version of the twin-cam six. This example has non-standard alloy wheels.

Driving an E-type: pure performance

Perhaps the first thing you notice when you clamber into an E-type is the enormous length of bonnet. The view is an exciting one, even if the seating on the earlier cars is not exactly comfortable. With the right smells from the interior, a traditional bank of instruments, and a good throaty exhaust note, the E-type promises much, and does not disappoint.

Being a Jaguar the power comes in smoothly, and the flexibility is remarkable. The E-type still feels a fast car in a straight line as it accelerates swiftly, and it does not run out of steam at 100 mph or even 120 mph. You can floor the accelerator at the magic 'ton' and watch the bonnet come up!

Roadholding, though utterly predictable, is not of the 'glued to the road' variety. E-types can be thrown around with abandon provided you remember that considerable notice will be required of any emergency stops! Braking gradually improved throughout the life of the model, but can prove exciting on the earlier examples, even though they were equipped with disc brakes.

However, these earlier cars exude a character that the later V12s never possessed. With their silent smoothness, power steering and even automatic transmission, the Series III had gone a bit soft . . . but it could still exceed 140 mph!

was equally rapturous and the stand was permanently engulfed in a sea of people. The E-type was just one of the 400 models on show from 80 manufacturers on three floors covering three acres! In spite of this, the Jaguars were clearly the stars of the show.

Orders flooded in from around the world, but in particular from Jaguar's most important market, the United States. Even in 1962 the car was a rare sight in Britain. In 1961 the few examples to be seen were virtually mobbed whenever they stopped. The 'E' was not just looks, however; that had been comprehensively proven when Graham Hill raced one to victory

against the Ferraris and Astons first time out.

In 1964 several of the shortcomings were addressed. Visually unchanged, the new model was fitted with an enlarged 4.2-litre version of the trusty XK engine in place of the 3.8. Opinions vary as to the relative merits of these two engines, but certainly the 4.2 produced more torque. The

Road-test cars managed the magic 150 mph

brakes and, in particular, the gearbox were significantly improved, as was the interior.

The range was supplemented in 1966 by the less attractive but more practical Two Plus Two model, and in 1967 the dreaded US Federal Safety Regulations began to take their toll on the pure E-type shape. An intermediate stage has come to be known, retrospectively, as the Series 1½ model, before a more comprehensive package of changes resulted in the Series II.

Less stylish, the Series II was more civilised and kept the model selling well. The updating was particularly appreciated in the States, where the earlier examples, with overheating problems and a lack of air conditioning, had sometimes made ownership frustrating.

By the late 1960s the E-type needed an

Jaguar E-type

T he E-type was introduced in March 1961 as a replacement for the XK150S. The styling was mainly the work of aerodynamicist Malcolm Sayer but with the usual input from Jaguar boss William Lyons, who had a perfect eye for what looked right and for what would sell. The E-type was powered by the same 3.8-litre straight-six twin-cam as the XK150, but broke new ground in having independent rear suspension and torsion bar front suspension. E-type evolution saw a 4.2-litre version introduced in 1964 and then a V12 in 1971. Production ended in 1974 after 72,517 had been built.

From the start of production the E-type was built as a roadster or convertible and as a coupé. The range broadened out to include a 2+2 coupé and a 4.2-litre version of the twin-cam engine replaced the 3.8 in 1964.

Semi-monocoque construction

The E-type followed the racing D-type in having monocoque (i.e. chassis-less) construction for the centre section of the body. Separate subframes were used for the engine and rear suspension.

Classic interior

The E-type interior changed over time, but the Series 1 cars, such as this one, were characterised by the elegant wood-rim steering wheel and detail such as the row of toggle switches on the dashboard which safety legislation eventually outlawed.

Triple windscreen wipers

The solution to clearing the E-type's shallow screen was to fit three, rather than two, wipers. It was an approach used on some other British sports cars exported to the American market, such as the MGB.

Aerodynamic body

The perfect shape of the E-type was a combination of the work of aerodynamicist Malcolm Sayer (who designed the Le Mans-winning D-types) and the styling input from Jaguar boss William Lyons.

Short wheelbase

Although the E-type looks long and sleek, its wheelbase (i.e. the distance between the centres of front and rear wheels) was actually shorter than that of the XK family (the 120, 140 and 150) that preceded it.

Torsion bar front suspension

The E-type's front wire wheel and disc brake were carried on a classic double wishbone independent front suspension system. But whereas most rivals used coils springs, Jaguar used the more space-efficient longitudinal torsion bars, a feature more often found on Continental cars than British.

Inboard rear brakes

Not only did the E-type boast disc brakes all round at a time when rivals like Ferrari still used drums, but they were mounted inboard at the rear to save the unsprung weight of a drum attached to the hub in the conventional way.

Knock-off wheels

Wire-spoked wheels with knock-off hubs were standard equipment on the first E-types. Later in the car's life, steel disc wheels were fitted.

image and performance boost to maintain its pre-eminent status. The various regulations were stifling the performance, and a radical answer was once more needed. The answer was the V12, Jaguar's superb new 5.3-litre powerplant. It was fitted into the long-wheelbase chassis of the 2×2, with the necessary adjustments to suit the bigger engine, and it produced the Series III.

The Series III E-type was altogether softer and less of a sports car. Perhaps the market was changing, or people were becoming accustomed to greater sophistication. The engine was silky smooth, the power steering effortless, the new ventilated brakes efficient, and the wider tyres improved roadholding. Paradoxically this E-type was, not surprisingly, the most sophisticated but it lacked the 3.8's great character.

The E-type was not perfect, but the pure driving pleasure and the intoxicating beauty made the car uniquely satisfying and sensational fun. To many the E-type was, and still is, the ultimate sports car.

Above: E-types of two eras show excitement giving way to refinement. The Roadster is a straight six, using a classic engine that first saw action in 1948. The Fixed Head Coupé is a Series III, with its power coming from the silky-smooth 5.3-litre V12 that went on to power its even more refined successor, the XJS.

PERFORMANCE & SPECIFICATION COMPARISON	Engine	Displacement	Power	Torque (lb/ft)	Max speed	0-60 mph	Length (in/mm)	Wheelbase (in/mm)	Track front/rear	Production total	Price
Series I Roadster (1961)	Straight-six twin-cam	3781 cc	265 bhp 5500 rpm	260 lb ft 4000 rpm	149 mph 240 km/h	7.1 secs	175.3 in 4453 mm	96 in 2438 mm	50/50 in	7,815	£1,480
Series I Coupé (1961)	Straight-six twin-cam	3781 cc	265 bhp 5500 rpm	260 lb ft 4000 rpm	150 mph 242 km/h	6.9 secs	175.3 in 4453 mm	96 in 2438 mm	50/50 in	7,667	£1,550
Series I 4.2 Roadster (1964)	Straight-six twin-cam	4235 cc	265 bhp 5400 rpm	283 lb ft 4000 rpm	149 mph 240 km/h	7.4 secs	175.3 in 4453 mm	96 in 2438 mm	50/50 in	9,548	£1,568
Series I 4.2 Coupé (1964)	Straight-six twin-cam	4235 cc	265 bhp 5400 rpm	283 lb ft 4000 rpm	150 mph 242 km/h	7.0 secs	175.3 in 4453 mm	96 in 2438 mm	50/50 in	7,770	£1,648
Series I 4.2 2+2 (1966)	Straight-six twin-cam	4235 cc	265 bhp 5400 rpm	283 lb ft 4000 rpm	139 mph 224 km/h	7.4 secs	184.5 in 4686 mm	105 in 2667 mm	50.25/ 50.25 in	5,572	£1,857
Series II Roadster (1968)	Straight-six twin-cam	4235 cc	246 bhp 5400 rpm	263 lb ft 3000 rpm	142 mph 228 km/h	7.2 secs	175.3 in 4453 mm	96 in 2438 mm	50/50 in	5,132	£1,655
Series III Coupé (1971)	V12	5343 cc	272 bhp 6000 rpm	304 lb ft 3600 rpm	146 mph 235 km/h	6.4 secs	184.5 in 4686 mm	105 in 2667 mm	53/53 in	7,985	£2,510
Series III Roadster (1971)	V12	5343 cc	272 bhp 6000 rpm	304 lb ft 3600 rpm	142 mph 228 km/h	6.8 secs	184.5 in 4686 mm	105 in 2667 mm	53/53 in	7,298	£2,708
Aston Martin DB4 GT (1958-63)	Straight-six twin-cam	3670 cc	240 bhp 5500 rpm	240 lb ft 4250 rpm	141 mph 227 km/h	8.5 secs	171.75 in 4362 mm	98 in 2489 mm	54/53 in	1,110	£5,470 (1962)
Ferrari 250 GT SWB (1959-64)	V12	2953 cc	280 bhp 7000 rpm	N/A	140 mph 225 km/h	6.5 secs	164 in 4165 mm	94.7 in 2400 mm	53.3/ 53.3 in	582	£5,607 (1963)

Jaguar E-type Data File

The origins of Jaguar Cars can be traced back to 1922, when 21-year-old William Lyons and William Walmsley started the Swallow Sidecar Company. From making most stylish sidecars, the company progressed to building similarly stylish bodies for Austin 7s. In 1931 the SS models were introduced, with rakish Lyons-designed bodies mounted on specially-built Standard chassis. Aping the Bentleys of the time at a fraction of the cost, the model name Jaguar was adopted for a new range in 1935.

Post-war, the company became known as Jaguar Cars and soon launched the XK engine. This first appeared in the brilliant XK120 sports car introduced in 1948 and then in a superb large saloon, the Mk VII, in 1950. Five Le Mans wins in the 1950s established the company internationally, and a new small saloon increased production considerably.

The E-type continued the success story and led the export charge started by the XK120. In 1968 Jaguar introduced the world-beating XJ saloons, Sir William Lyons' finest creation. This model sustained the company until the present XJ40 model was introduced in 1986.

1961 Series I 3.8 Roadster and Fixed Head Coupé

Launched in March 1961, the E-type was offered in two body styles. Both the Open Two-Seater (roadster) model and the Fixed Head were strictly two-seaters and mechanically identical. The bodies were of monocoque construction, featuring front and rear bulkheads joined together by large tubular sills. To the front bulkhead was attached a front tubular sub-frame that carried the engine and front suspension. Suspension was independent all round, and disc brakes were fitted front and rear. The rear suspension unit was fitted into a separate cage that was attached to the underbody via rubber insulation.

Above: The E-type's 3.8-litre straight-six engine dated back to 1948 and featured twin overhead cams. In 1961 it produced 265 bhp.

Above: The row of toggle switches on the dashboard indicates that this is an early E-type; they were replaced by rockers in 1967.

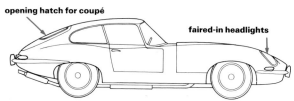

opening hatch for coupé

faired-in headlights

Above: Covered lights show this is a Series I car.

1964 Series I 4.2 Roadster and Fixed Head Coupé

The 4.2 engine was developed for the large Mk X saloon and fitted at the same time to the E-type. Its main virtue was increased torque, and performance remained similar. The 4.2 benefitted from a considerably improved, all-synchromesh gearbox developed in-house by Jaguar. A Dunlop tandem inline vacuum-type servo replaced the previous Kelsey Hayes bellows type. The body shape and exterior trim fittings remained largely unchanged, and externally the new model could only be recognised by the addition of chrome-plated emblems, on the bootlid and tailgate of the roadster and Fixed Head models respectively, reading '4.2' and 'E-Type'. The interior was considerably changed, with new seats, and the previous aluminium consoles were now trimmed.

1966 Series I 4.2 2+2 Fixed Head Coupé

An addition to the range, the 2+2 E-type was lengthened by 9 inches and was 2 inches higher. This enabled two small seats to be created in the rear, suitable for children or for adults over short distances. The new model could be distinguished by its higher roofline and very tall, rather upright windscreen. The car was 2 cwt heavier and consequently had uprated rear springs. The greater length allowed automatic transmission to be offered for the first time on an E-type, as an option.

By lengthening the E-type by nine inches and making it a couple of inches higher, the 2+2 was created with room (just) for four.

1967 Series I½ 4.2 2+2, Roadster and Coupé

All three models were changed somewhat in 1967 to meet the first of the changes demanded by US Federal Regulations. It was an interim model and several minor changes were made during its brief life, dependent upon the country to which the car was destined. The major external change was the removal of the glass covers over the headlamps. Under the bonnet, changes were made to meet the US emission control regulations and the familiar polished cam covers were replaced by black items with silver ribs. Export cars were fitted with Zenith-Stromberg carburettors rather than the triple SUs of the UK market. Inside the car the door handles were recessed into the doors, and during the life of the model the toggle switches were superseded by rocker switches.

Left: Headlights were uncovered on the so-called Series I½. The faired-in lights of the Series 1 were not acceptable in some markets, so the design was standardised.

Below: Uncovered lights distinguish the Series I½ models.

engine given emission controls

internal door handle recessed

headlight covers removed

Below: In 1963 Jaguar built a small series of racing E-types, the 'lightweight', but despite its D-type heritage the E-type was never intended as a racing car. It gained a few victories but was outclassed by Ferrari's famous 250 GTO.

Twin-cam engine

Power for the E-type came from Jaguar's well proven 3.8-litre twin-cam engine. That had been designed during World War II and made its debut in the XK120 sports car in 1948, in 3.4-litre form. By the time it appeared in the E-type it had taken Jaguar to five Le Mans 24-Hours wins, in the C- and D-type.

SPECIFICATION

1961 E-type Jaguar

ENGINE

Type:	inline six-cylinder twin-cam
Construction:	cast-iron block and light-alloy head; seven main bearings
Bore×stroke:	3.43 in×4.17 in (87 mm×106 mm)
Displacement:	3781 cc
Compression ratio:	9.0:1
Valve gear:	two valves per cylinder operated by twin-chain driven overhead camshafts in hemispherical combustion chambers
Fuel system:	three 2-in SU HD8
Ignition:	mechanical distributor
Maximum power:	265 bhp at 5500 rpm (SAE gross)
Maximum torque:	260 lb ft at 4000 rpm

TRANSMISSION

Type:	four-speed manual with synchromesh on top three ratios	
Ratios:	1st	3.377:1
	2nd	1.86:1
	3rd	1.283:1
	4th	1.00:1
Final drive:	hypoid bevel with limited slip differential	
Ratio:	3.33:1 or 3.07:1	

BODY/CHASSIS

Type:	steel monocoque centre section with square tube front subframe and pressed steel rear subframe; convertible or coupé two-seater bodywork

RUNNING GEAR

Steering:	rack and pinion
Suspension:	front: independent with double wishbones, longitudinal torsion bars, telescopic dampers and anti-roll bar rear: independent with one lower lateral link and one lower radius arm per side with driveshaft acting as upper lateral link; two telescopic coil/spring damper units per side
Brakes:	discs front and rear; rears mounted inboard; servo assisted
Wheels:	wire spoked 5 in×15 in
Tyres:	Dunlop 6.40×15 RS5 crossply

DIMENSIONS AND WEIGHT

Length:	175.5 in (4457 mm)
Width:	65.3 in (1658 mm)
Height:	48 in (1220 mm)
Wheelbase:	96 in (2438 mm)
Track:	50 in (1270 mm) front and rear
Turning circle:	37 ft (11.3 m)
Dry weight:	2446 lb (1117 kg) roadster; 2520 lb (1143 kg) coupé

PERFORMANCE

Acceleration:	0-30mph 2.8 secs
	0-40mph 4.4secs
	0-50mph 5.6secs
	0-60mph 6.9secs
	0-70mph 8.5secs
	0-80mph 11.1secs
	0-90mph 13.2secs
	0-100mph 16.2secs
	0-110mph 19.2secs
	0-120mph 25.9secs
	0-130mph 33.1secs
Standing ¼ mile:	14.7 sec

Acceleration in gear:	mph	fourth	third
	30-50	5.4	4.3
	40-60	5.5	4.3
	50-70	5.4	4.1

Maximum speed:	150 mph (242 km/h)
Overall fuel consumption:	17.9 mpg
Price (1961):	£2,196 19s 2d (including tax)

Performance figures from AUTOCAR

Independent rear suspension

The E-type was the first Jaguar to have independent rear suspension. It was mounted on a separate subframe and featured inboard disc brakes. Unusually, the driveshaft doubled as the upper suspension link.

Narrow track

One of the few things to date the E-type, even 30 years on, is the narrow track of only 50 in, which is emphasised by the overhanging bodywork. It was increased on the V12 models to 53 in front and rear.

Louvred bonnet

The twin-cam engine under that low bonnet generated a considerable amount of heat. The escape route for it was provided by a double row of bonnet louvres just in front of the windscreen.

Forward-hinged bonnet

The E-type's bonnet is a very long, complicated fabrication that hinges forward to reveal the classic straight-six 3.8-litre twin-cam. The shape of the bonnet changed somewhat to accommodate the later V12 engine.

Faired-in headlights

The headlights on the Series 1 cars were covered by a clear plastic screen for aerodynamic efficiency. Covered lights were illegal in the United States and they were discontinued for the Series 1½ cars.

Crossply tyres

Originally Dunlop crossplies were fitted to the E-type because their behaviour was far more consistent than the early radial tyres. The sudden breakaway characteristics of Michelin Xs, for example, would have been disastrous in a 150-mph car. Few E-types today, however, still wear crossplies, and this car is no exception.

1968 Series II 4.2 Roadster, 2+2 and Coupé

The Series II models were more radically altered. The open headlamps were now more prominent, and the bonnet mouth was increased in size to aid cooling and the fitting of air conditioning, a new optional extra. The front bumpers and motif bar were heavier items and gave the appearance of being one-piece. At the rear a new three-piece wraparound bumper was mounted higher, and below it was sited a new stainless-steel finisher to which was affixed the square number plate. Larger sidelight units were fitted front and rear. The 2+2 model was further revised, with the windscreen base being moved forward to increase the angle. Braking was changed from Lockheed to Girling and power steering became an option.

Above: The Series II saw new and larger rear lights fitted.

Below: On the Series II the indicators were larger and mounted below the bumper.

1971 Series III 5.3 Roadster and 2+2 Coupé

The V12 engined cars were the most radically altered. Appearance differed considerably as the result of the fitting of a grille in the bonnet mouth and giving the wings small flares to clear the wider wheels and tyres. Only Roadster and 2+2 models were offered, and the open car was now based on the same longer wheelbase as the four-seater. A 'V12' badge was added to the rear in place of the '4.2' one, and a ventilator grille was fitted to the closed car's tailgate. The front suspension was altered by inclining the wishbones to give anti-dive characteristics and the ride height was now adjustable. The front sub-frame was altered to take the new, wider engine. Ventilated front disc brakes and Girling Monotube dampers were introduced.

The V12s, the Series III cars, are immediately recognisable thanks to the large air intake with its chrome grille.

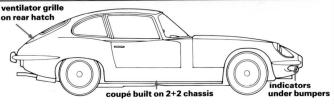

coupé built on 2+2 chassis · *indicators under bumpers*

ventilator grille on rear hatch

Above and below: Series III cars were built on the long 2+2 wheelbase.

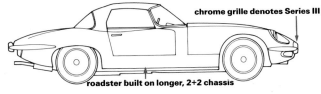

chrome grille denotes Series III

roadster built on longer, 2+2 chassis

Inside the E-type

In designing the E-type, Jaguar applied much of what they had learned building the D-type racers that dominated the Le Mans 24 Hours race in the 1950s, and the E-type used a similar centre monocoque (i.e. chassis-less) construction. Note the height and depth of the door sills, a feature that helped to provide a rigid structure. That was far more important on the open roadsters than on the coupé shown here, which was stiffened by its roof. The straight-six engine was carried on its own separate tubular subframe, which bolted to the monocoque, while the rear suspension was held in a pressed steel carrier or subframe.

The rear suspension was one of the

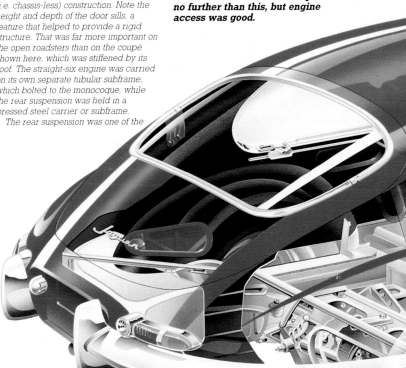

Above: The length of the E-type's bonnet meant that it could open no further than this, but engine access was good.

most interesting technical features of the E-type. Just like today's Testarossa, the E-type had twin coil spring and damper units mounted on each side of the driveshaft. The driveshaft itself was used as the upper transverse link and the disc brakes were mounted inboard to reduce unsprung weight (the lower the weight of wheel, tyre and brake the suspension has to control, the better). The system was good enough to form the basis for that used in the XJ6.

The racing D-type had pioneered the use of disc brakes, and the E-type had discs all round, but the early E-types did not stop nearly as well as they went.

Right: By 1971, with the introduction of the V12 Series III cars, the early wood-rim steering wheel had been replaced with a leather-covered wheel. Its diameter was smaller too, as the V12s had power steering. More luxury tourers than sports cars, many V12s, like this one, had automatic transmission.

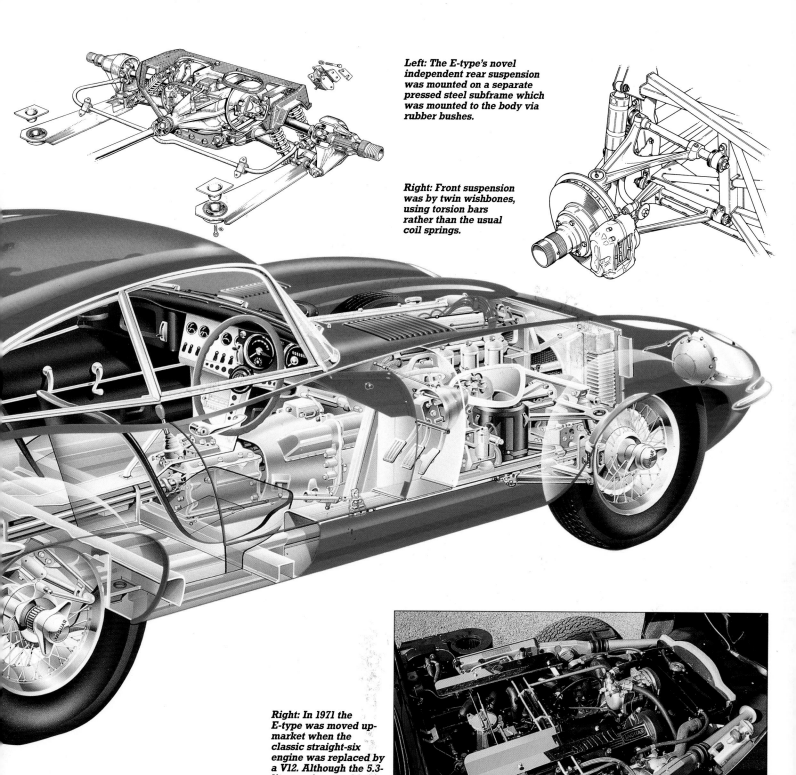

Left: The E-type's novel independent rear suspension was mounted on a separate pressed steel subframe which was mounted to the body via rubber bushes.

Right: Front suspension was by twin wishbones, using torsion bars rather than the usual coil springs.

Right: In 1971 the E-type was moved up-market when the classic straight-six engine was replaced by a V12. Although the 5.3-litre engine was bigger, alloy construction meant that there was little weight penalty. On this example fuel is supplied by four Stromberg carburettors.

Below: The E-type's wide, low windscreen was cleared by three, rather than the conventional two, wipers.

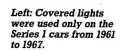

Left: Covered lights were used only on the Series 1 cars from 1961 to 1967.

Right: Exposed lights with heavy chrome surround were introduced with the Series II cars in 1968. The indicator repeater above the bumper shows that this is a left-hand-drive US car.

AC Cobra

A blend of a 1950s British chassis and American V8 muscle gave "the last of the hairy-chested sports cars" acceleration to rival any modern supercar. Carroll Shelby was the man who made it happen; the car was the Cobra.

Below: At Le Mans in 1963 this hard-topped Cobra 289 was driven to seventh place overall by Peter Bolton and Ninian Sanderson. The engine was fitted with four twin-choke Weber carburettors but was otherwise only mildly tuned, giving an output of about 300 bhp.

The Cobra is perhaps the ultimate example of that rare breed of car, built from the simplest of ingredients but which magically adds up to so much more than the sum of its parts. Barely 1,000 examples of all variants were built, but the Cobra's reputation as one of the most fearsomely fast and beautiful of all sports cars goes way beyond the numbers. On the road, it set totally new standards for straight-line performance – figures that still look awesome even against today's quickest supercars. On the racetrack, it dominated production sports racing for many years, especially in the USA, and in Daytona coupé form it snatched the Sports Car Manufacturers' World Championship from Ferrari in 1965.

Today, a real Cobra is one of the most desirable of all classic cars, and the variety of replicas available all round the world proves that imitation *is* the sincerest form of flattery. Yet whatever else the Cobra is, it is hardly sophisticated. Below the muscular curves of its aluminium skin is a simple tubular chassis which dates from the early 1950s, and a basically cheap, rugged yet highly effective production-line V8 engine. And that's about all there is – just sledgehammer power in minimum weight.

It was a well-tried theme, putting affordable and

Left: Both 289- and 427-engined Cobras had electrifying performance. In 1965 a roadgoing 427 was timed at just 4.2 seconds from 0-60 mph.

Inset left: The name 'Cobra' came to Carroll Shelby in a dream, apparently. Shelby owned the rights to the name, and later used it on the Shelby Mustangs.

Above: The Daytona featured a streamlined fastback body designed by Pete Brock on a stiffened version of the leaf-spring 289 frame.

uncomplicated US V8 engines into light and nimble European-style sporting chassis. Allards with Ford and Cadillac V8s had started the trend in the early 1950s; US gentleman-racer Briggs Cunningham had tried a Cadillac-powered Healey Silverstone and then his own line of Cunningham Le Mans entries; and a couple of people had even attempted putting V8 power in AC Ace chassis before 1960, but the Cobra represented the big jump from one-offs to a successful production car.

It was different because of the determination and imagination of one man, Carroll Shelby – the man who invented the Cobra.

Shelby is the son of a Texas mailman, born in 1923 and crazy about cars from childhood. He has been a military flying instructor, a haulage contractor, an oil-field wrangler and a failed chicken farmer. He has also been a hugely successful racing driver and a Le Mans winner (for Aston Martin in 1959). He was in the right place at the right time with his easy-going Texan charm to bring Ford's new engine and AC's old chassis together and create the Cobra early in 1962.

He turned car constructor after heart problems forced him to retire as a racing driver in 1960, with two ambitions. The first was to build a *successful* V8-powered, European-style sports car; the second was to use it to beat Enzo Ferrari in racing. That was a personal thing; Shelby had once been approached by Ferrari with the offer of a works drive, then, when he went to discuss terms, treated with the sort of off-handed scorn for which Ferrari was infamous. Shelby promised

Ferrari that one day he would be back to "beat his ass" on the racetrack.

He set out with only the vague notion of somebody's V8 in somebody else's chassis. He spoke to General Motors, to Healey, to Aston Martin and to Jensen. Some, like GM, were too buried in bureaucracy to cope with Shelby's get-things-done attitude, and GM didn't need an in-house competitor for their Corvette; Donald Healey, an old friend of Shelby's through racing and record-breaking, was enthusiastic but was prevented from going ahead by his new backers at BMC, who didn't need competition for the big Austin-Healeys. And then Shelby heard about AC.

Shelby promised Ferrari he'd be back to beat him

AC, based in Thames Ditton, Surrey, had a tradition as sporting car manufacturers dating back to before World War I, but they had a problem. Their Ace had been in production since 1953, first with an ageing AC six-cylinder engine, then with a six-cylinder Bristol engine from 1956, and then a six-cylinder Ford from early 1961, each looking for a bit more power. The Ford six was tried because supplies of the pre-war BMW-based Bristol engine were in any case about to dry up (as Bristol were about to launch a new generation using US Chrysler V8s), but in spite of being relatively cheap and very tuneable the Ford engine was only barely able to keep the Ace compet-

itive. Shelby heard of the problem from a journalist friend, contacted AC in September 1961 to suggest a so-far unnamed V8, and AC agreed.

Almost simultaneously, Shelby found his engine, from Ford. Earlier in 1961 he had met Dave Evans, at the Pike's Peak hill climb. Evans was in charge of Ford's NASCAR racing engine programme; Shelby was a Goodyear tyre distributor. In October, another journalist friend put Shelby back in touch with Evans, whom he knew had an interesting new engine. It was an all-iron V8, but its new thin-wall castings made it almost as light as an aluminium engine, without the usual costs or technical problems. It had been drawn up in 1958 and launched in the mid-sized Fairlane for 1961, and was the smallest V8 Ford had ever made, the lightest, and with the shortest stroke of any engine in its class, which gave it great performance potential. Shelby immediately contacted Evans, who quickly sent two examples of the engine.

From there, the Cobra happened very rapidly. The Ace chassis had been developed from a design by John Tojeiro, a few examples of which had been sold for sports racing cars in Britain in the early 1950s. It was a simple tubular ladder with two big tubes set quite close together and linked by smaller cross-members and fabricated mounts for the suspension – which was by transverse leaf springs with lower wishbones, much like a Fiat 500. A light tubular superstructure carried the alloy body panels. The new Ford V8 was a relatively easy fit, virtually as light as the old Bristol six and coming complete with an ideal

AC Cobra

The Cobra can trace its ancestry back a long way, to the pretty AC Ace, introduced in 1953. There was fundamentally little difference visually between the Ace and the first Cobra, the 260-cu in version from 1962. The big difference was under the bonnet, where the Ace's two-litre AC or Bristol engine had been replaced by the American Ford 260-cu in (4263-cc) V8 engine. Over the years, engine sizes varied but it was the introduction of the big-block 427-cu in (6998-cc) V8 in 1965 that brought about the distinctive shape of the Cobra 427, which radiated power and performance.

wheels, but as
increased
made to alloy
sed on the racing

Roll-over hoop

A rear roll-over hoop was fitted to the 427 S/C model (S/C standing for street/competition). The S/C was a halfway house, tamer than the pure race Cobras but more potent than the normal road cars, and was a development aimed at using up and selling off unwanted competition cars.

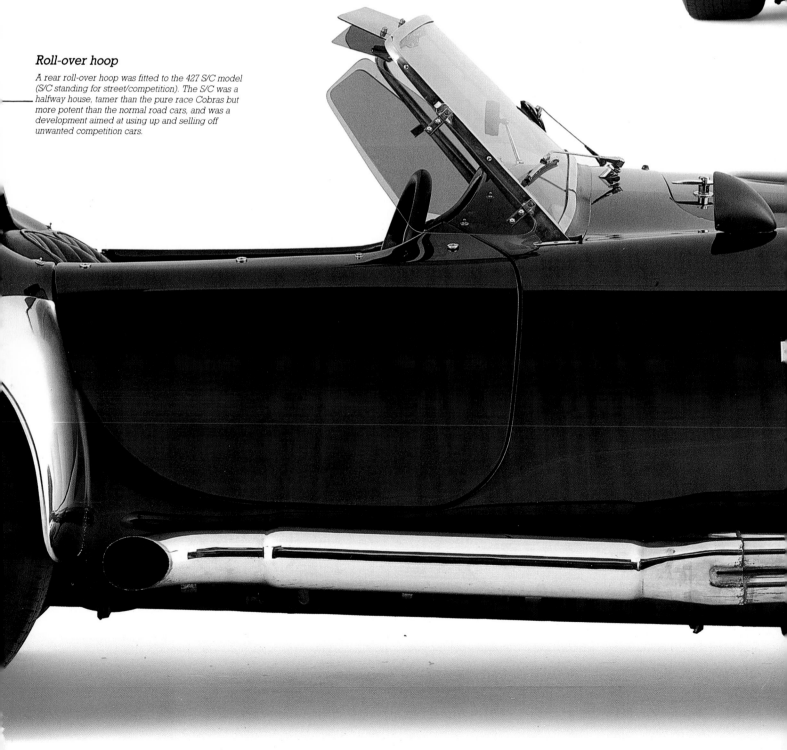

427-cu in big-block engine

The American Ford 427-cu in (seven-litre) V8 engine was first fitted to the Cobra in 1965; it was a very well-proven over-square design with 107.4 mm bore and 96 mm stroke. Although as much as 200 lb heavier than the 289-cu in (4736-cc) engine it could generate far more power, and had years of successful competition in NASCAR to its credit.

Side exhausts

Side exhausts, mounted on both sides of the car, were a feature of the S/C model; they were intended to provide the minimum restriction to the engine, increasing power. Routing the pipes outside also helped reduce the very considerable heat soak from the big engine and transmission into the cockpit, which could make the interior uncomfortably hot.

Halibrand alloy wheels

Original Cobras ran on wire-spo[k] power outputs rose and wheel w accordingly the sensible switch wheels, in this case Halibrands a GT40s.

Alloy body

All Cobras had alloy bodies, hand-crafted in very small numbers by AC at Thames Ditton, Surrey.

Tubular steel chassis

To cope with the extra power of the 427 engine, the Cobra's chassis was strengthened considerably. The two main chassis rails were thick-wall steel tube with tubular steel cross-members. Rigid subframes were used front and rear to support the suspension.

By January 1963 it had won its first races and gained the definitive 289-cu in engine, after just 75 260s had been built. The car was sold through Ford dealerships and Shelby had already moved to larger premises, but sales were really only ever enough to gain racing homologation, rather than the 1,000 cars per year that Shelby had once envisaged. For all that, the Cobra had to be seen as a success. It won races and it attracted people into Ford showrooms, even if they then bought some lesser car; it was the perfect front for Ford's new 'Total Performance' image.

The 427s were staggeringly fast

In March 1963 the leaf-spring chassis was improved by rack-and-pinion steering in place of the old worm and roller, and there had been many other improvements, from new electrics to different gearing for better flexibility. The next change was dramatic. In October 1963, looking for more power for racing, Shelby tried a Ford 427 NASCAR engine in a modified leaf-spring chassis, and although the first prototype proved virtually undriveable with so much power, it set the scene for the big-block Cobra.

Shelby and AC finally made it work by designing a more modern chassis, still with a ladder layout but much strengthened and now with coil-spring suspension, developed with the aid of Ford's computers. The production 427 was announced in January 1965 and although most used the milder 428 engine rather than the true 427 racer, they were still staggeringly fast. In May 1966, AC added a 289 version of the coil-spring chassis for Europe, and one of these was the final Cobra built, in February 1969. Meanwhile, Shelby had built a handful of Daytona coupés on leaf-spring 289 chassis, chasing speed through aerodynamics, and finally kept his promise to Ferrari to beat his cars on the track. The Cobra legend was complete.

Above: In early trials the power and weight of the 427 engine proved too much for the AC Ace-derived leaf-spring chassis. When the Cobra 427 entered production in 1965, it had a much stronger coil-spring frame and greatly improved handling.

Above: The first version of the Cobra entered production in 1962 with Ford's new lightweight small-block V8 in 260-cu in form. By January 1963 it had graduated to the 289 version of the engine, and in March of the same year it gained rack-and-pinion steering: this was the Cobra Mk II. The small wheel-arch lips denote the car's vintage. Most Cobras were built for the American market, but a few right-hand-drive examples were sold by AC in the UK from 1964.

Borg-Warner four speed manual gearbox. The chassis had to be strengthened and a lot of details tidied up, but the prototype Cobra was completed by January 1962 – by which time Shelby had also arranged engine supplies from Ford and chassis from AC, both on credit.

The prototype was sent without the engine to Shelby's California works in February 1962, given the latest 260-cu in V8 tuned to produce 260 bhp, improved at the Riverside circuit, then shown to the public at the New York show in April 1962. In May the first magazine test appeared and it became apparent that the Cobra (a name which came to Shelby in a dream) was a winner. First production cars were built by July, with the chassis shipped from England, the engines fitted and details finished in the USA, with further development taking place virtually car by car. More lessons were learned when the Cobra was first raced – at Riverside in October 1962, where it led comfortably against GM's racing Corvettes before mechanical failure forced its retirement.

Driving the Cobra: *a friendly monster*

In spite of its reputation, the Cobra is really quite a friendly monster. The first thing you notice about a 289 is how small it seems. It has maximum instrumentation and minimum trim (even cord door-pulls), and no possibility of an extra passenger or even cockpit luggage space. A 427 is bigger inside, but even a 289 has room for a fairly straight-arm driving position. Standard seats are simple buckets with very low backs, but they are comfortable and grip well enough if helped by full-harness belts. The controls aren't as heavy as you might expect from a 1960s sports car with 350 bhp, but the power is obvious from the moment you start it; a rumbling, uneven tickover that turns into a spine-tingling howl.

In any Cobra, the power and acceleration are ferocious, with 0-60 mph in typically close to five seconds and 0-100 mph in barely over 10 seconds. The mid-range flexibility from so much power is awesome. Treat the car with respect and remember its simple chassis and relatively skinny tyres. The Cobra will be predictable, and forgiving up to a point. With a big V8 up front it will naturally understeer, but power oversteer is available almost anywhere, any time; just make sure you are ready for it.

PERFORMANCE & SPECIFICATION COMPARISON	Engine	Displacement	Power	Torque (lb ft)	Max speed	0-60 mph	Length (in/mm)	Wheelbase (in/mm)	Track front/rear	Weight total (lb/kg)	Price
AC Cobra 289 (1963)	V8, overhead-valve	4727 cc	271 bhp 6000 rpm	314 lb ft 3400 rpm	138 mph 222 km/h	5.5 sec	156.0 in 3962 mm	90.0 in 2286 mm	55.0 in 54.0 in	2354 lb 1068 kg	£2,400 (1963)
Austin-Healey 3000 (1959)	Straight-six, overhead-valve	2912 cc	124 bhp 4750 rpm	162 lb ft 2700 rpm	115 mph 185 km/h	10.8 sec	157.3 in 3995 mm	92.0 in 2337 mm	48.8 in 50.0 in	2520 lb 1143 kg	£1,175 (1959)
Chevrolet Corvette (1963 fuel-injected)	V8, overhead-valve	5359 cc	360 bhp 5000 rpm	295 lb ft 3200 rpm	135 mph 217 km/h	5.9 sec	175.3 in 4453 mm	98.0 in 2489 mm	56.3 in 57.0 in	3150 lb 1429 kg	$4,687 (1963)
Ferrari 250 GT SWB (1959)	V12, overhead-cam	2953 cc	280 bhp 7000 rpm	N/A	140 mph 225 km/h	6.5 sec	164.0 in 4165 mm	94.5 in 2400 mm	53.3 in 53.3 in	2804 lb 1272 kg	£5,607 (1963)
Jaguar E-type Series I (1961)	Straight-six, twin-cam	3781 cc	265 bhp 5500 rpm	260 lb ft 4000 rpm	149 mph 240 km/h	7.1 sec	175.3 in 4453 mm	96.0 in 2438 mm	50.0 in 50.0 in	2625 lb 1191 kg	£1,480 (1961)

AC Cobra Data File

T he AC Cobra showed just what can be done with the most basic of traditional sports car chassis when allied to a tremendously powerful engine. The Ace, from which the Cobra was developed, was powered by either a straight-six AC engine or a straight-six Bristol unit. Both were good engines, but had long since reached the end of their development potential when Carroll Shelby decided to turn Ace into Cobra. The first Cobra appeared in 1961 and, for such an ancient design, lived a long while. By the time the last Cobra was built, in 1969, the original leaf springs had given way to coils, the chassis was much improved and the steering had become rack and pinion, but the product was still recognisably the same fearsome cross-breed that was the original Cobra.

Above: AC were the right firm at the right time for Carroll Shelby.

Left: You can't always believe what you read – a Cobra '427' might have the heavier, longer-stroke 428 engine under its bonnet.

1961 Cobra prototype

Based on an uprated Ace chassis and probably using one of Shelby's original 221-cu in 'sample' engines, the prototype was built at AC's Thames Ditton works during the winter of 1960-61, with help from Shelby, and first tested at Silverstone in January.

Unlike any subsequent Cobra, it had inboard rear disc brakes – a strange choice for ease of maintenance on what was always likely to be a racing car. It was sent to Shelby in February, fitted with a 260-cu in engine, and used as a test-bed.

1962 Cobra 260

Having been exhibited at the New York show in April and featured in magazine tests by May, the Cobra went into production (slowly at first) in July 1962. It now had outboard rear

discs, a 260-bhp 260-cu in V8, and worm-and-roller steering on its Ace-based leaf-spring chassis. Minor improvements were constantly being made to the design.

1963 Cobra 289

Following Ford's engine updating programme, the Cobra switched to the 289-cu in engine from January 1963, gaining little by way of power but much better flexibility and even more long-term tuning potential.

Briefly, the chassis was largely unchanged, but in March it was much improved by the introduction of rack-and-pinion steering with some suspension retuning, and shortly after by adding slightly wider wheels.

bodyshell virtually as original AC Ace

alloy body on separate tubular steel chassis

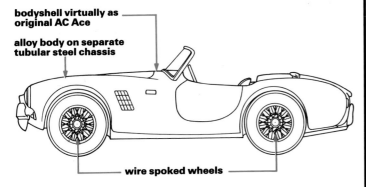

wire spoked wheels

1963-66 Cobra 427 prototypes

The first 427 prototype, built in October 1963, used a 427 Ford NASCAR V8 in a modified 289 leaf-spring chassis, but proved almost undriveable. The next prototype, also based on a 289, used a full-race all-alloy Ford 390-cu in V8 in a very lightweight car with bodywork split

across the middle and hinged for easy access. That gave it the nickname 'Flip-Top', but its "evil" handling led its testers to call it 'The Turd'. By December it had a 427 engine but still needed some serious chassis changes which were to entail the development of a new suspension layout.

1964 Daytona coupé

The Daytona coupés were developed from leaf-spring 289 chassis, with coupé bodies for better aerodynamics – for European Championship-type racing and especially for Le Mans. They also had a lot more chassis

tubing, allegedly only to support the body but really adding a lot more strength without actually breaking the racing rules. In 1965 the Daytonas took six class wins and took the World Championship from Ferrari.

Below: Outwardly like the Daytona, but with a more highly-developed spaceframe chassis underneath: this is the Willment Cobra.

1965 Cobra 427

The production 427 was announced in January, with the all-new coil-spring chassis and heavily revised bodywork, making it an altogether bigger car. It was slow to sell and many were sold as 'Semi-Competition'

roadsters, to move stock and help Shelby try to reach homologation targets. Most subsequent 427s actually used the milder-tuned and cheaper Ford 428 V8 engines which still produced dramatic performance.

air intake for bigger engine

flared wheel arches for larger wheels

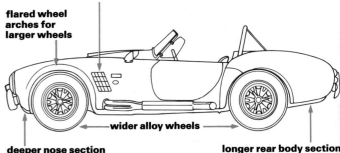

wider alloy wheels

deeper nose section

longer rear body section

Above: The S/C variant of the 427 was an intermediate street/track car, offered to the public so as to clear excess stocks of racers built in an effort to homologate the car for the GT Manufacturers' Championship.

1966 AC 289

In May, AC combined the excellent new coil-spring chassis with the lighter 289-cu in engine to produce a car specifically for Europe, and one of the best-balanced Cobras of all. Production of the leaf-spring cars was

ended in March 1965 shortly after the introduction of the 427. The last 427s were made as late as 1968, but the last Cobra (not counting the AC Mk IV) was a European-spec coil-spring 289, built in February 1969.

Above: The leaf-spring Cobra Mk II can be identified by its less curvaceous 'hips', less bulbous wings, central fuel filler, multi-bar grille and absence of front vent slots. The AC 289 gained the wider and far more rigid coil-spring Mk III chassis of the 427 (as in the main cutaway drawing), which was 50 lb heavier but three times as strong.

SPECIFICATION
1965 AC Cobra 427

ENGINE

Type:	V8, overhead-valve
Construction:	cast-iron block and alloy heads, five main bearings
Bore×stroke:	107.4 mm×96 mm
Displacement:	6997 cc
Compression ratio:	10.5:1
Valve gear:	two valves per cylinder operated via pushrods and rockers by single block-mounted camshaft
Fuel system:	Holley four-barrel 750CFM carburettor
Ignition:	mechanical, by coil and distributor
Maximum power:	410 bhp at 5,600 rpm
Maximum torque:	462 lb ft at 2,800 rpm

TRANSMISSION

Type:	Borg-Warner four-speed manual	
Ratios:	1st	2.20:1
	2nd	1.66:1
	3rd	1.31:1
	4th	1.0:1
Final drive ratio:	3.54:1 (options ranged from 4.1:1 to 2.9:1)	

BODY/CHASSIS

Type:	ladder frame tubular steel chassis with aluminium alloy two-seater convertible body

RUNNING GEAR

Steering:	rack and pinion
Suspension:	front: independent with unequal-length wishbones, coil springs and telescopic dampers rear: independent with unequal-length wishbones, coil springs and telescopic dampers
Brakes:	Girling discs front and rear, 11.63-in diameter front, 10.75-in diameter rear
Wheels:	alloy or wire, 15-in diameter
Tyres:	185 in×15 in front, 195 in×15 in rear

DIMENSIONS AND WEIGHT

Length:	156.0 in (3962 mm)
Width:	68.0 in (1727 mm)
Height:	48.0 in (1219 mm)
Wheelbase:	90.0 in (2286 mm)
Track:	55.0 in (1397 mm) front, 54.0 in (1372 mm) rear
Kerb weight:	2,529 lb (1147 kg)

PERFORMANCE

Acceleration:	0-30 mph 1.8 sec
	0-40 mph 2.6 sec
	0-50 mph 3.4 sec
	0-60 mph 4.5 sec
	0-70 mph 5.7 sec
	0-80 mph 6.8 sec
	0-90 mph 8.5 sec
	0-100 mph 10.3 sec
	0-110 mph 13.1 sec
	0-120 mph 16.4 sec
Standing ¼ mile:	12.4 sec

Acceleration in gear:	mph	fourth
	30-50	3.4
	40-60	3.6
	50-70	3.9

Maximum speed:	165 mph (266 km/h)
Overall fuel consumption:	14 mpg
Price (1965):	£3,750

Performance figures from MOTOR

AC Cobra 427 kindly supplied by the National Motor Museum

Lipped wheel arches

Another distinguishing feature of the 427 S/C was the small lips on the edges of the wheel arches; these were added to cover the enormous tyres fitted to this model.

Coil-spring suspension

The early 260 and 289 Cobras used the same suspension design as the Ace, with transverse leaf springs front and rear. That was discarded for the 427, which used a more modern system of double wishbones with coil springs front and rear. Anti-dive and anti-squat geometry was built into the design. Anti-roll bars front and rear were also standard equipment on the S/C.

Flared wheel arches

Widening the car to allow for the 427's wider track and far larger wheels and tyres gave the 427 its distinctive bulging wheel arches. At the same time the rear of the car was restyled, leaving little of the original AC Ace 'look'.

Wide track

In a move to give the Cobra 427 roadholding to match its immense power, the track front and rear was widened considerably compared with the 289, by 4½ inches at the rear and 3½ inches at the front.

Up to 600 bhp

With all the modifications that could be made to the Cobra 427 (which included a long-dwell, high-lift camshaft, mechanical valve-lifters and compression ratios as high as 14:1), as much as 600 bhp at 8,500 rpm could be extracted in racing trim.

The AC Mk IV

In 1982, the Cobra was 'reborn', with blessings from both Ford and AC, as the AC Mk IV (assuming that the 260 was the Mk I, the rack-and-pinion 289 the Mk II and the coil-spring 427 the Mk III). The Mk IV was built with original jigs and tooling to be very like an original 427. Its creator is Brian Angliss, one of the most respected of Cobra restorers, who began to make many otherwise unavailable parts, and eventually to build complete new cars virtually from scratch. He built his first around 1974, and followed it with more, clearly identified as his own and with no intention of being regarded as originals. His business changed its name from Cobra Parts to Autokraft and moved to premises near the old AC works, at Brooklands. In 1978 Angliss arranged with an American classic car dealer to import his Cobra copies into the USA. A few had been imported by 1980, but ran into type approval problems. He then worked to have the car federalised, and found a good deal of help from Ford themselves, who are usually very sensitive about Cobra 'replicas' or use of the name. In 1982 AC granted Angliss a 25-year licence to use the AC name and logo, and to build Cobra-shaped cars, which were in limited production by 1984. Angliss also bought control of the ailing AC Cars. In 1990, Ford moved to wind up AC, but, contrary to some reports, the company still exists and Angliss has continued to build the Mk IV in limited numbers.

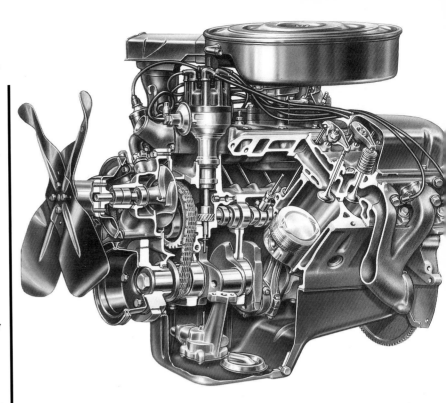

Left and below: Brian Angliss has made the Mk IV something close to the perfect Cobra, even gaining American type approval. The use of original tooling and jigs means that the Mk IV is far more desirable than the numerous replicas available.

Chassis

All Cobra chassis share the common layout of a massive twin-tube ladder; in that, they date back to the Ace and beyond that to John Tojeiro's hand-built sports-racers, sold in tiny numbers in the early 1950s. 'Toj' built the first for himself, with two three-inch main tubes linked by a similar cross-tube and steel box-sections at each end to carry the suspension. It was light, cheap and took a variety of engines. In 1953, AC were introduced to Tojeiro and in his chassis saw the basis of the sports car they badly needed to revive their image. A couple of Tojeiros had bodies very like the 1949 Le Mans-winning Ferrari barchetta, and as LOY 500 and JOY 500 were to be prolific winners; a third model became the Ace prototype. For the Cobra, AC and Shelby retained the Ace's layout of lower wishbones and transverse leaf springs whose free ends acted as upper links. The main tubes were of the same diameter and spacing as on the Ace but with thicker walls, and the engine mounts were changed and other mounts generally beefed up. On the prototype, the rear discs were mounted inboard, but production cars used outboard discs all round. Rack-and-pinion steering was adopted in 1963, but the big change came in 1965, to cope with the added power, weight and size of the 427 engine. The main tubes were bigger, thicker-walled and positioned further apart, and the suspension towers were tubular rather than sheet fabrications. Conventional coil springs and wishbones replaced the leaf springs, stronger driveshafts and hubs were used, and Ford claimed that their computer had worked out the geometry and springing for the fully adjustable suspension to give a more compliant ride yet with much better location and control – just what a full-race 427 with close to 500 bhp needed!

Below right: The compact V8 engine, whether 427 as here or 289, is set well back behind the front axle line, giving good weight distribution.

Below: Autokraft production employs many original AC tools and drawings, but the Mk III-type chassis has been further strengthened and the body skin is made of hand-rolled 16-gauge aluminium alloy.

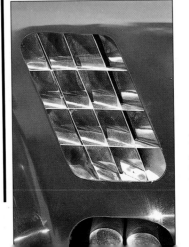

Above and left: Side air vents were first used on the 1963 Le Mans Cobras. Most, on both 427s and 289s, are simple, slatted louvres but the 'chip-cutter' style (left) appears on some 427s, along with sill-mounted side exhausts.

Engine

Alongside the light and compact 289-cu in V8 of the original Cobra (as also used in the majority of Ford GT40s), the mighty 427 is a heavyweight in every respect. The big-block started in 1958, at 352 cu in, and grew through 390 and 406 cu in before reaching 427 in 1963. From 1960 it had many power options, from four-barrel carbs to special heads, cams and manifolds. As well as it being their biggest street option, Ford used the big-block for NASCAR racing, and outright power. The 427 had wedge-shaped combustion chambers, huge

Left: The Ford small-block V8 was derived from Robert Stirrat's 1958 'Challenger' design. Although of cast iron, it drew on the latest foundry techniques and was very light by the standards of its time. It went through 221- and 260-cu in incarnations before the definitive 289-cu in (4736-cc) displacement was arrived at. The stock unit produced 271 bhp but Shelby offered up to 400 bhp in full-race tune.

rectangular ports, high compression, and two four-barrel carbs. For the road it gave 425 bhp and 480 lb ft of torque. For racing, it was strong enough to be tuned much further, thanks to a forged crank with very strong bearings, and a high-capacity lubrication system, particularly in 'side-oiler' form with an additional oil feed from the side of the crankshaft. Even with an alloy sump, timing cover and inlet manifold it was 150 lb heavier than a 289-cu in engine, but probably 150 bhp more powerful. For racing, Shelby quoted 480 bhp and 510 lb ft of torque, off the shelf. That said, most 427 Cobras didn't have the 427 engine at all, but the 428 from the Galaxie. That was much milder than the racing 427. It had a longer stroke and a less robust crank, a single four-barrel carb, lower compression and some 390 bhp in Cobra trim; it was heavier even than the 427, but much cheaper – less than half the price. Strangely, the 427's actual capacity was 425 cu in, but Ford called it a 427 because Oldsmobile already sold a 425; and the 428 really was a 427 . . . but Ford had to call it something!

Above: The 427-cu in big-block weighed some 150 lb more than the 289 but was stupendously strong. Even in street form, power output could be as much as 425 bhp; tuned for competition, it could deliver anything up to 600 bhp.

Right: The 289 was a short-stroked as well as light and rigid engine, as can be seen in this end-on cutaway. These features contributed greatly to its potential for performance applications.

Below: Some early Mk IIs were fitted with British-made Smith's gauges, but later Cobras were equipped with American Stewart-Warner instrumentation.

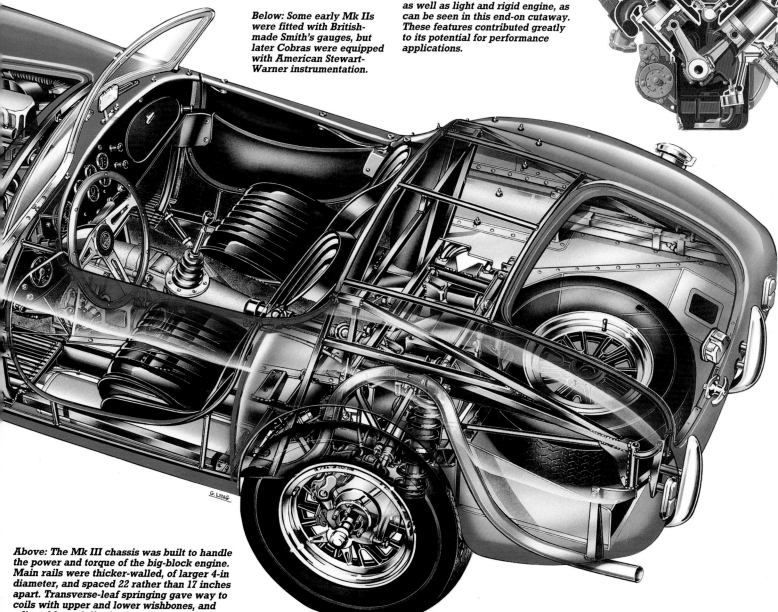

Above: The Mk III chassis was built to handle the power and torque of the big-block engine. Main rails were thicker-walled, of larger 4-in diameter, and spaced 22 rather than 17 inches apart. Transverse-leaf springing gave way to coils with upper and lower wishbones, and adjustable anti-dive/anti-squat geometry.

Chevrolet Corvette

Corvettes have been built since 1953. There have been several generations in that time; one of the best was built from 1956 to 1962. With its glassfibre body and powerful 360-bhp V8 engine, the fastest could exceed 150 mph.

As a first effort, the Corvette of 1953 proved that America could build a sports car, and, perhaps even more surprising, that Chevrolet, makers of reliable sedans for the millions, could make a sports car.

It was novel, not for its wraparound windscreen which was the norm in the 1950s, but for its pioneering glassfibre body. Its performance was pretty good too – with 150 bhp from its straight-six engine it could reach 107 mph and get from 0-60 mph in 11 seconds – but it lacked impact. That was fixed at a stroke in 1956 with a redesign inspired by General Motors' most famous stylist, Harley Earl.

Earl's genius did not preclude his gaining inspiration from others, and from other eras, and the Corvette's most distinctive feature, those scalloped front wings, was an idea developed from one used on the mighty Duesenbergs before the war. A more easily recognised influence came from the Mercedes 300SL Gullwing with elements like the double bulged bonnet. It didn't really matter where the design came from; the '56 Corvette was clearly a genuine sports car – just one look told you it meant business.

Luckily the last of the first generation Corvettes had been given a V8 engine to replace the heavy and truck-like pushrod 'Blue Flame' straight-six of the first cars, so the new model did not have to convince a doubting public. The Corvette's foreign rivals had more sophisticated engines; the Jaguar XK120 had the superb twin-cam six that was later used in the E-type and the esoteric Mercedes Gullwing and Roadster had a fuel-injected overhead-cam six, but still the Corvette had no reason to feel ashamed. Chevrolet engineers didn't care that their engine was just a cast-iron V8, with only one camshaft to operate all its valves; what was more important was that it

. . . a 0-60 mph time of 5.9 seconds

performed, producing 210 bhp at 5,200 rpm from its 265 cubic inches (4344 cc).

The sheer size of the engine meant there was even more torque available, a massive 272 lb ft at 3,600 rpm. That was just the start; through the life of the second-generation Corvette, until its replacement by the equally dramatic Sting Ray in 1963, improvements were made to the engine and the rest of the car to make it in many respects actually better than some of its far more expensive European competitors. That was demonstrated to good effect on North America's race tracks. In 1957 Chevrolet took the Corvette to Sebring to contend the GT class against the Jaguars, Ferraris and Mercedes and finished 1-2. These were production cars, but with the factory options with which any keen club racer could order his 'Vette. Most important was the handling suspension kit of an anti-roll bar for the front, stiffer springs and dampers all round, a Positraction limited-slip differential, and a quicker steer-

ing ratio to make the car more responsive. You could even order 'ventilated' brakes . . . although these were large finned drums rather than discs.

If there was a major Corvette weakness it was the brakes, which faded dreadfully. Chevrolet persevered with drums until 1965 and the option of sintered metal linings in the late '50s did go some way to fixing the problem. But, as a designer from another time and country once put it, "I make cars to go, not stop," and the Corvette was performance personified.

If Mercedes could offer fuel injection, so could Chevrolet. Their system was built by the Rochester Carburetor Co and rejoiced in the

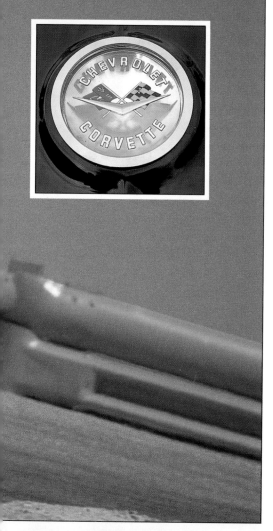

grand name of Ramjet. That helped give the Corvette 290 bhp, a 0-60mph time of 6.9 seconds and a standing quarter-mile time of only 15.6 seconds. By 1961 output from the fuel-injected engine was up to 315 bhp, and by '62 a 'fuellie' Corvette was pumping out no less than 360 bhp. These are gross rather than the more accurate and conservative net figures quoted today, but even so, it meant that 150-mph plus performance was no trouble, nor was a 0-60 time of 5.9 seconds, fearsomely quick even by today's standards.

Rochester's injection was unreliable, though, suffering from an awkward flat spot and poor idling, and relatively few cars were fitted with it. That didn't matter too much as pouring fuel through a four-barrel carburettor had virtually the same effect.

Still built in plastic after 38 years

To European eyes the Corvette represented sheer brute force, but in reality it showed what could be achieved with simple and conventional engineering well applied. All American cars of that era had a separate chassis, or frame, as it's termed there, and the Corvette was no exception. But the X-braced perimeter frame was stiff enough for the job, and the engine was mounted as low as possible to give a good centre of gravity and as far back as practical to give good weight distribution. Despite all that cast-iron engine up front, the weight distribution was an excellent 52/48 front/rear. Front suspension was by double wishbones – nothing wrong in that, and Chev-

rolet were hardly alone in supporting the rear axle on simple semi-elliptic leaf springs. The first Corvette started off with only automatic transmission, and the Powerglide system was only a two-speed in any case, but that was soon changed with a three-speed manual and the option of a four-speed. Mechanically, pretty well everything was conventional; the exception was the one thing most people know about the Corvette, that it was made of glassfibre.

It's almost impossible to realise how revolutionary that was in the early 1950s. Glassfibre had been used in boats (some thought that's why the car was given its nautical name) and on some low-volume sports cars, but it was years before even Colin Chapman had thought of using it for his Lotus Elite. Why would a major manufacturer like Chevrolet opt for it? Harley Earl liked the early glassfibre sports cars (like the quaintly named Woodhill Wildfire) and GM wanted to experiment with glassfibre to see if it might be the material to use in mass production for the future. The Corvette, which might have stayed in production for only a couple of years, was a good way of evaluating it. It soon became clear that glass fibre could never replace steel panels for high volume, but the Corvette had proved its point and carried on to be the longest-running glassfibre production car in the world.

If it's a miracle the Corvette ever existed, it's almost as great a one that it survived the wild styling excesses of the '50s when fins grew to truly bizarre proportions and the chrome the cars carried weighed as much as the engine. Yet because the Corvette programme was run by real sports car enthusiasts, like chief engineer Zora Arkus Duntov, it retained its classic shape. It did grow three inches wider and 10 inches longer for 1958, its two headlights gave way to four, it gained a garish heavily-chromed front grille and rear bumper, and towards the end of the second generation of cars new stylist Bill Mitchell gave it a revised rear end. But America's sports car stayed essentially true to its roots until the advent of the spectacular Sting Ray.

Above: By the early 1960s even the Corvette had more than its fair share of chrome embellishments, although nothing like the amount adorning the contemporary saloons.

Left: The 1956 Corvette was a vast improvement over the first generation of Corvettes, with such luxuries as wind-up windows with optional power assistance and even a transistorised radio.

Above: These rather aggressive-looking rear bumpers were added in 1958, when chrome was taking a firm hold over the American car. Chevrolet built 9,168 1958 models, almost 3,000 more than in 1957.

Chevrolet Corvette

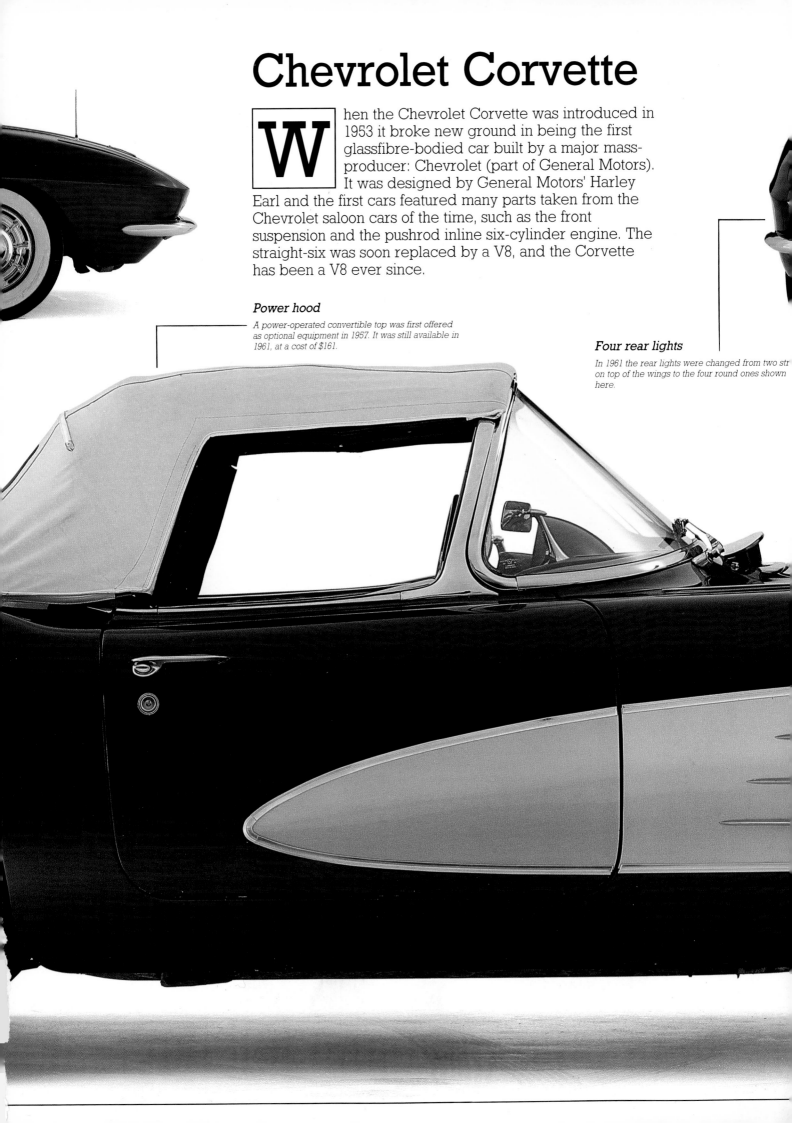

W hen the Chevrolet Corvette was introduced in 1953 it broke new ground in being the first glassfibre-bodied car built by a major mass-producer: Chevrolet (part of General Motors). It was designed by General Motors' Harley Earl and the first cars featured many parts taken from the Chevrolet saloon cars of the time, such as the front suspension and the pushrod inline six-cylinder engine. The straight-six was soon replaced by a V8, and the Corvette has been a V8 ever since.

Power hood

A power-operated convertible top was first offered as optional equipment in 1957. It was still available in 1961, at a cost of $161.

Four rear lights

In 1961 the rear lights were changed from two str on top of the wings to the four round ones shown here.

Concealed hood

When not in use the convertible's hood folded away out of sight under a lockable cover behind the seats, in marked contrast to some of the Corvette's rivals.

Colour schemes

In 1961 the Corvette was available in a choice of seven colours: Tuxedo Black, Ermine White, Roman Red, Sateen Silver, Jewel Blue, Fawn Beige and Honduras Maroon. For an extra $16 you could have the side cove picked out in either Sateen Silver, as here, or white.

Limited-slip differential

To help the Corvette cope with some of its higher power outputs a Positraction limited-slip differential was an option. First offered in 1957, by 1961 it was a $43 option.

'Duck-tail' rear

In 1961, when the second generation of Corvettes was coming to an end, new Corvette stylist Bill Mitchell revised the rear of the car, going from the smooth curved back to the so-called duck-tail back, which lasted one season until replaced by the Sting Ray.

Glassfibre body

The Corvette was the first mass-produced glassfibre-bodied car, and glassfibre has been used for the Corvette body every year since 1953 to the present day. On the early cars there were no fewer than 46 separate glassfibre panels, but by the time of the '61 model shown here production had become more sophisticated.

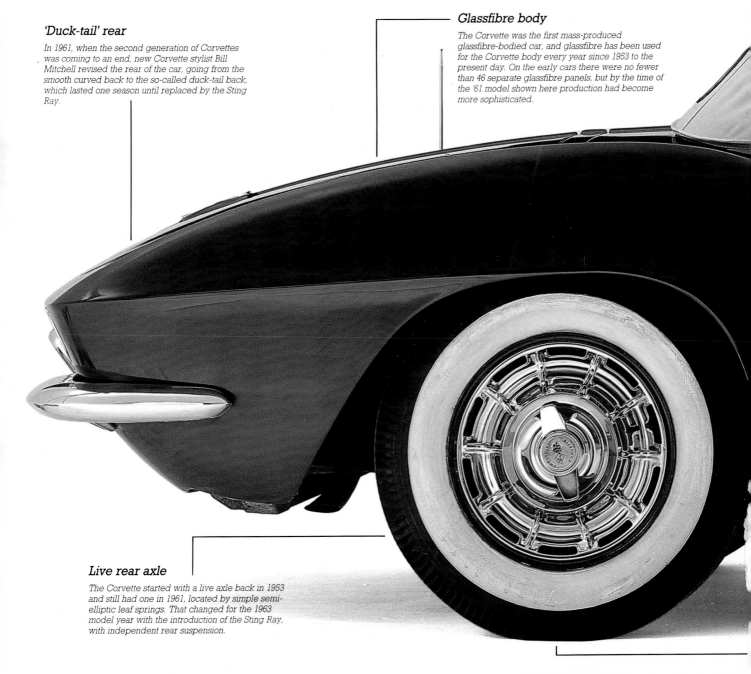

Live rear axle

The Corvette started with a live axle back in 1953 and still had one in 1961, located by simple semi-elliptic leaf springs. That changed for the 1963 model year with the introduction of the Sting Ray, with independent rear suspension.

Above: On the track in California. It made more sense to race the Corvette with its factory-option hardtop in place, as it reduced aerodynamic drag considerably. In 1962, when this model was built, the hardtop cost $236.75, and 8,065 customers bought one.

Inset: A 1961 Corvette in its natural habitat, the sunshine of Florida.

Driving a Corvette: *a civilised savage*

With so many power and handling options, the Corvette could be just what you wanted it to be. For the majority it was an almost civilised sports car, with a reasonable ride, good performance and relaxed three-speed automatic. But for the more adventurous who took advantage of Chevrolet's option list, the car was as fearsome a device as any on the market. Take the '57 model with the 283-cu in fuel-injected engine that offered 1 bhp for every cubic inch and savage acceleration, best achieved through the optional Borg Warner close-ratio four-speed, which would see you reach 60 mph in 6.6 seconds if you shifted gears quick

enough and go on to at least 135 mph if you could hang on.

For that performance you would opt for the uprated stiff suspension that turned the ride from acceptable to almost solid but gave excellent handling for a live-axle car, with power-assisted steering that actually let you know what the front wheels were doing. Despite these advantages, you can't take liberties with the more powerful Corvettes; using all the power and torque transforms its normal determined understeer into a spin from which the quickest of steering will not save you if the brakes fade away to nothing!

PERFORMANCE & SPECIFICATION COMPARISON	Engine	Displacement	Power	Torque (lb ft)	Max speed	0-60 mph	Length (in/mm)	Wheelbase (in/mm)	Track front/rear	Weight total (lb/kg)	Price
Chevrolet Corvette (1961)	V8, overhead-valve	5353 cc	340 bhp 6000 rpm	N/A	135 mph 217 km/h	5.9 sec	177.2 in 4501 mm	102.0 in 2591 mm	57.0 in 59.0 in	2850 lb 1293 kg	$3,934 (1961)
AC Cobra 289 (1962)	V8, overhead-valve	4727 cc	271 bhp 6000 rpm	314 lb ft 3400 rpm	138 mph 222 km/h	5.5 sec	156.0 in 3962 mm	90.0 in 2286 mm	55.0 in 54.0 in	2315 lb 1050 kg	£2,070 (1962)
Jaguar E-type (1961)	Straight-six, twin-cam	3442 cc	265 bhp 4000 rpm	260 lb ft 4000 rpm	149 mph 240 km/h	7.1 sec	175.3 in 4453 mm	96.0 in 2438 mm	50.0 in 50.0 in	2625 lb 1191 kg	£1,480 (1961)
Austin-Healey 3000 (1959)	Straight-six, overhead-valve	2912 cc	124 bhp 4750 rpm	162 lb ft 2700 rpm	115 mph 185 km/h	10.8 sec	157.3 in 3995 mm	92.0 in 2337 mm	48.8 in 50.0 in	2520 lb 1143 kg	£1,175 (1959)
Ferrari 250 GT SWB (1959)	V12, overhead-cam	2953 cc	280 bhp 7000 rpm	N/A	140 mph 225 km/h	6.5 sec	164.0 in 4165 mm	94.5 in 2400 mm	53.3 in 53.3 in	2804 lb 1272 kg	£5,607 (1963)

Chevrolet Corvette Data File

he Corvette was the first sports car built by Chevrolet, a division of General Motors. Chevrolet was formed in 1911, and became part of GM in 1919. By the mid-1920s it was the biggest division of GM and it has been ever since. The first really successful Chevrolet was the four-cylinder 490 of 1915, which eventually overtook the legendary Ford Model T on the annual sales charts.

The mainstay of Chevrolet production was always affordable mass-produced saloons, and by 1941 Chevrolet sales were over one million for the year. Although Chevrolet introduced innovations like their Powerglide auto transmission and more interesting cars like the Bel Air coupé in the early 1950s, the Corvette was a real breakthrough, with its glassfibre body and the impressive performance from its straight-six engine.

Initial Corvette sales were very poor, but after the introduction of the V8 engine the model has never looked back and has existed in various forms ever since. For many years the nearest Chevrolet came to building another sports car was the Camaro, but that was introduced as a mass-production competitor for the Ford Mustang, and it's the Corvette that still deserves the tag of 'America's sports car'.

Above: In 1958 the Corvette was made 10 inches longer and three inches wider. The extra width allowed space for the new four-headlight treatment.

Left: The wraparound rear bumper, extending as far as the back of the rear wheel arch, was another styling feature added for the 1958 model year.

1958 model year

The Corvette was significantly restyled in '58. The car was lengthened by 10 inches and made three inches wider. Following the fashion of the time, the 1958 model was given four rather than two headlights and a far heavier and clumsier-looking front grille treatment, with a lot more chrome. Vents were incorporated behind the front bumpers to the side of the main grille. Chrome strakes and a vent were fitted to the side scallops. Fake louvres were incorporated on the bonnet. Chrome bands were added to the boot lid, and heavier chrome rear bumpers fitted.

The interior was restyled, with a 160-mph speedo, and the rev counter was moved in front of the driver.

Above: The dashboard of the 1957 models was an ergonomic disaster, although the rather optimistic 140-mph speedo was right in front of the driver. The passenger had to suffer the hideous air vent.

Right: Single headlights and the row of chrome teeth in the grille show that this is a 1957 model.

1957 model year

The most important change for the '57 model was the use of the larger, 283-cu in (4639-cc) V8. The 1956 model was powered by a 210 bhp, 4344-cc V8. The greater displacement was achieved by increasing the bore of the 265 engine by ⅛ in to 3.875 in (98 mm). The 283 could be bought in five states of tune – standard was 220 bhp, then 245 or 270 bhp with a four-barrel carburettor and 250 or 283 bhp with the Rochester Ramjet mechanical fuel injection.

Fitting the optional injection gave the Corvette one of the earliest injected engines and made the Corvette a very fast car, with a 0-60 time of 6.5 seconds (with the lowest of the optional final drives, that could be reduced to 5.5 seconds) and a top speed of over 120 mph. In all, 1,040 fuel-injected models were produced.

A four-speed manual gearbox was added to the option list, as was option 684, the stiffer handling suspension and quicker steering ratio.

Below: The 1958 Corvette was longer and wider.

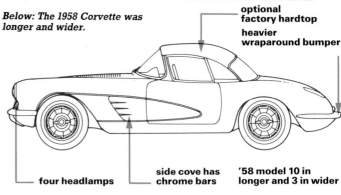

optional factory hardtop

heavier wraparound bumper

four headlamps

side cove has chrome bars

'58 model 10 in longer and 3 in wider

Below: The 1957 Corvette was visually almost identical to the 1956 model.

first year for optional factory hardtop

wind-up windows with optional power assist

optional power-operated hood

side coving, available in three colours

top-mounted rear lights

1961 model year

The changes in the '59 and '60 models were minor, although the fake louvres on the bonnet were deleted. Greater change came in 1961 from designer Bill Mitchell, with a heavily revised 'ducktail' back end with four lights. The front was changed too, the heavy chrome look giving way to a wire mesh grille, while the headlight surrounds were painted, not chrome.

An alloy radiator became standard. Alloy cylinder heads had been offered on the '60 models but were discontinued due to warping.

Power options on the 283-cu in engine range from 230 bhp through to 315 bhp. Other options include a power folding convertible top, a Positraction limited-slip differential rear axle and a 24-gallon fuel tank.

Left: The 1961 model can be told from the '58, '59, and '60 models by the lack of the distinctive chrome teeth in the front grille. Behind that grille Chevrolet had introduced a new alloy radiator to cool a range of 4.6-litre V8 engines, producing from 230 bhp to 315 bhp. The fastest of the 1961s was capable of 140 mph.

Four headlights

The trend in the mid-1950s in America was towards a four-headlight system, and the Corvette fell into line in 1957 and maintained this four-light design until the end of the second generation in 1962.

Fuel injection

The Corvette was one of the earliest cars to have fuel injection, first appearing on the '57 model. The mechanical Ramjet system was built by the Rochester Carburetor Co. and on the '61 model helped produce 315 bhp. Most powerful of all the injected early Corvettes was the 375-bhp V8, first fitted in 1964.

SPECIFICATION

1961 Chevrolet Corvette

ENGINE

Type:	V8 with cast-iron block and heads; five main bearings
Bore×stroke:	102 mm×82 mm
Displacement:	5353 cc
Compression ratio:	11.25:1
Valve gear:	two valves per cylinder operated by single block-mounted camshaft in centre of vee, via pushrods and rockers
Fuel system:	single Carter AFB four-barrel carburettor; Rochester Ramjet fuel injection optional
Ignition:	mechanical by coil and distributor
Maximum power:	340 bhp at 6,000 rpm
Maximum torque:	N/A

TRANSMISSION

Type:	four-speed manual (optional)	
Ratios:	1st	2.20:1
	2nd	1.66:1
	3rd	1.31:1
	4th	1.00:1
Final drive:	hypoid bevel with optional Positraction limited slip differential	
Final drive ratio:	3.70:1	

BODY/CHASSIS

Type:	X-braced steel perimeter frame with separate glassfibre body

RUNNING GEAR

Steering:	worm and ball
Suspension:	front: independent with double unequal length wishbones, coil springs, telescopic dampers and anti-roll bar rear: non-independent with live rear axle, semi-elliptic leaf springs and telescopic dampers
Brakes:	drums front and rear: 11-in diameter; optional sintered metallic linings
Wheels:	steel disc, 15-in diameter
Tyres:	crossply 6.70×15 in

DIMENSIONS AND WEIGHT

Length:	177.2 in (4501 mm)
Width:	70.5 in (1791 mm)
Height:	51.9 in (1318 mm)
Wheelbase:	102.0 in (2591 mm)
Track:	57.0 in (1448 mm) front, 59.0 in (1499 mm) rear
Kerb weight:	2,850 lb (1293 kg)

PERFORMANCE

Acceleration:	0-30 mph 2.5 sec 0-40 mph 3.4 sec 0-50 mph 4.5 sec 0-60 mph 5.9 sec 0-70 mph 7.5 sec 0-100 mph 16.5 sec
Standing ¼ mile:	14.9 sec
Maximum speed:	135 mph
Overall fuel consumption:	14.5 mpg
Price (1961):	$3,934

Chevrolet Corvette kindly supplied by M.A. Hutton-Williams

Corvette badge

Chevrolet was named after a Frenchman. If you look closely at the round badge on the boot you'll see the crossed flag emblem of the Corvette, and one of those flags has the French fleur de lys on it as well as the famous Chevrolet 'bow tie' emblem.

Vents

In 1958 the Corvette was made three inches wider (and 10 inches longer) and the wider front accommodated the two almost oval vents behind the bumper, purely for styling.

Model identification

American cars changed design every single year. Although the Corvette changed far less than many other models, there were still differences. The absence of chrome bars on the grille shows that this is a '61 model.

V8 engine

Since 1955 every Corvette has had a V8 engine. There have been various displacements and usually a range of power outputs to choose from for each model year. The '61 model, for example, had a 327-cu in (5.3-litre) cast-iron pushrod V8 with a choice of four power outputs: 245, 270, 275 and 315 bhp.

Power windows

Electrically operated windows were available on the Corvette as early as 1956. In 1961 they were an option that would have cost you just under $60.

Jaguar wheelbase

When the Corvette was introduced one of its main rivals was the Jaguar XK120. Chevrolet evaluated the Jaguar while the Corvette was developed and ended up with the same 102-in wheelbase. Otherwise the two cars had little in common.

Left: The side vent with its chrome surround was a feature that first appeared on the 1958 models when the car was widened by three inches.

Below: The chrome strip along the front wings or fenders is yet another distinguishing feature of the 1961 cars. More significant was the redesigned 'duck tail' rear of the car, shown more clearly in the side drawing below.

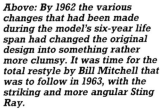

Above: By 1962 the various changes that had been made during the model's six-year life span had changed the original design into something rather more clumsy. It was time for the total restyle by Bill Mitchell that was to follow in 1963, with the striking and more angular Sting Ray.

Above left: By 1962 the interior had become very stylish indeed. Contrast this view with the interior of the 1957 model on the previous page.

Left: It would be hard to claim you didn't know how fast you were driving!

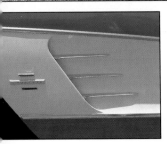

Left: The first- and second-generation Corvettes had unadorned side coves, but from 1958 to 1961 all models had this dummy vent and three chrome ribs. In 1961 the plain Chevrolet badge replaced the crossed flag side emblem of previous Corvettes.

Below: From 1956 all Corvettes had a pushrod overhead-valve V8 engine with displacements ranging from 4.3 to a peak of 7.4 litres in 1970. The engine was set well back in the chassis to give as even a weight distribution as possible with a front-mounted engine. Designed by Ed Cole, the 'small-block' V8 was one of Chevrolet's best engines.

Below: The '61 Corvette had a 'duck tail' rear.

'duck tail' rear styling

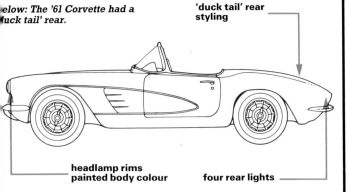

headlamp rims painted body colour

four rear lights

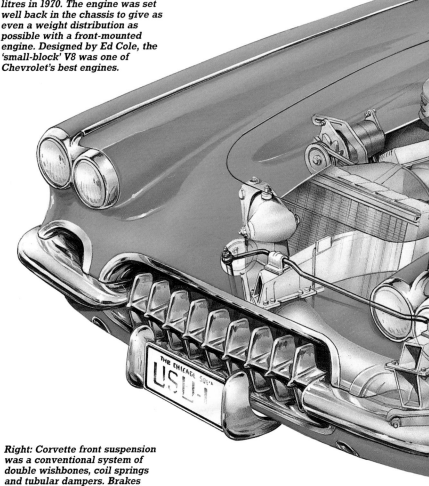

1962 model year

The larger, 327-cu in V8 was added to the range and the 283 dropped. The extra displacement came from increasing the bore to 4 in (102 mm) and the stroke to 3.25 in (83 mm). The bigger engine's greater torque increased the Corvette's mid-range performance considerably and it meant that higher rear axle ratios could be used, giving more relaxed performance with no sacrifice in acceleration. Power options ranged from the base 250 bhp through 300, 340 and 360 bhp with the manual four-speed transmission, and either 250 or 300 bhp with the three-speed automatic transmission.

The main visual changes were to the side scallops or coves, which lost their chrome outline and were no longer picked out in a separate colour.

Above: In 1962 the three bars were removed in favour of this chrome grille treatment. A further difference is the removal of the chrome surround for the cove, which was now available in body colour only.

Right: Corvette front suspension was a conventional system of double wishbones, coil springs and tubular dampers. Brakes were drums; discs were not introduced until 1965.

Left: Behind the seats can be seen the cover under which the convertible top folds neatly out of sight.

Above: A 1960 model in Roman Red, one of eight colours offered in 1960, including Tasco Turquoise and Honduras Maroon.

Above: Rochester Ramjet mechanical fuel injection was an option on the 1962.

Below: The Corvette was built on an X-braced perimeter frame with a non-structural, glassfibre body. That made the Corvette the world's first glassfibre car from a major mass manufacturer.

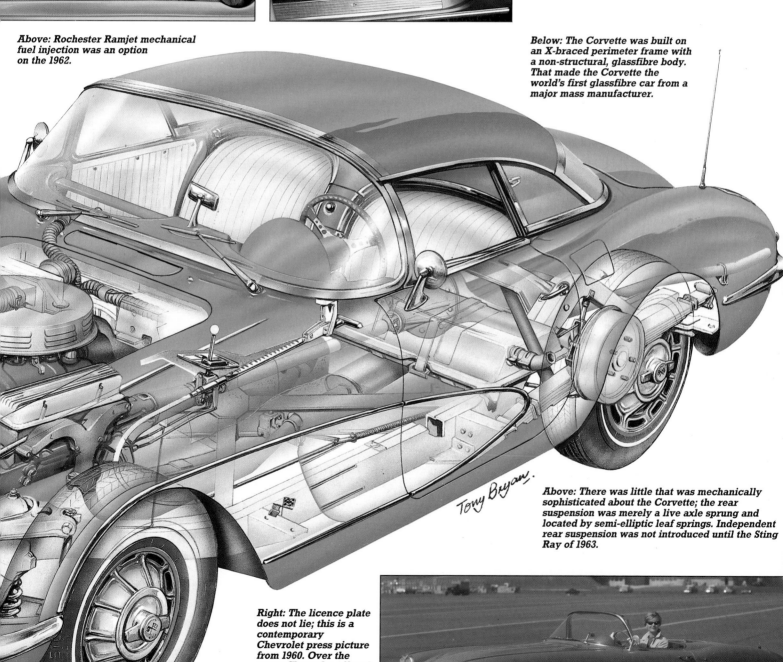

Tony Bryan.

Above: There was little that was mechanically sophisticated about the Corvette; the rear suspension was merely a live axle sprung and located by semi-elliptic leaf springs. Independent rear suspension was not introduced until the Sting Ray of 1963.

Right: The licence plate does not lie; this is a contemporary Chevrolet press picture from 1960. Over the years Chevrolet offered wide-band whitewall tyres, as here, and thin-band type, as on the cutaway above.

Corvette ZR-1

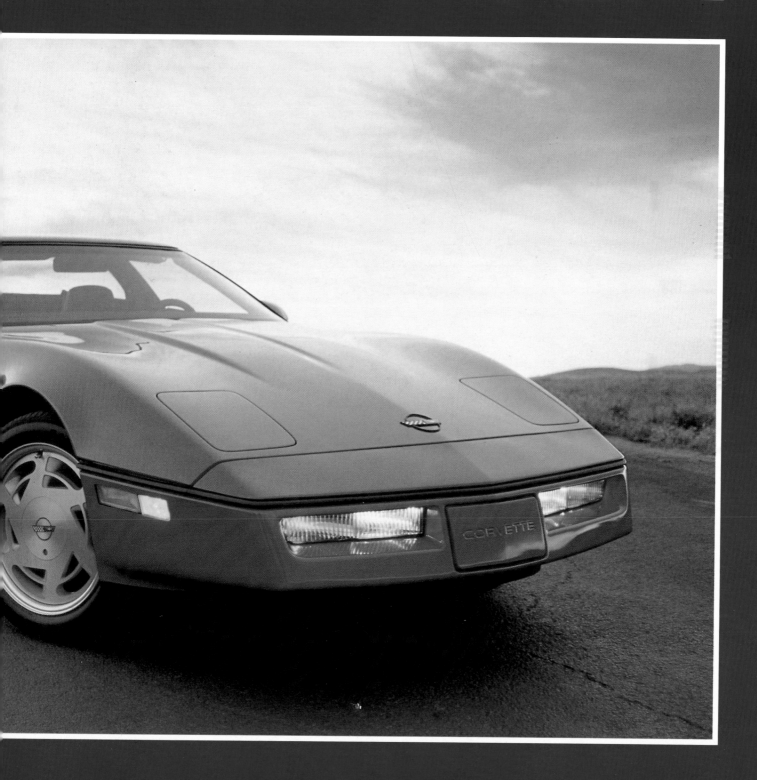

What does it take to turn the latest incarnation of "America's most-stolen" automobile into a Ferrari-beating 170-mph supercar? It starts with a 375-bhp 32-valve all-aluminium V8 designed by Lotus and goes on from there . . .

Above: Hints of the muscular styling bulges of previous-generation Corvettes remain, and the Chevrolet badging is familiar, but the latest ZR-1 is a lean, aerodynamically-refined product of many hours in the wind tunnel. The high-performer looks like any other contemporary Corvette, though.

T he Corvette has always stood out, from the very first model of 1953, when it was a status symbol for the country club set, to the awesome high-performance big-block cars of the late 1960s. It was then, and remains, America's only true two-seat sports car, but there's more to it than that. If you've ever looked for innovation in American automobiles, you've seen it first in a Corvette. While the typical American sedan still used a live rear axle with drum brakes, Corvettes had four-wheel disc brakes and four-wheel independent suspension since the mid-1960s.

Nonetheless, the Corvette has had its share of detractors over the years, saying that it's too big and heavy, or that its quality and workmanship leave a lot to be desired. When it comes to performance, it has been a very long time since the Corvette has lived up to its all-conquering image of the 1960s. During the 1980s you could buy a rather antiquated Buick GSX or Pontiac Turbo Trans Am that would leave it behind – at least in a straight line. And the Corvette is, by no

stretch of the imagination, an exotic. This changed dramatically with the introduction of the Lotus-engined ZR-1.

General Motors have been accused of a lot of things over the past decade, and most of them have not been good: unimaginative styling, antiquated engineering, continual foot-dragging when it comes to innovation, and major quality-control lapses. GM had been used to dictating to the American public, and as long as there were no alternatives (read Japanese cars) everything was fine, but during the 1980s, GM even lost their technological and styling edge to Ford. Clearly, the world's largest corporation was in serious trouble. To those who follow the automotive industry, this had been obvious for some time, but by the mid-1980s it became obvious to the American public as well. GM badly needed to revamp their image and product line. New styling, new engines and new engineering were needed and the Corvette would play its part in revitalising GM's image.

Chevrolet's aims were ambitious – the ZR-1

must be the best-performing production car in the world, bar none; at the same time, it must meet driveability standards equal to those of the regular L98-powered Corvette; and it should meet current EPA (Environmental Protection Agency) fuel-economy standards in order to avoid incurring the 'gas guzzler' tax.

"A spectacular level of performance . . ."

According to Corvette chief engineer David R. McLellan, "The ZR-1 is a statement that we can do things today that no-one even dreamed could be done 10 or 20 years ago. We've achieved a spectacular level of performance and still are able to meet or exceed all government standards for fuel economy, safety, noise and emissions."

At first glance, and maybe even after several, the ZR-1 doesn't look too different from any other current Corvette. You'd think that, with

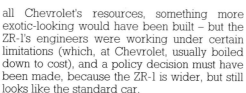

Right: The chisel-nosed frontal styling of this 1990 ZR-1 has been superseded by the softer, cleaner, and more elegant look of the 1992-spec car on the left.

Below: The convex upper tail panel with its recessed, almost rectangular, rear lights was unique to the ZR-1 in the 1990 model year. Now this feature is shared with lesser Corvettes.

all Chevrolet's resources, something more exotic-looking would have been built – but the ZR-1's engineers were working under certain limitations (which, at Chevrolet, usually boiled down to cost), and a policy decision must have been made, because the ZR-1 is wider, but still looks like the standard car.

Originally, Chevrolet wanted to use the existing small-block V8 along with two four-valve twin-cam cylinder heads. In this way, the engine would fit within the existing chassis rails and under the production Corvette bonnet. Lotus, who had previously worked with General Motors on other projects, were chosen to develop the new cylinder heads in April 1985 (a year later, GM bought a controlling interest in the British company). The problem, given all of Chevrolet's parameters, was that the venerable small-block V8 couldn't meet the performance goals, which at that time were set at 400 bhp, along with the necessary high level of refinement. Certainly, a modified Chevrolet small-block V8 could easily produce 400 bhp but it could not meet the drive-ability and fuel-economy standards. Lotus convinced Chevrolet that a totally new engine was needed, and this was codenamed LT5.

While the engine was designed by Lotus, it is produced and assembled by Mercury Marine, the world's largest manufacturer of boat engines, in Stillwater, Oklahoma. This was the first time Chevrolet had entered into such an arrangement – obviously in order to ensure that there wouldn't be any quality-control problems; by comparison, the typical Chevrolet engine is slapped together. According to Chevrolet, the ZR-1's introduction was delayed several times until they were certain that the LT5 was totally reliable.

The final result wasn't 400 bhp, but it was close enough. The LT5 produces 375 bhp at 5,800 rpm with 370 lb ft of torque at 4,800 rpm – enough to propel the ZR-1 to a top speed exceeding 170 mph, with acceleration to match: 0-60 mph comes in the mid-five-second range, while the standing quarter-mile is reached in

the low 13-second range. This is serious performance; the ZR-1 is quicker (albeit not by much) than cars such as the Ferrari Testarossa and Porsche Carrera 4. Yes, there are faster cars, such as the Lamborghini Diablo and the Ferrari F40, but these aren't regular production models, and they cost an incredible amount of money.

Razor-sharp race-car handling

As for the rest of the car, the regular Corvette already has excellent handling and braking – there is little that could be done to improve these aspects of the ZR-1. When required, the ZR-1 exhibits razor-sharp race-car handling. Everything – engine, suspension, brakes, transmission – works in such a satisfying way that you're willing to overlook minor deficiencies. One of the Corvette's bugaboos over the years has been its noisy, creaking bodywork – the 1991 model is noticeably quieter than the 1990 one and initial reports indicate that the 1992 version is even better built. That's how it has been with the Corvette: every year it gets a little better.

As you would expect, the ZR-1 comes with a full complement of luxury features: leather interior; air conditioning; solar glass roof panel; power windows, door locks and seats; cruise control; heated, power side-view mirrors; tilt steering wheel; a Delco/Bose cassette/CD player system; and an airbag supplemental restraint device.

Perhaps the most unusual thing about the ZR-1 is that it isn't unusual. Unless you know what to look for, the ZR-1 is almost identical to the regular production Corvette. All 1991 Corvettes now use the ZR-1 tail-light treatment (which was almost the only way to tell the difference on the 1990 model). The ZR-1 is the least visible exotic, but that's what makes it unique.

Chevrolet Corvette ZR-1

The Chevrolet Corvette ZR-1 is the latest, and undoubtedly the greatest, in the long Corvette line. Introduced in 1990, it marked a new age in the Corvette story. It demonstrated Chevrolet's determination to prove that they could produce a technologically advanced car good enough to live with the best of the European exotics from the likes of Porsche, Ferrari and Lamborghini. To that end, Chevrolet used the same quad-cam, multi-valve approach. The Corvette 'muscle car' tradition was maintained, however, as the engine was still a large, 5.7-litre, V8.

SRCS Selective Ride Control System

The ZR-1 driver can choose one of three suspension settings: Touring, Sport and Performance. Within each setting the damping is stiffened as road speed rises, with the computer making 10 adjustments per second.

Quad-cam V8 engine

Although this V8 has 5.7 litres, like that in the standard Corvette, in the ZR-1 it's an all-alloy unit developed by Lotus, with four valves per cylinder and double overhead camshafts per bank of cylinders rather than the standard two valves per cylinder and pushrod valve gear.

TUNED PORT INJECTI

Knock sensor

Although the ZR-1's engine is a conventional normally-aspirated unit rather than a turbo, it's still fitted with a knock sensor. That prevents engine detonation (or 'pinking') and enables the car to run on low, 87-octane, fuel if required.

CAGS Computer-Aided Gear Selection

As an aid to fuel economy, the transmission automatically switches from first to fourth gear when pulling away, depending on throttle opening and coolant temperature.

Glassfibre bodywork

Every Corvette has had a glassfibre body, and the ZR-1 is no exception. In addition to conventional glassfibre, other composite materials are used for the front and rear bumpers.

Tyre-pressure monitoring system

Another first for the Corvette was the fitment of pressure sensors in each tyre to warn when tyre pressures fell below an acceptable level. The sensor activates a warning light on the dashboard.

Top and above: Both these angles emphasise the pre-1991-pattern sharp-edged nose treatment. Like all the 1984-on generation of Corvettes, ZR-1s have never had a conventional radiator grille – cooling air is taken from beneath the 'bumper' moulding (this applies to the new shape as well). Flip-up headlights set back in the bonnet are another front-end feature common to all variants, although the side lights and indicators have now changed.

Driving the ZR-1: brutally fast

There is little to warn you of what the ZR-1 is all about. Once you're inside, if feels like any other Corvette. The adjustable leather seats are comfortable, if snug.

Turning the ignition key, you'll find that the big V8 sounds much like that of a standard L98 Corvette – deep and throaty. You know there's power there, but not how much. Accelerating with the output selection key in the 'Normal' position, the ZR-1 feels like the regular production L98: nice, but nothing special. Twist the key to the 'Full' position, however, and the quad-cam LT5 engine changes from a well-mannered Dr Jekyll to a roaring Mr Hyde, with brutal acceleration

accompanied by a wonderful scream from the V8.

The rest of the ZR-1 is up to the LT5's power. Few cars can corner and brake as well as a Corvette. Going through the gears is a pleasure; the clutch, the power brakes and the steering are just right, transmitting the desired feedback without being either too light or too heavy.

Now you know what the ZR-1 is all about. It is an absolute rush that puts a smile on your face – after your heart slows down a bit. But that rush continues as long as you dare to keep the accelerator pedal on the floor, and it's addictive.

PERFORMANCE & SPECIFICATION COMPARISON	Engine	Displacement	Power	Torque (lb ft)	Max speed	0-60 mph	Length (in/mm)	Wheelbase (in/mm)	Track front/rear	Weight total (lb/kg)	Price
Chevrolet Corvette ZR-1	V8, quad-cam, 32-valve	5727 cc	375 bhp 5800 rpm	370 lb ft 4800 rpm	171 mph 275 km/h	5.6 sec	178.5 in 4534 mm	96.2 in 2443 mm	60.0 in 62.0 in	3519 lb 1596 kg	$64,138 (1991)
De Tomaso Pantera GT5S	V8, overhead-valve	5763 cc	350 bhp 6000 rpm	333 lb ft 3800 rpm	165 mph 266 km/h	5.4 sec	168.1 in 4270 mm	99.0 in 2515 mm	59.5 in 62.1 in	3219 lb 1460 kg	£47,621 (1986)
Lotus Esprit Turbo SE	Inline-four, 16-valve, turbo	2174 cc	264 bhp 6500 rpm	261 lb ft 3900 rpm	161 mph 259 km/h	4.9 sec	171.0 in 4343 mm	96.0 in 2438 mm	60.0 in 61.2 in	2650 lb 1202 kg	£47,310 (1991)
Nissan 300 ZX	V6, quad-cam, 24-valve, twin-turbo	2960 cc	280 bhp 6400 rpm	274 lb ft 3600 rpm	155 mph 249 km/h	5.6 sec	178.1 in 4525 mm	101.2 in 2570 mm	58.9 in 60.4 in	3485 lb 1581 kg	£31,250 (1991)
Porsche 944 Turbo	Inline-four, overhead-cam, turbo	2479 cc	250 bhp 6000 rpm	258 lb ft 4000 rpm	154 mph 248 km/h	5.7 sec	165.4 in 4200 mm	94.5 in 2400 mm	58.2 in 57.1 in	2698 lb 1224 kg	£43,648 (1991)

Corvette ZR-1 Data File

The Corvette was introduced in 1953. Although only 300 were initially built, it represented Chevrolet's attempt to change their staid, conservative image by producing a 'sports car', but sales failed to reach expectations and one-third of the first year's production was left unsold. The next year proved to be the turning point, as the then-new 265-cu in small-block Chevrolet V8 (the same basic engine that powers today's Corvette) was introduced, transforming the Corvette into a true performance car.

The 1956 model got a new body, along with a larger, 283-cu in, engine. In 1963 the Corvette finally received a major mechanical and styling overhaul, and the resulting 'mid-year' design continued until 1967. Prior to 1963, all Corvettes used a solid rear axle and all were convertibles; in 1963, a split-window coupé was offered and an all-new chassis with four-wheel independent suspension became standard. This chassis lasted until 1982; the coupé's split window lasted for one year only.

The Corvette was totally redesigned in 1984. New aerodynamic styling, a new 'uniframe' chassis and new front and rear suspension systems brought GM's sports car into the 1980s. The car was smaller in every dimension except width, and, through extensive use of aluminium, it was several hundred pounds lighter as well. From 1985, the standard Corvette engine has been the L98 350-cu in small-block V8, rated between 230 and 245 bhp, but the Callaway twin-turbo 350, rated at 382 bhp, could also be ordered since 1987 for those wanting more power.

The convertible was re-introduced in 1986; in the same year, anti-lock brakes became standard equipment on all models. The latest development was the introduction of the ZR-1 Special Performance Package in 1990.

Above: Better-integrated, wrap-around side and turn-signal lamp units were part of the 1991 Corvette facelift.

Left: There's still a vestige of shark-like reference in the looks of the Corvette – but four horizontal rather than two vertical 'gills' were another revision for 1992-spec cars, plus new wheels.

Below: A 'clamshell' front end gives superb engine access.

Above: In profile, even the latest Corvette shape is quite old-fashioned, with its long bonnet, and cabin set well to the rear.

Styling

There isn't a styling theme that can be attributed specifically to the ZR-1, but its bodywork changes made it slightly wider and one inch longer than the regular production Corvette. The flare in the ZR-1's body from the door and extending rearward is there to accommodate its wider rear tyres. This flare adds three inches across the rear at its widest point, and requires different doors, rear quarters, rockers, rear fascia and rear upper panel.

The current Corvette's basic shape dates from 1984. Whereas the previous model was curvy and sensuous, the current Corvette's wedge shape reflects more of an emphasis on aerodynamics. A product

of considerable wind-tunnel testing, the 1984-onward Corvette shows a smaller frontal area, a much more sharply raked rear window and a rear section that is as aerodynamically 'correct' as the front of the car. You'll note that its nose doesn't have the usual grille opening for air to flow through to the radiator; air intake is through an opening underneath the bumper.

The 1990 ZR-1 came with its own, distinctive upper rear panel – convex with rectangular tail-lights. At least you could tell the 1990 ZR-1 from production Corvettes by looking at the back. However, the standard models thereafter also utilise this rear panel treatment.

Below: Despite looking near-identical, the ZR-1 is three inches wider than the standard Corvette, necessitating many new panels.

Above and below: All the usual options are standard in the ZR-1 interior. The instruments look neat, but can be hard to read.

SPECIFICATION

1991 Chevrolet Corvette ZR-1

ENGINE

Type:	V8, quad-cam, 32-valve
Construction:	aluminium-alloy block and heads
Bore × stroke:	99 mm × 93 mm
Displacement:	5727 cc
Compression ratio:	11.0:1
Valve gear:	four valves per cylinder, operated by twin overhead camshafts per bank of cylinders
Fuel system:	electronic fuel injection
Ignition:	electronic
Maximum power:	375 bhp at 5,800 rpm
Maximum torque:	370 lb ft at 4,800 rpm

TRANSMISSION

Type:	six-speed manual	
Ratios:	1st	2.68:1
	2nd	1.80:1
	3rd	1.29:1
	4th	1.00:1
	5th	0.75:1
	6th	0.59:1
Final drive ratio:	3.45:1	

BODY/CHASSIS

Type:	steel chassis with glassfibre and composite body

RUNNING GEAR

Steering:	rack and pinion
Suspension:	front: independent with upper and lower wishbones, transverse monofilament plastic leaf spring and three-position electronically-controlled dampers
rear: independent with upper and lower trailing arms, transverse monofilament plastic leaf spring, three-position electronically-controlled dampers and anti-roll bar
Brakes:	ventilated discs front and rear; 13-in (330-mm) diameter front, 12-in (305-mm) diameter rear with three-channel anti-lock braking
Wheels:	aluminium-alloy; 9.5-in diameter front, 11-in diameter rear
Tyres:	Goodyear Eagle ZR40; 275/40 ZR17 front, 315/35 ZR17 rear

DIMENSIONS AND WEIGHT

Length:	178.5 in (4534 mm)
Width:	73.2 in (1859 mm)
Height:	46.7 in (1186 mm)
Wheelbase:	96.2 in (2443 mm)
Track:	60.0 in (1524 mm) front, 62.0 in (1575 mm) rear
Kerb weight:	3,519 lb (1596 kg)

PERFORMANCE

Acceleration:	0-30 mph 2.4 sec		
	0-40 mph 3.3 sec		
	0-50 mph 4.3 sec		
	0-60 mph 5.6 sec		
	0-70 mph 6.9 sec		
	0-80 mph 9.2 sec		
	0-90 mph 11.0 sec		
	0-100 mph 13.5 sec		
	0-110 mph 16.0 sec		
Standing ¼ mile:	13.2 sec		
Acceleration in gear:	mph	fifth	fourth
	30-50	—	4.2
	50-70	6.9	—
Maximum speed:	171 mph (275 km/h)		
Overall fuel consumption:	18 mpg		
Price (1991):	$64,138		

Performance figures from CAR AND DRIVER

Chevrolet Corvette ZR-1 kindly supplied by Taylor Gee

Plastic transverse springs

Chevrolet have long used the Corvette to test new materials, and for years the car has had single-element transverse leaf springs made of an almost indestructible composite material with a far longer fatigue-life than spring steel.

Six-speed manual gearbox

The Corvette was the first production car in the world to feature a six-speed transmission. This appeared first as an option on the 1989 model and is used on the current ZR-1. It's made by ZF in Germany, rather than Chevrolet.

Variable fuel injection

Under normal use, the engine uses only eight primary ports and injectors. When the electronic control module senses that the accelerator pedal has been floored and engine speed is above 3,500 rpm, a vacuum actuator opens the secondary throttles and an additional eight injectors come onstream to give a huge power boost.

Driver-operated 'power key'

A key located under the dashboard can be turned to disable the vacuum actuator and prevent the extra injectors being used.

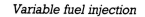

Anti-lock brakes and traction control

Not only has the ZR-1 excellent ventilated discs all round, fitted with an anti-lock system, but there's also an anti-wheelspin device to increase driver control in snow or ice.

Transmission

All ZR-1s are equipped with a six-speed manual transmission, designed by ZF (Zahnradfabrik Friedrichshafen AG) and Chevrolet, and built by ZF in Germany, which also became a no-cost option on the standard Corvette. Specifically designed for use with the ZR-1, the transmission has a torque capacity of 425 lb ft.

What makes the ZF gearbox interesting is its CAGS (Computer-Aided Gear Selection) feature, which is partially responsible for the LT5 engine meeting EPA emission standards. Under certain conditions –

specifically when water temperature is 120 degrees or more, the car is moving at between 12 and 19 mph, and the throttle opening is not more than 35 per cent – during the first to second gear change a solenoid blocks out second gear and the gear lever is forced into fourth instead. This can be unnerving if you don't expect it – it's easy to imagine that there is something wrong with the transmission – but as long as you drive the ZR-1 with some gusto, you'll never have a problem with CAGS or the six-speed transmission.

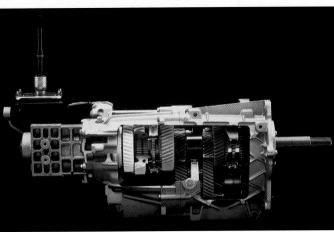

Above: Designed specifically to handle the ZR-1's power and torque, the six-speed gearbox is built by ZF in Germany.

Chassis, suspension and brakes

Unlike the previous generation, the current Corvette uses plastic transverse springs front and rear. The ZR-1 comes as standard with the Z51 Performance Handling Package and the FX3 Selective Ride Control suspension equipment, both of which are available on the regular Corvette.

The Z51 package consists of higher-rate springs, a power-steering oil cooler and larger front brake calipers and discs (at 13 inches, one inch larger than the stock units). All Corvettes since 1986 have been equipped with Bosch ABS II.

The Selective Ride Control System (developed jointly between GM and Bilstein Engineering, and not exclusive to the ZR-1) is a computer-controlled damping system that operates in three modes: Touring, Sport and Performance, driver-set via a dial located on the console. A small electric motor opens and closes a rotary valve on each damper, thereby controlling compression and rebound strokes at a rate of 10 adjustments per second, allowing the driver to tailor the ZR-1's ride to a wide range of road

surfaces. Within each of the three modes, the shock absorbers' damping action automatically increases as road speed rises. Adjustments are programmed to occur at 25, 50, 75, 100, 125 and 150 mph, but, to prevent the computer from hunting up and down when the car is cruising at one of these speeds, the point at which the damping action is reduced is set 5 mph lower. The system does work, but even in its lowest setting (Touring), the ZR-1's suspension is extremely stiff. This poses no problems when the road surface is flat and smooth, but over an uneven surface the ride is unforgiving. That, coupled with the car's extremely sensitive steering, means the ZR-1 can dart back and forth during high-speed cornering on less-than-ideal road surfaces.

Another interesting feature is the ZR-1's low-tyre-pressure warning system. Inside each wheel is a pressure sensor: if inflation falls below a certain point, it is signalled to a receiver in the car which actuates a warning lamp on the dash.

Below: A Bosch ABS II anti-lock braking system has been standard on the Corvette since the 1986 model year. For 1992 the ZR-1 also has ASR, which limits wheelspin under acceleration.

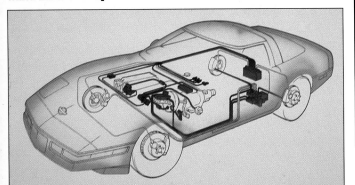

Engine

It is the LT5 engine which makes the ZR-1 what it is; transforms the Corvette from an excellent car into a great one. The all-aluminium LT5 engine weighs approximately 39 lb more than a comparable cast-iron L98. Although the use of aluminium cuts 89 lb from the cylinder block alone, the LT5's extra componentry weighs more – 10 lb more of camshaft, 17 lb more of connecting rod mass, an extra 31 lb in the cylinder heads, 20 lb additional exhaust manifold mass, a 25-lb crankshaft saddle and 26 lb of injector housings and cylinder liners. In addition, the LT5 holds more oil.

The aluminium block is cast in sand, with a deck height of 9.03 inches with 4.40-in bore-centre spacing. It features a wet-sleeve, open-deck construction with Nikasil-plated aluminium liners seated on a shoulder forming the bottom of the water jacket. At the top of the cylinder liners there is a 1-mm-tall flame guard to protect the cylinder head gasket.

One of the specifications called for was to maintain a 5.7-litre (350-cu in) displacement. With a bore centre of 4.40 inches (identical to that of the 60 million or so Chevrolet small-block V8s built to date), the bore had to be reduced from 4.00 to 3.90 inches and the stroke increased from 3.48 to 3.66 inches. Chevrolet insisted on a 4.40-in bore spacing in case they decided to use these cylinder heads on a production small-block V8. That's an

option that Chevrolet have not yet taken up.

The Nikasil coating on the cylinder walls allows the use of aluminium cylinder liners instead of the more common cast iron. Not only does this save weight, but the coating also permits the running of very close piston-to-cylinder-wall tolerances for optimum ring sealing, resulting in greater output and durability.

The crankshaft is a cross-drilled, forged-steel unit and the connecting rods are also made of a forged-steel alloy.

Power output is 375 bhp at 5,800 rpm with 370 lb ft of torque at 4,800 rpm.

Chevrolet insisted that Lotus made the LT5 engine fit between the standard engine-compartment chassis rails. The LT5 thus has a very narrow, 22-degree-included angle between the intake and exhaust valves. The four overhead camshafts are driven by a series of three chains and the valves are actuated by direct-acting hydraulic lifters.

The combustion chambers are cloverleaf shaped with a centrally-located spark plug. Each lip of the cloverleaf forms a small quench area that directs the air/fuel mixture towards the spark plug while imparting turbulence in the cylinder. This allows for the high compression ratio of 11:1 and the capability of running on 87-octane unleaded fuel.

Below right: The large, gently-tapering rear window lifts up for access to a stowage area behind the seats. The 'boot' is filled by a petrol tank . . .

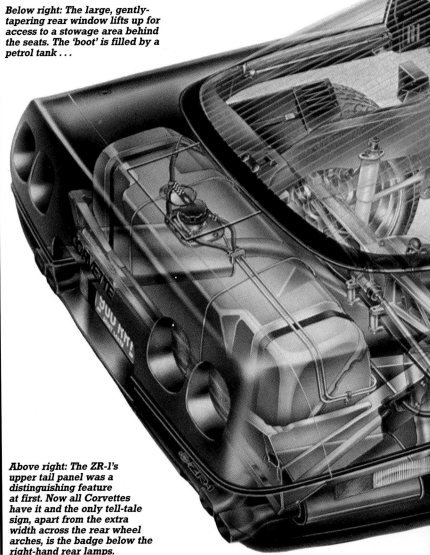

Above right: The ZR-1's upper tail panel was a distinguishing feature at first. Now all Corvettes have it and the only tell-tale sign, apart from the extra width across the rear wheel arches, is the badge below the right-hand rear lamps.

Above: Almost a work of art ... the Lotus-designed LT5 engine. The quadruple-overhead-camshaft all-aluminium V8 has four valves per cylinder, a 5.7-litre displacement and an output of 375 bhp at 5,800 rpm with 370 lb ft of torque at 4,800 rpm. The unusual aluminium casting on top is for the fuel injection system, with a separate runner to each inlet valve.

Below: The fuel injection system on the LT5, with a two-stage, three-valve throttle body and separate tracts for each of the engine's 16 inlet valves, allows the fitting of a 'power key' on the ZR-1. When switched to 'Full' it supplies fuel to all 16 inlet valves. When set at 'Normal' only the primary port valves and injectors operate, making the engine much more docile; the key can be removed to lock it into this position, e.g. when the car is left with parking attendants.

Above: The Corvette's suspension uses a transverse plastic 'monoleaf' spring at each end.

Above left: The ZR-1's rear wheels are 11 inches wide, against 9½-in fronts; the rear tyres are massive 315/35 ZR-rated Goodyear Eagles.

Right: Lotus engineered the LT5 for flexibility as well as power, but its 375 bhp gives performance that makes the ZR-1 faster than a Lamborghini Countach or Ferrari Testarossa in 'federalized' form.